Neil. Edinburgh 1973

SCOTTISH REMINISCENCES

PUBLISHED BY

JAMES MACLEHOSE AND SONS, GLASGOW,

𝔓𝔲𝔟𝔩𝔦𝔰𝔥𝔢𝔯𝔰 𝔱𝔬 𝔱𝔥𝔢 𝔘𝔫𝔦𝔟𝔢𝔯𝔰𝔦𝔱𝔶.

——

MACMILLAN AND CO., LTD., LONDON.

New York, · ·	*The Macmillan Co.*
London, · · ·	*Simpkin, Hamilton and Co.*
Cambridge, · ·	*Macmillan and Bowes.*
Edinburgh, · ·	*Douglas and Foulis.*

——

MCMIV.

SCOTTISH·REMINIS-CENCES ❧ ❧ ❧ ❧ BY
SIR · ARCHIBALD · GEIKIE

GLASGOW · JAMES · MACLEHOSE
AND · SONS · PUBLISHERS · TO
THE · UNIVERSITY · 1904 ❧ ❧

First Edition April 1904.
Reprinted April 1904.

GLASGOW: PRINTED AT THE UNIVERSITY PRESS
BY ROBERT MACLEHOSE AND CO. LTD.

PREFACE.

ONE who has sojourned in every part of a country and for sixty years has mingled with all classes of its inhabitants; who has watched the decay and disappearance of old, and the uprise of new usages; who has been ever on the outlook for illustrations of native humour, and who has been in the habit all along of freely recounting his experiences to his friends, may perhaps be forgiven if he ventures to put forth some record of what he has seen and heard, as a slight contribution to the history of social changes.

Literature is rich in Scottish reminiscences of this kind, so rich indeed that a writer who adds another volume to the long list runs great risk of repeating what has already been told. I have done my best to avoid this danger by turning over the pages of as many books of this class as I have been able to lay hands upon. In the course of this reading I have discovered that not a few of the 'stories' which I picked up long ago have found their way into print. These I have generally excluded from the present volume, save in cases where my version seemed to me better than that which had been published. But with all my care I cannot hope to have wholly escaped from pitfalls of this nature.

No one can have read much in this subject without discovering the perennial vitality of some anecdotes. With slight and generally local modification, they are told by generation after generation, and always as if they related to events that had recently occurred and to persons that were still familiarly known. Yet the essential basis of their humour may occasionally be traced back a long way. As an example of this longevity I may cite the incident of snoring in church, related at p. 86 of the following chapters, where an anecdote which has been told to me as an event that had recently happened among people now living was in full vigour a hundred years ago, and long before that time had formed the foundation of a clever epigram in the reign of Charles II. Another illustration of this persistence and transformation may be found in the anecdote of the wolf's den (p. 292). The same recurring circumstances may sometimes conceivably evoke, at long intervals, a similar sally of humour; but probably in most cases the original story survives, undergoing a process of gradual evolution and local adaptation as it passes down from one generation to another.

CONTENTS.

CHAPTER I.

CHAPTER II.

CHAPTER III.

CHAPTER IV.

CHAPTER V.

CHAPTER VI.

CHAPTER VII.

CHAPTER VIII.

CHAPTER IX.

CHAPTER X.

CHAPTER XI.

CHAPTER XII.

CHAPTER XIII.

CHAPTER I.

WHEN on the 5th of April, 1603, James VI. left Edinburgh with a great cavalcade of attendants, to ascend the throne of England, a series of social changes was set in motion in Scotland which has been uninterruptedly advancing ever since. Its progress has not been uniform, seeing that it has fluctuated with the access or diminution of national animosities on the two sides of the Tweed, until, as these sources of irritation died away, the two nations were welded into one by the arts of peace. Looking back across the

A

three centuries, we can recognise two epochs when the progress of change received a marked impetus.

The first of these dates from the failure of the Jacobite cause in 1746. At Culloden, not only were the hopes of the Stuarts finally extinguished, but a new period was ushered in for the development of Scotland. The abolition of the heritable jurisdictions, the extension of the same organised legal system over every part of the kingdom, the sup- pression of cattle-raids and other offences by the Highlanders against their lowland neighbours, the building of good roads, and the improvement of the old tracks, whereby easy communication was provided across the country, and especially through the Highlands between the northern and southern districts —these and other connected reforms led to the gradual breaking down of the barrier of animosity that had long kept Highlander and Lowlander apart, and by thus producing a freer intercourse of the two races, greatly strengthened the community as a whole, whether for peace or for war. On the other hand, the landing of Prince Charles Edward, the uprise of the clans, the victory of Preston- pans, and the invasion of England could not fail to revive and intensify the ancient enmity of the English against their northern neighbours. This animosity blazed out anew under the Bute administration, when fresh fuel was added to it from the literary side by Wilkes and Churchill. Nevertheless the leaven of union was quietly at work all the time. Not only did Scot commingle more freely with Scot, but increasing facilities of communication allowed the southward tide of migration to flow more freely across the Border. English travellers also found their way in growing numbers into that land north of the Tweed which for centuries had been at once scorned and feared, but which could now be everywhere safely visited. What had been satirised as

> The wretched lot
> Of the poor, mean, despised, insulted Scot,

came to be the subject of banter, more or less good humoured. The Englishman, while retaining a due sense of his own superiority, learnt to acknowledge that his northern neighbour did really possess some good qualities which made him not unworthy of a place in the commonwealth, while the Scot, on his side, discovered that his 'auld enemies' of England were far from being all mere 'pock-

puddings.' As the result of this greater inti-
macy of association, the smaller nation was
necessarily drawn more and more to assimilate
itself to the speech and ways of its larger,
wealthier, and more advanced partner.

But the decline in Scottish national peculiarities during the hundred years that followed
Culloden was slow compared with that of the
second epoch, which dates from the first half
of last century, when steam as a motive power
came into use, rapidly transforming our manu-
facturing industries, and revolutionising the
means of locomotion, alike on land and sea.
Scott in his youth saw the relics of the older
time while they were still fairly fresh and
numerous, and he has left an imperishable
memorial of them in his vivid descriptions.
Cockburn beheld the last of these relics
disappear, and as he lived well on into the
second of the two periods, he could mark
and has graphically chronicled the accelerated
rate of change.

Those of us who, like myself, can look
back across a vista of more than three score
years, and will compare what they see and
hear around them now with what they saw
and heard in their childhood, will not only
realise that the social revolution has been

marching along, but will be constrained to admit that its advance has been growing perceptibly more rapid. They must feel that the old order has indeed changed, and though they may wish that the modern could establish itself with less effacement of the antique, and may be disposed with Byron to cry,

> Out upon Time! who for ever will leave
> But enough of the past for the future to grieve,

they have, at least, the consolation of reflecting that the changes have been, on the whole, for the better. Happily much of the transformation is, after all, external. The fundamental groundwork of national character and temperament continues to be but little affected. The surface features and climate of the country, with all their profound, if unperceived, influences on the people, remain with no appreciable change. Even the inevitable wave of evolution does not everywhere roll on with the same speed, but leaves outlying corners and remote parishes unsubmerged, where we may still light upon survivals of an older day, in men and women whose ways and language seem to carry us back a century or more, and in customs that link us with an even remoter past.

It would be far beyond my purpose to enter into any discussion of the connection between the causes that have given rise to these social changes and the effects that have flowed from them. The far-reaching results of the introduction of steam-machinery in aggregating communities around a few centres, in depopulating the country districts, and in altering the habits and physique of the artizans, open up a wide subject on which I do not propose to touch. My life has been largely passed in the rural and mountainous parts of the country, where increased facilities for locomotion have certainly been the most obvious direct source of change to the inhabitants, though other causes have undoubtedly contributed less directly to bring about the general result. It has been my good fortune to become acquainted with every district of Scotland. There is not a county, hardly a parish, which I have not wandered over again and again. In many of them I have spent months at a time, finding quarters in county towns, in quiet villages, in wayside inns, in country houses, in remote manses, in shepherds' shielings, and in crofters' huts. Thrown thus among all classes of society, I have been brought in contact with each varying phase of life of the people. During the last twenty years, though no longer permanently resident in Scotland, I have been led by my official duties to revisit the country every year, even to its remotest bounds. I have also been enabled, through the kindness of a yachting friend, to cruise all through the Inner and Outer Hebrides. These favourable opportunities have allowed me to mark the gradual decline of national peculiarities perhaps more distinctly than would have been possible to one continuously resident. As a slight contribution to the history of the social evolution in Scotland, I propose in the following chapters to gather together such reminiscences as may serve to indicate the nature and extent of the changes of which I have been a witness, and to record a few illustrations of the manners and customs, the habits and humour of the people with whom I have mingled.

My memory goes back to a time before railways had been established in Scotland, when Edinburgh and Glasgow were connected only by a coach-road and a canal, and when stage-coaches still ran from the two cities into England. I may therefore begin these reminiscences with some reference to modes of travel.

Probably few readers are aware how recently roads practicable for wheeled carriages have become general over the whole country. In the seventeenth century various attempts were made to run stage-coaches between Edinburgh and Leith, between Edinburgh and Haddington, and between Edinburgh and Glasgow. But these efforts to open up communication, even with the chief towns, appear to have met with such scant support as to be soon abandoned. The usual mode of conveyance, for ladies as well as gentlemen, was on horseback. A traveller writing in 1688 states that there were then no stage-coaches, for the roads would hardly allow of them, and that although some of the magnates of the land made use of a coach and six horses, they did so 'with so much caution that, besides their other attendance, they have a lusty running footman on each side of the coach, to manage and keep it up in rough places.' It was probably not until after the suppression of the Jacobite rising in 1715 that roadmaking and road-repair were begun in earnest. For strategic purposes, military roads were driven through the Highlands, and this important work, which continued until far on in the century, not only opened up the Highlands to wheeled traffic, but reacted on the general lines of communication throughout the country.[1] By the time that railways came into operation the main roads had been well engineered and constructed, and were fitted for all kinds of vehicles.

Before the beginning of the railroad period, the inhabitants of Scotland had three means of locomotion into England. Those who were wealthy took their own carriages and horses, or hired post-horses from stage to stage. For the ordinary traveller, there were stage-coaches on land and steamboats on the sea.

With a comfortable carriage, and the personal effects of the occupants strapped on behind it, posting to London was one of the pleasant incidents of the year to those who had leisure and money at command. Repeated season after season, the journey brought the travellers into close acquaintance with every district through which the public road passed.

[1] In 1773, when Mrs. Grant of Laggan, as a girl, had to make the journey from Inveraray to Oban there was 'no road but the path of cattle,' 'an endless moor, without any road, except a small footpath, through which our guide conducted the horses with difficulty.'—*Letters from the Mountains*, 5th edit., vol. i., p. 4. Half a century later the conditions do not seem to have altered much in that region, as shown in Dr. Norman Macleod's *Reminiscences of a Highland Parish*.

They had a far greater familiarity with the
details of these districts than can now be
formed in railway journeys. They knew every
village, church, and country-house to be seen
along the route, and could mark the changes
made in them from year to year. At the
inns, where they halted for the night, they
were welcomed as old friends, and made to
feel themselves at home. This pleasant mode
of travelling, so graphically described in
Humphry Clinker, continued in use among
some county families long after the stage-
coaches had reached the culmination of their
speed and comfort. My old friend, T. F.
Kennedy of Dunure, used to describe to me
the delights of these yearly journeys in his
youth. Posting into England did not die
out until after the completion of the continuous railway routes, when the failure of
travellers on the road led to the giving up
of post-horses at the inns.

One of my early recollections is to have
seen the London coaches start from Princes
Street, Edinburgh. Though railways were
beginning to extend rapidly over England, no
line had yet entered Scotland, so that the
first part of the journey to London was made
by stage-coach. There was at that time no

line of railway, with steam locomotives, leading out of Edinburgh. Stage-coaches appear
to have been tried between London and
Edinburgh as far back as 1658, for an ad-
vertisement published in May of that year an-
nounces that they would 'go from the George
Inn without Aldersgate to Edinburgh *in Scotland*, once in three weeks for £4 10s., with
good coaches and fresh horses on the roads.'
In May, 1734, a coach was advertised to
perform the journey between Edinburgh and
London 'in nine days, or three days sooner
than any other coach that travels the road.'
An improvement in the service, made twenty
years later, was thus described in an adver-
tisement which appeared in the *Edinburgh
Evening Courant* for July 1st, 1754 :

'The Edinburgh Stage-Coach, for the better accommodation of Passengers, will be altered to a new genteel
two-end Glass Machine, hung on Steel Springs, exceeding
light and easy, to go in ten days in summer and twelve
in winter; to set out the first Tuesday in March, and
continue it from Hosea Eastgate's, the *Coach and Horses*
in Dean Street, Soho, London, and from John Somerville's
in the Canongate, Edinburgh, every other Tuesday, and
meet at Burrow-bridge on Saturday night, and set out from
thence on Monday morning, and get to London and
Edinburgh on Friday. In the winter to set out from
London and Edinburgh every other Monday morning and
to go to Burrow-bridge on Saturday night; and to set out

thence on Monday morning and get to London and
Edinburgh on Saturday night.   Passengers to pay as usual.
Performed, if God permits, by your dutiful servant,

'HOSEA EASTGATE.

'Care is taken of small parcels according to their
value.'

Before the end of the century the frequency,
comfort, and speed of the coaches had been
considerably increased.   Palmer, of the Bath
Theatre, led the way in this reform, and in
the year 1788 organised a service from London
to Glasgow, which accomplished the distance
of rather more than 400 miles in sixty-five
hours.   Ten years later, Lord Chancellor
Campbell travelled by the same system of
coaches between Edinburgh and London, and
he states that in 1798 he 'performed the
journey in three nights and two days, Mr.
Palmer's mail-coaches being then established ;
but this swift travelling was considered dangerous as well as wonderful,—and I was gravely
advised to stop a day at York, "as several
passengers who had gone through without
stopping had died of apoplexy from the
rapidity of the motion."   The whole distance
may now (1847) be accomplished with ease
and safety in fourteen hours.'[1]

[1] *Lives of the Lord Chancellors*, vol. vi., p. 50.   This was
written in the early years of railway enterprise.   The journey

Passengers between Edinburgh and Glasgow before the days of railways had a choice of two routes, either by road or by canal. As far back as the summer of 1678, an Edinburgh merchant set up a stage-coach between the two cities to carry six passengers, but it appears to have had no success. In 1743, another Edinburgh merchant offered to start a stage-coach on the same route with six horses, to hold six passengers, to go twice a week in summer and once in winter. But his proposal does not appear to have met with adequate support. At last, in 1749, a kind of covered spring-cart, known as the ' Edinburgh and Glasgow Caravan,' was put upon the road and performed the journey of forty-four miles in two days. Nine years later, in 1758, the ' Fly,' so called on account of its remarkable speed, actually accomplished the distance in twelve hours. The establishment of Palmer's improved stage-coaches led to a further advance in the communications between Edinburgh and Glasgow, but it was not until 1799 that the time taken in the journey was reduced to six hours. In my

is now performed every day in seven hours and three quarters, and the time will probably be further shortened in the not distant future.

boyhood, before the stage-coaches were driven
off by the railway, various improvements on
the roads, the carriages, and the arrangements
connected with the horses, had brought down
the time to no more than four hours and a
half.[1]

Much more leisurely was the transit on the
Union Canal. The boats were comfortably
fitted up and were drawn by a cavalcade of
horses, urged forward by postboys. It was
a novel and delightful sensation, which I can
still recall, to see fields, trees, cottages, and
hamlets flit past, as if they formed a vast
moving panorama, while one seemed to be
sitting absolutely still. For mere luxury of
transportation, such canal-travel stands quite
unrivalled. Among its drawbacks, however,
are the long detentions at the locks. But as
everything was new to me in my first expedition to the west, I remember enjoying
these locks with the keenest pleasure, sometimes remaining in the boat, and feeling it
slowly floated up or let down, sometimes
walking along the margin and watching the
rush of the water through the gradually
opening sluices.

Both the stage-coaches and the passenger

---

[1] Chambers' *Domestic Annals of Scotland*, vols. ii. and iii.

boats on the canal were disused after the opening of the Edinburgh and Glasgow Railway in the spring of 1842. A few weeks subsequent to the running of the first trains, the *Glasgow Courier* announced that 'the whole of the stage-coaches from Glasgow and Edinburgh are now off the road, with the exception of the six o'clock morning coach, which is kept running in consequence of its carrying the mail bags.'

Steamboats had not yet been introduced upon the large freshwater lakes of Scotland, except upon Loch Lomond, when I visited the Trossachs region for the first time in 1843. I was rowed the whole length of Loch Katrine in a boat by four stout Highlanders, who sang Gaelic songs, to the cadence of which they kept time with their oars. It was my first entry into the Highlands, and could not have been more impressive. The sun was almost setting as the boat pushed off from Stronachlachar and all the glories of the western sky were cast upon the surrounding girdle of mountains, the reflections of which fell unbroken on the mirror-like surface of the water. As we advanced and the sunset tints died away, the full autumn moon rose above the crest of Ben Venue, and touched off the higher crags with light, while the shadows gathered in deepening black along the lower slopes and the margin of the water. Before we reached the lower end of the lake the silvery sheen filled all the pass of the Trossachs above the sombre forest. The forms of the hills, the changing lights in the sky, and the weird tunes of the boatmen combined to leave on my memory a picture as vivid now as when it was impressed sixty years ago.

No more remarkable contrast between the present tourist traffic in this lake region and that of the early part of last century could be supplied than that which is revealed by an incident recorded as having occurred about the year 1814, four years after the publication of Scott's *Lady of the Lake*. An old Highlander, who was met on the top of Ben Lomond, said he had been a guide from the north side of the mountain for upwards of forty years; 'but that d——d Walter Scott, that everybody makes such a work about!' exclaimed he with vehemence—'I wish I had him to ferry over Loch Lomond: I should be after sinking the boat, if I drowned myself into the bargain; for ever since he wrote his *Lady of the Lake*, as they call it, everybody goes to see that filthy hole Loch Katrine, then comes round by Luss, and I have had only two gentlemen to guide all this blessed season, which is now at an end. I shall never see the top of Ben Lomond again!—The devil confound his ladies and his lakes, say I!'[1]

If this indignant mountaineer could revisit his early haunts, his grandchildren would have a very different story to tell him of the poet's influence. For one visitor to his beloved mountain in his day there must now be at least a hundred, almost all of whom have had their first longing to see that region kindled by the poems and tales of Scott. No man ever did so much to make his country known and attractive as the Author of *Waverley* has done for Scotland. His fictitious characters have become historical personages in the eyes of the thousands of pilgrims who every year visit the scenes he has described. In threading the pass of the Trossachs, they try to see where Fitz James must have lost his 'gallant grey.' In passing Ellen's Isle, they scrutinise it, if haply any

[1] *Letters from a Gentleman in the North of Scotland* [Captain Burt], 5th edit., vol. i., p. 203, footnote by Editor R. Jamieson.

B

relics of her home have survived. At Coilan-
togle Ford they want to know the exact spot
where the duel was fought between the King
and Roderick Dhu. At Aberfoyle they look
out for the Clachan, or some building that
must stand on its site, and their hearts are
comforted by finding suspended to a tree on
the village green the veritable coulter with
which Bailie Nicol Jarvie burnt the big
Highlander's plaid. So delighted indeed
have the tourists been with this relic of the
past that they have surreptitiously carried it
off more than once, and have thus compelled
the village smith each time to manufacture
a new antique.

Before steam navigation was introduced,
packet ships sailed between Leith and London
carrying both passengers and goods. But as
the time taken on the journey depended on
winds and waves, these vessels supplied a
somewhat uncertain and even risky mode
of transit. Thus in November, 1743, an
Edinburgh newspaper announced that the
Edinburgh and Glasgow packet from London,
'after having great stress of weather for twenty
days, has lately arrived safe at Holy Island
and is soon expected in Leith harbour.'

The first steamboats that plied between

Leith and London were much smaller in size and more primitive in their appointments than their successors of to-day. Mineral oil had not come into use, and animal and vegetable oils were dear. Hence the saloons and cabins were lighted with candles, and, as wicks that require no snuffing were not then in vogue, it may be imagined that the illumination could not be brilliant, and that candle grease was apt to descend in frequent drops upon whatever happened to lie below. The Rev. Dr. Lindsay Alexander used to tell that when he once accompanied a brother clergyman in the steamboat to London, they were unable to obtain berths in any of the state-rooms, and had to content themselves each with a sofa in the saloon. In the middle of the night he was awakened by a groaning which seemed to come from the sofa of his elderly friend. Starting up, he enquired if the doctor was in pain. The answer came in a shaky voice : ' I'm afraid—I've had—a stroke—of paralysis.' In an instant the younger man was out of bed, calling for a light, as the candles had all burnt themselves into their sockets. When the light came, the reverend gentleman was seen to have been lying immediately below the drip of a guttering candle, and the drops of tallow, falling on his cheek, had congealed there into a cake that had gradually spread up to his eye. As he could not move the muscles of his face, the poor man's imagination had transferred the powerlessness to the rest of his side. With the help of the steward, however, the hardened grease was scraped off, and the doctor, recovering the use of his facial muscles, was able once more to drop off to sleep.

Railroads have been unquestionably the most powerful agents of social change in Scotland. From the opening of the first line down to the present time, I have watched the yearly multiplication of lines, until the existing net-work of them has been constructed. Had it been possible, at the beginning, to anticipate this rapid development, and to foresee the actual requirements of the various districts through which branch-lines have been formed, probably the railway-map would have been rather different from what it now is. Some local lines would never have been built, or would have followed different routes from those actually chosen. The competition of the rival companies has led to a wasteful expenditure of their capital, and to the construction of lines which either do not pay their expenses, or yield only a meagre return for the outlay disbursed upon them. A notable instance of the effects of this rivalry was seen in the competition of two great companies for the construction of a line between Carnwath on the Caledonian system and Leadburn on the North British. The country through which the route was to be taken was sparsely peopled, being partly pastoral, partly agricultural, but without any considerable village. When the contest was in progress, a farmer from the district was asked to state what he knew of traffic between Carnwath and Dolphinton, a small hamlet in Lanarkshire. His answer was, 'Od, there's an auld wife that comes across the hills ance in a fortnicht wi' a basket o' ribbons, but that's a' the traffic I ken o'.' The minister of Dolphinton, being eager to have a railway through his parish, set himself to ascertain the number of cattle that passed along the road daily in front of his manse. He was said to have counted the same cow many times in the same day. The result of the competition was a compromise. Each railway company obtained powers to construct a new line which was to run to Dolphinton and there terminate. And these two lines to this hamlet of a few cottages,

and not as many as 300 people, were actually
constructed and have been in operation for
many years.   Each of them has its terminal
station at Dolphinton, with station-master and
porters.   But there were not, and so far as I
know, there are not now, any rails connecting
the two lines across the road.   This diminutive village thus enjoys the proud preemin-
ence of being perhaps the smallest place in the
three kingdoms which has two distinct terminal
stations on each side of its road, worked by
two independent and rival companies.

Not long after the opening of the North
British line to Dolphinton, I spent a day at
the southern end of the Pentland Hills, and
in the evening, making my way to the village,
found the train with its engine attached.   The
station was as solitary as a churchyard.   After
I had taken my seat in one of the carriages,
the guard appeared from some doorway in
the station, and I heard the engine-driver shout
out to him, 'Weel, Jock, hae ye got your
passenger in?'

The opening of a railway through some of
these lonely upland regions was a momentous
event in their history.   Up till then many
districts which possessed roads were not traversed by any public coach nor by many

private carriages, while in other parishes, where roads either did not exist or were extremely bad and unfit for wheeled traffic, the sight of a swiftly-moving train was one that drew the people from far and near. Some time, however, had to elapse before the country-folk could accustom themselves to the rapidity and (comparative) punctuality of railroad travelling. When the old horse-tramways ran, it was a common occurrence for a train to be stopped in order to pick up a passenger, or to let one down by the road-side, and it is said that this easy-going prac-tice used to be repeated now and then in the early days of branch-railways. An old lady from Culter parish, who came down to the railway not long after it was opened, arrived at the station just as the train had started When told that she was too late, for the trai had already gone beyond the station, she ex claimed, 'Dod, I maun rin then,' and pro ceeded at her highest speed along the plat form, while the station-master shouted after her to stop. She was indignant that he would not whistle for the train to halt or come back for her.

Railway construction in the Highlands came later than it did in the Lowlands, and entered among another race of people with different habits from those of their southern fellow-countrymen. The natural disposition of an ordinary Highlander would not often lead him to choose the hard life of a navvy, and volunteer to aid in the heavy work of railway construction. The following anecdote illustrates a racial characteristic which probably could not have been met with in the Lowlands. During the formation of one of the lines of railway through the Highlands a man came to the contractor and asked for a job at the works, when the following conversation took place :

'Well, Donald, you've come for work, have you? and what can you do?'

''Deed, I can do onything.'

'Well, there's some spade and barrow work going on ; you can begin on that.'

'Ach, but I wadna just like to be workin' wi' a spade and a wheelbarrow.'

'O, would you not? Then yonder's some rock that needs to be broken away. Can you wield a pick?'

'I wass never usin' a pick, whatefer.'

'Well, my man, I don't know anything I can give you to do.'

So Donald went away crestfallen. But

being of an observing turn of mind, he walked along the rails, noting the work of each gang of labourers, until he came to a signal-box, wherein he saw a man seated, who came out now and then, waved a flag, and then resumed his seat. This appeared to Donald to be an occupation entirely after his own heart. He made enquiry of the man, ascertained his hours and his rate of pay, and returned to the contractor, who, when he saw him, good-naturedly asked :

'What, back again, Donald? Have you found out what you can do?'

''Deed, I have, sir. I would just like to get auchteen shullins a week, and to do that' —holding out his arm and gently waving the stick he had in his hand.

A desire to select the lightest part of the work, however, is not peculiar to the Celtic nature, but comes out, strongly enough, some-times, in the Lowlands, as was illustrated by the proposal of a quarryman to share the labour with a comrade. 'If ye ram, Jamie,' said he, 'I'll pech'; that is, if his friend would work the heavy iron sledge-hammer, he himself would give the puff or pant with which the workmen accompany each stroke they make.

The unpunctuality of the railways, the dirtiness of the carriages on branch lines, and the frequent incivility of the officials are only too familiar to all who have to travel much upon the system of at least one of the Scottish companies. A worthy country-man who had come from the north-east side of the kingdom by train to Cowlairs, was told that the next stoppage would be Glasgow. He at once began to get all his little packages ready, and remarked to a fellow-passenger, ' I'm sailin' for China this week, but I'm thinkin' I'm by the warst o' the journey noo.'

It must be confessed, however, that the railway officials often have their forbearance sorely tested, especially in the large mining districts, where the roughness and violence of the mob of passengers can sometimes hardly be held in check, and where the temptation to retaliate after the same fashion may be difficult to resist. Having also to be on the watch for dishonesty, they are apt to develop a suspiciousness which sometimes, though perhaps needlessly, exasperates the honest traveller. Occasionally their sagacity is scarcely a match for the knavery of a dishonest Scot. Thus, a man, when the ticket collector came round, was fumbling in all his pockets for his ticket, until the official, losing patience, said he would come back for it. When he returned, noticing that the man had the ticket between his lips, he indignantly snatched it away. Whereupon a fellow-passenger remarked, 'You must be singularly absent-minded not to remember that you had put your ticket in your mouth.' 'No sae absent-minded as ye wad think,' was the answer; 'I was jist rubbin' oot the auld date wi' my tongue.'

Perhaps the most striking evidence of the effect of increased facilities for locomotion and traffic upon the habits of the population is presented by the western coast of the country, or the region usually spoken of as the West Highlands and Islands. Few parts of Britain are now more familiar to the summer tourist than the steamboat tracks through that region. Every year thousands of holiday-makers are carried rapidly and comfortably in swift and capacious vessels through that archipelago of mountainous land and blue sea. They have, as it were, a vast panorama unrolled before them, which changes in aspect and interest at every mile of their progress. For the most part, however, they obtain and carry away with them merely a kind of general and superficial impression of the scenery, though the memory of it may remain indelibly fixed among their most delightful experiences of travel. They can have little or no conception of the interior of those islands or of the glens and straths of the mainland, still less of the inhabitants and their ways and customs. Nor, as they are borne pleasantly along past headland and cliff, can they adequately realise what the conditions of travel were before the days of commodious passenger-steamers.

When Johnson and Boswell landed in Skye in the year 1773, there was not a road in the whole island practicable for a wheeled carriage. Locomotion, when not afoot, was either on horseback or by boat. The inland bridle-tracks lay among loose boulders, over rough, bare rock, or across stretches of soft and sometimes treacherous bog. The boats were often leaky, the oars and rowlocks unsound, the boatmen unskilful; while the weather, even in summer, is often boisterous enough to make the navigation of the sea-lochs and sounds difficult or impossible for small craft. And such continued to be the conditions in which the social life of the West Highlands was carried on long after Johnson's time. During the first thirty or more years of last century the voyage from the Clyde to Skye was made in sailing packets, and generally took from ten to fifteen days. It was not until steamboats began to ply along the coast that the scattered islands were brought into closer touch with each other and with the Lowlands. To the memory of David Hutcheson, who organised the steamboat service among the Western Highlands and Islands, Scotland owes a debt of gratitude. The development of this service has been the gradual evolution of some seventy years. Half a century ago it was far from having reached its present state of advancement. There were then no steamers up the West Coast to Skye and the Outer Hebrides, save those which carried cargo and came round the Mull of Cantyre. During the herring season, and about the times of the cattle-markets, the irregularities and discomfort of these vessels can hardly be exaggerated. When the decks were already loaded perhaps with odoriferous barrels of herring, and when it seemed impossible that they could hold anything more, the vessel might have to make a long detour to the head of some mountain-girdled sea-loch to fetch away a flock of sheep, or a herd of

Highland cattle. At most of the places of call there were no piers. Passengers had accordingly to disembark in small boats, sometimes at a considerable distance from high-water mark, to which, perhaps in the middle of the night, they scrambled across sea-weed and slippery shingle.

As a steamboat called at each place in summer only once, in later years twice, in a week, and in winter only once in a fortnight, the day of its arrival was eagerly looked forward to by the population, in expectation of the supplies of all kinds, as well as the letters and newspapers, which it brought from the south. You never could be sure at what hour of the day or night it might make its appearance, and if you expected friends to arrive by it, or if you proposed yourself to take a passage in it, you needed to be on the watch, perhaps for many weary hours. In fine weather, this detention was endurable enough; but in the frequent storms of wind and rain, much patience and some strength of constitution were needed to withstand the effects of the exposure. The desirability of having waiting-rooms or places of shelter of any kind is even yet not fully realised by the Celtic mind.

The native islander, however, seemed never to feel, or at least would never acknowledge these various inconveniences. It was so great a boon to have the steamers at all, and he had now got so used to them that he could not imagine a state of things different from that to which he had grown accustomed. Nor would he willingly allow any imperfections in David Hutcheson's arrangements, on which he depended for all his connection with the outer world. I remember a crofter in the island of Eigg, who, when asked when the steamer would arrive, replied at once, 'Weel, she'll be comin' sometimes sooner, and whiles earlier, and sometimes before that again.' The idea of lateness was a reproach which he would not acknowledge.

William Black, the novelist, used to tell of an English clergyman who, having break-fasted and paid his bill at Tobermory, was anxious for the arrival of the steamboat that was to take him north. He made his way to the pier, and walked up and down there for a time, but could see no sign of the vessel. At last, accosting a Highlander, who, leaning against a wall, was smoking a cutty-pipe, he asked him when the Skye steamer would call. Out came the pipe, followed by the laconic answer, 'That's her smoke,' and the speaker pointed in the direction of the Sound of Mull. The traveller for a time could observe nothing to indicate the expected vessel, but at last noticed a streak of dark smoke rising against the Morven Hills on the far side of the island that guards the front of the little bay of Tobermory. When at last the steamer itself rounded the point and came fully into sight, it seemed to the clergyman a much smaller vessel than he had supposed it would be, and he remarked to the Highlander, 'That the Skye steamer! that boat will surely never get to Skye.' The pipe was whisked out again to make way for the indignant reply, 'She'll be in Skye this afternoon, if nothin' happens to Skye.' The order of nature might conceivably go wrong, but Hutcheson's arrangements could be absolutely depended upon.

The captains of these steamers were personages of some consequence on the west coast. Usually skilful pilots and agreeable men, they came to be on familiar terms with the lairds and farmers all along their route, whom they were always glad to oblige and from whom they received in return many tangible proofs of recognition and good-will. At the end of a visit which I had been paying to friends on the south coast of Mull, the captain, to whom my kind host had previously written, brought his vessel a little out of his way in order to pick me up. The shore being full of rocks and reefs, my boat had to pull some distance out to the steamer, so that the tourist passengers had time to gratify their curiosity by crowding to one side to see the cause of this unusual stoppage. When the boat came alongside its cargo was transhipped in the following order : first a letter for the captain, next a live sheep, then a portmanteau, and lastly myself. There were many inquisitive glances at the scantiness of my flock, but the sheep had been sent as a present from my host to the captain, in recognition of some little services which he had lately been rendering to the family.

I have known a number of these captains, and have often been struck with their quiet dignity and good nature in circumstances that must have tried their temper and patience. They had much responsibility, and must often have had anxious moments in foggy or stormy weather. Now and then a vessel met with an accident, or was even shipwrecked, but the rarity of such always possible mishaps afforded good proof of the skilful seamanship with which

c

the Hutcheson fleet was handled. There was always a heavy traffic in goods. Scores of cases, boxes, barrels, and parcels of all conceivable shapes and sizes had to be taken on board and distributed at the various places of call. Live stock had to be adequately accommodated, and the varying times and direction of the tides had to be allowed for. Then there was the tourist traffic, which, though small in those days compared with what it has now grown to, required constant care and watchfulness. Not improbably the human part of his cargo gave a captain more trouble than the rest. The average tourist is apt to be selfish and unreasonable, ready to find fault if everything does not go precisely as he wished and expected. He is usually inquisitive, too, and doubtless asks the same questions that are put to the captain and seamen of the ship season after season. He has formed certain anticipations in his own mind of what he is to see, and when these are not quite realised he wants to know why. A common hallucination among travellers south of the Tweed clothes every Highlander in a kilt, and surprise is often expressed that the 'garb of old Gaul' is so seldom seen. The answer of one of David Hutcheson's officers should suffice for all who give vent to this surprise : ' Oh no, nobody wears the kilt here but fools and Englishmen.'

Various anecdotes are in circulation about the passengers and crew of these western steamboats. One of these narratives, of which different versions have been told, relates how on a dull, drizzling, and misty evening, when every attention had to be given to the rather intricate navigation, a lady began to ask questions of the man at the wheel. He answered her as briefly as possible for a time ; but, as she still plied him with queries, he at last lost his temper and abruptly desired her to go to the nether regions. She retired in high dudgeon and sought out the captain, insisting that the man should be discharged, and that she would report the matter to Mr. Hutcheson. The captain tried to soothe her, expressing his own regret at the language that had been used to her, and assuring her that he would make the man apologise to her for his conduct. She thereupon went down to the saloon and poured out her indignation to some of her fellow-passengers. In the midst of her talk, a man in dripping oilskins and cap in hand appeared at the door, and, after some hesitation and looking round the company, advanced to the irate lady and said, 'Are you the leddy I tellt to gang to hell? Weel, the captain says ye needna gang yet.' Such was the apology.

I well remember, when as a lad of eighteen I first visited Skye, that the steamer carrying the usual miscellaneous cargo in the hold and on deck, after rounding the Mull had made so many calls, and had so much luggage and merchandise to discharge at each halt, that it was past midnight of the second day before we came into Broadford Bay. The disembarkation was by small-boat, and as we made our way shorewards, the faces of the oarsmen were at every stroke lit up with the pale, ghostly light of a phosphorescent sea. The night was dark, but with the aid of a dim lantern one could mount the rough beach, where I was met by a son of the Rev. John Mackinnon of Kilbride, with whom I had come to spend a few weeks. We had a drive of some five miles inland, enlivened with Gaelic songs which my young friend and his cousin screamed at the pitch of their voices. At a certain part of the road they became suddenly silent, or only spoke to each other in whispers. We were then passing the old graveyard at Kilchrist; but when we had got to what was judged a safe distance beyond it and its ghosts, the hilarity began anew, and lasted until we came to our destination between two and three o'clock in the morning.

The introduction of the electric telegraph naturally aroused much curiosity in the rural population as to how the wires could carry messages. A West Highlander who had been to Glasgow and was consequently supposed to have got to the bottom of the mystery, was asked to explain it. 'Weel,' said he, 'it's no easy to explain what you will no be understandin'. But I'll tell ye what it's like. If you could stretch my collie dog frae Oban to Tobermory, an' if you wass to clap its head in Oban, an' it waggit its tail in Tobermory, or if I wass to tread on its tail in Oban an' it squaked in Tobermory—that's what the telegraph is like.'

CHAPTER II.

THE social history of Scotland has been inti-
mately linked with the successive ecclesiastical
polities which have held sway in the country.
Nowhere can the external and visible records
of these polities be more clearly seen than
among the Western Isles, for there the political revolutions have been less violent, though
not less complete, than in other parts of the
country, and the effacement of the memorials
of the past has been brought about, more
perhaps by the quiet influence of time, than
by the ruthless hand of man. First of all we
meet with various lingering relics of Paganism;
then with abundant and often well-preserved
records of the primitive Celtic Church; next

with evidence of the spread of the Roman Catholic faith; further with the establishment of Protestantism, but without the complete eradication of the older religion; and lastly with the doings of the various religious sects into which the inhabitants are now unhappily divided.

Various memorials of Paganism may be recognised, to some of which further reference will be made in a later chapter. Of these memorials, the numerous standing stones are the most conspicuous, whether as single mono-liths, marking the grave of some forgotten hero or dedicated to some unknown divinity, or as groups erected doubtless for religious purposes, like the great assemblage at Caller-nish in the Lewis. Besides these stones, many burial mounds, resting-places of the pagan dead, have yielded relics of the Stone and Bronze Ages. In some respects more impressive even than these relics, are the superstitious customs which still survive amongst us, and have probably descended uninterruptedly from pagan times; such, for instance, as the practice of walking around wells and other places three times from east to west, as the sun moves, and the practice of leaving offerings at the springs which are resorted to for curative purposes. Some of these customs were continued by the early Celtic Church, persisted afterwards through the Roman Catholic period, and even now, in spite of all the efforts of Protestant zeal, they have not been wholly extirpated.

The vestiges of the early Celtic Church, by which Paganism was superseded, are specially abundant in the Highlands. Even where all visible memorials have long since vanished, the name of many a devoted saint and missionary still clings to the place where he or she had a chapel or hermitage, or where some cell was dedicated to their memory. The names of Columba, Bridget, Oran, Donan, Fillan, Ronan, and others are as familiar on the lips of modern Highlanders as they were on those of their forefathers, although the historical meaning and interest of these names may be unknown to those who use them now. When, besides the name attached to the place, the actual building remains with which the name was first associated in the sixth or some later century, the interest deepens, especially where the relic stands, as so many of them do, on some small desolate islet, placed far amid the melancholy main, and often for weeks together difficult or impossible of approach, even now, with the stouter boats of the present day. Such places, like those off the west coast of Ireland, were sought for retirement from the work and worry of the world, where the missionary devoted himself to meditation and prayer. The numerous Deserts, Diserts, Dysarts, and Dyserts in Ireland and Scotland are all forms of the Gaelic word *Disert*, derived from the Latin *Desertum*, a desert or sequestered place, and mark retreats of the early propagandists of Christianity. It fills one with amazement and admiration to contemplate the heroism and self-devotion which could lead these men in their frail coracles to such sea-washed rocks, where there is often no soil to produce any vegetation, and where, except by impounding rain, there can be no supply of fresh water.

Perhaps the most striking of these 'deserts' in Scotland is to be found on the uninhabited rock known as Sùla Sgeir, which rises out of the Atlantic, about forty miles to the north of the Butt of Lewis. Though much less imposing in height and size than the Skellig off the coast of Kerry, it is at least four times further from the land, and must consequently have been still more difficult to reach in primitive times. I had a few years ago an opportunity of landing on this rock, during a yachting cruise to the Faroe Islands. With some little difficulty, on account of the heavy swell, I succeeded in scrambling ashore, and found the rock to consist of gneiss, like that of the Long Island. My arrival disturbed a numerous colony of sea-fowl. The puffins emerged from their holes, and sat gazing at me with their whimsical wistful look. Flocks of razorbills and guillemots circled overhead, filling the air with their screams, while the gannets, angry that their mates should be disturbed from their nests, wheeled to and fro still higher, with mocking shouts of ha! ha! ha! A dank grey sea-fog hung over the summit of the islet. Everything was damp with mist and clammy with birds' droppings, which in a dry climate would gather as a deposit of guano. Loathsome pools of rain-water and sea-spray, putrid with excrement, filled the hollows of the naked rock, while the air was heavy with the odours of living and dead birds. The only things of beauty in the place were the tufts of sea-pink that grew luxuriantly in the crannies. Some traces of recent human occupation could be seen in the form of a few rude stone-huts erected as shelters by the men who now and then come to take off the gannets and their eggs, and who when there lately had left some heaps of unused peat behind them.

Yet this desolate, bird-haunted rock, with the heavy surf breaking all round it and re-sounding from its chasms and caves, was the place chosen by one of the Celtic saints as his 'desert.' His little rude chapel yet remains, built of rough stones and still retaining its roof of large flags. It measures inside about fourteen feet in length by from six to eight in breadth, with an entrance doorway and one small window-opening, beneath which the altar-stone still lies in place. There could hardly ever have been a community here ; one is puzzled to understand how even the saint himself succeeded in reaching this barren rock, and how he supported himself on it during his stay. He came, no doubt, in one of the light skin-covered coracles, which could con-tain but a slender stock of provisions. When these were exhausted, if the weather forbade his return to Lewis or to the mainland, he had no fuel on the rock to fall back upon, with which to cook any of the eggs or birds of the islet, and there was no edible vegetation, save the dulse or other sea-weeds growing between tide-marks.

With the decay and dissolution of the Celtic

Church, probably many of the chapels erected by that community were forsaken and allowed to fall into ruin. But some continued to be used, and were even enlarged or rebuilt, when the Church of Rome established its rule over the whole country. Architecture had meanwhile made an onward step. The buildings erected by the emissaries of Rome presented a strong contrast to those which they replaced, for they were solidly built with lime, in a much more ornate style, with a freer use of sculpture and on a much larger scale. The old church of Rodil, in Harris, for example, belonging perhaps to the thirteenth century, is full of sculptured figures; while the Cathedral of Iona would hold some dozens of the primitive cells.

In various parts of the country evidence may be seen that the Celtic sculptured stones had ceased to be respected, either as religious monuments or as works of art, when the Roman Catholic churches were erected. At St. Andrews, for example, the old chapel of St. Regulus, probably built between the tenth and twelfth centuries, was allowed to remain, and it still stands, roofless indeed, but in wonderful preservation as regards the masonry of its walls. But of the crosses that rose above the sward around it, many of them delicately carved with interlaced work in the true Celtic style, some were broken up and actually used as building material for the great Cathedral which was begun in the year 1160. Again, at St. Vigeans, in Forfarshire, a large quantity of similar sculptured stones of the Celtic period was built into the masonry of the twelfth-century church erected there under the Latin hierarchy.

The Roman Catholic faith, which once prevailed universally over the country, still maintains its place on some of the islands, particularly Barra, Benbecula, and South Uist, and in certain districts of the mainland. In Eigg, about half of the population is still Catholic, the other half being divided between the Established and Free Churches. The three clergymen, Protestant and Roman Catholic, when I first visited the island, were excellent friends, and used to have pleasant evenings together over their toddy and talk. The Catholic memorial chapel to the memory of Lord Howard of Glossop was determined 'to be erected in one of the Catholic islands,' and Canna was chosen as its site. The building has been placed there, and with its high Norman tower now forms a conspicuous landmark for leagues to east and west. But the crofter population is gone, and with it Catholicism has disappeared from Canna, though some five crofter families still live on the contiguous island of Sanday.

In my peregrinations through the Catholic districts of the west of Scotland I have often been struck with some interesting contrasts between them and similar regions in Ireland, where Catholic and Protestant live together. The Scottish priests have always seemed to me a better educated class and more men of the world than their brethren in Ireland. Students who have been trained abroad have their ideas widened and their manners polished, as is hardly possible in the case of those who leave their villages to be trained at Maynooth, whence they are sent to recommence village life as parish priests. Again, there has always appeared to me to be in the West Highlands far less of the antagonism which in Ireland separates Catholics and Protestants. They live together as good neighbours, and, unless you actually make enquiry, you cannot easily discriminate between them.

No feature in the social changes which Scotland has undergone stands out more conspicuously than the part played in these changes by the clergy since the Reformation. This clerical influence has been both beneficial and baneful. On the one hand, the clergy have unquestionably taken a large share in the intellectual development of the people, and in giving to the national character some of its most distinctive qualities. For many generations, in face of a lukewarm or even hostile nobility and government, they bore the burden of the parish schools, elaborating and improving a system of instruction which made their country for a long time the best educated community in Europe. They have held up the example of a high moral standard, and have laboured with the most unremitting care to train their flocks in the paths of righteousness.

On the other hand, the clergy, having from the very beginning of Protestantism obtained control over the minds and consciences of the people, have naturally used this powerful influence to make their theological tenets prevail throughout the length and breadth of the land. They early developed a spirit of intolerance and fanaticism, and with this same spirit they succeeded in imbuing their people, repressing the natural and joyous impulses of humanity, and establishing an artificial and exacting code of conduct, the enforcement of which led to an altogether hurtful clerical domination. While waging war against older forms of superstition, they introduced new forms which added to the terrors and the gloom of life. These transformations were longest in reaching their climax among the Highlands and Islands, but have there attained their most complete development, as will be further pointed out in a later chapter. Happily, in the Lowlands for the last two hundred years, their effects have been slowly passing away. The growth of tolerance and enlightenment is increasingly marked both among the clergy and the laity. But the old leaven is not even yet wholly eradicated, though it now works within a comparatively narrow and continually contracting sphere.

Nevertheless, even those who have least sympathy with the theological tenets and ecclesiastical system of the Scottish clergy must needs acknowledge that, as earnest and indefatigable workers for the spiritual and temporal good of their flocks, as leaders in every movement for the benefit of the community, and as fathers of families, these men deserve the ample commendation which they have received. Their limited stipends have allowed them but a slender share of the material comforts and luxuries of life, and comparatively few of them have enjoyed opportunities to 'augment their small peculiar,' yet they have, as a whole, set a noble example of self-denial, thrift, and benevolence. Secure at least of their manses, they have contrived 'to live on little with a cheerful heart,' respected and esteemed of men. While supplying the material wants of their people, as far as their means would allow, they have yet been able to provide a good education for their families, and to

> Put forth their sons to seek preferment out;
> Some to the wars, to try their fortune there;
> Some to discover islands far away;
> Some to the studious universities.

The 'sons of the manse' are found filling positions of eminence in every walk of life.

With all this excellence of character and achievement, the clergy of Scotland have maintained an individuality which has strongly marked them as a class among the other professions of the country. This peculiarity is well exemplified in the innumerable anecdotes which, either directly or indirectly con-

D

nected with clergymen, form so large a proportion of what are known as 'Scotch Stories.' If we seek for the cause of the prominence of the clerical element in the accepted illustrations of Scottish humour, we shall hardly find it in any exceptional exuberance of that quality among the reverend gentlemen themselves, taken as a body, though many of their number have been among the most humorous and witty of their countrymen. As they were long drawn from almost every grade in the social scale of the kingdom, they have undoubtedly presented an admirable average type of the national idiosyncrasies, though they are now recruited in diminishing measure from the landed and cultured ranks of society. Their number, their general dispersion over the whole land, their prominence in their parishes, the influence wielded by many of them in the church-courts and on public platforms, and the free intercourse between them and the people, have all helped to draw attention to them and to their sayings and doings. Moreover, since dissent from the National Church began, the clergy have been greatly multiplied. In each parish, where there was once only one minister, there are now two or even more.

A Scots proverb avers that 'A minister's legs should never be seen,' meaning that he should not be met with out of the pulpit. So long as he remains there, he stands invested with 'such divinity as doth hedge a king': unassailable, uncontradictable, and wielding the authority of a messenger from God to man. The very isolation and eminence of this position call attention to any merely human qualities or frailties which he may disclose in ordinary life. His parishioners, though inwardly glad if he can shed upon them 'the gracious dew of pulpit eloquence,' at the same time delight to find him, when divested of his gown and bands, after all, one of themselves; and while they enjoy his humour, when he possesses that saving grace, they are not unwilling sometimes to take his little peculiarities as subjects for their own mirthful but not ill-natured remarks. He may thus be like Falstaff, 'not only witty himself, but the cause that wit is in other men.' Hence the clerical stories may be divided into two kinds: those in which the humour is that of the ministers, and those in which it is that of the people, with the ministers as its object. In the first series, there is perhaps no particular flavour

different from that characteristic of the ordinary
middle-class Scot, though of course the many
anecdotes of a professional nature take their
colour from the calling of those to whom
they relate. In the second division, however,
a greater individuality may be recognised.
Whether it be from a sort of good-humoured
revenge for his incontestible superiority in the
pulpit, there seems to be a proneness to make
the most of any oddities in the minister's
manners or character. The contrast between
the preacher on Sunday and the same man
during the week—it may be absent-minded,
or irascible, or making mistakes, or getting
into ludicrous situations—appeals powerfully to
the Scotsman's sense of humour. He seizes
the oddity of this contrast, expresses it in some
pithy words, and thus, often unconsciously,
launches another 'story' into the world. His
humour, as in Swift's definition,

> Is odd, grotesque, and wild,
> Only by affectation spoiled;
> 'Tis never by invention got;
> Men have it when they know it not.

It is in the country, and more particularly
in the remoter and less frequented parishes,
that the older type of minister has to
some extent survived. We meet with him

rather in the Highlands than in the Lowlands. He cultivates his glebe, and sometimes has also a farm on his hands. He has thus some practical knowledge of agriculture, is often a good judge of cattle, and breeds his own stock.

The best example of a Highland clergyman I ever knew was the Rev. John Mackinnon, minister of the parish of Strath, Skye, to whose hospitable house of Kilbride I have already referred as my first home in the island. He succeeded to the parish after his father, who had been its minister for fifty-two years, and he was followed in turn by his eldest son, the late Dr. Donald, so that for three generations, or more than a hundred years, the care of the parish remained in the same family. Tall, erect, and wiry, he might have been taken for a retired military man. A gentleman by birth and breeding, he mingled on easy terms with the best society in the island, while at the same time his active discharge of his ministerial duties brought him into familiar relations with the parishioners all over the district. So entirely had he gained their respect and affections that, when the great Disruption of 1843 rent the Establishment over so much of

the Highlands, he kept his flock in the old
Church. He used to boast that Strath was
thus the Sebastopol of that Church in Skye.

The old manse at Kilchrist, having become
ruinous, was abandoned; and, as none was
built to replace it, Mr. Mackinnon rented the
farm and house of Kilbride. There had once
been a chapel there, dedicated to St. Bridget,
and her name still clings to the spot. Behind rises the group of the Red Hills; further
over, the black serrated crests of Blaven, the
most striking of all the Skye mountains,
tower up into the north-western sky, while
to the south the eye looks away down the
inlet of Loch Slapin to the open sea, out of
which rise the ridges of Rum and the Scuir
of Eigg. The farm lay around the house
and stretched into the low uplands on the
southern side of the valley. The farming
operations at Kilbride will be noticed in a
later chapter.

In the wide Highland parishes, where roads
are few and communications must largely be
kept up on foot, the minister's wife is sometimes
hardly less important a personage than her
husband, and it is to her that the social wants
of the people are generally made known.
Mrs. Mackinnon belonged to another family

of the same clan as the minister, and was in every way worthy of him. Tall and massive in build, with strength of character traced on every feature of her face, and a dignity of manner like that of a Highland chieftainess, she was born to rule in any sphere to which she might be called. Her habitual look was perhaps somewhat stern, with a touch of sadness, as if she had deeply realised the trials and transitoriness of life, and had braced herself to do her duty through it all to the end. But no Highland heart beat more warmly than hers. She was the mother of the whole parish, and seemed to have her eye on every cottage and cabin throughout its wide extent. To her every poor crofter looked for sympathy and help, and never looked in vain. Her clear blue eyes would at one moment fill with tears over the recital of some tale of suffering in the district, at another they would sparkle with glee as she listened to some of the droll narratives of her family or her visitors. She belonged to the family of Corriehatachan, and among her prized relics was the coverlet under which Samuel Johnson slept when he stayed in her grandfather's house. That house at the foot of the huge Beinn na Cailleach has long

ago disappeared; some fields of brighter
green and some low walls mark where it
and its garden stood.

The younger generation at Kilbride consisted of a large family of stalwart sons and
daughters, whose careers have furnished a
good illustration of the way in which the
children of the manses of Scotland have
succeeded in the world. The eldest son, as
above stated, followed his father as minister
of Strath; another became proprietor of the
Melbourne Argus; a third joined the army,
served in the Crimea, and in the later years
of his life was widely known and respected
as Sir William Mackinnon, Director-General
of the Army Medical Department, who left
his fortune to the Royal Society for the
furtherance of scientific research.[1] Most of
the family now lie with their parents under
the green turf of the old burial-ground of
Kilchrist. Miss Flora, the youngest daughter,

[1] Dr. Norman Macleod, writing in 1867, stated that since
the beginning of the last wars of the French Revolution the
island of Skye alone had sent forth 21 lieutenant-generals
and major-generals; 48 lieutenant-colonels; 600 commissioned
officers; 10,000 soldiers; 4 governors of colonies; 1 governor-
general; 1 adjutant-general; 1 chief baron of England; and
1 judge of the Supreme Court of Scotland. The martial tide
is now but feeble, though some additions could still be made
to the list.

was gathered to her rest not many months
ago. The later years of her life had been
spent by her at her beautiful home of Duisdale
in Sleat, looking across the Kyle to the heights
of Ben Screel and the recesses of Loch Hourn.
She was a skilled gardener and had transformed a bare hillside into a paradise of flowers
and fruit. She lent a helping hand to every
good work in the parish, managed the property
with skill and success, and knew the pedigree
and history of every family in the West Highlands. When I paid her my last visit, feeling
sure it would be the last, it was sad to see her
once tall muscular frame bowed down with
illness and pain, and to find her alone, the
last of her family left in Skye.

In former days, before inns had multiplied
in the Highlands, and especially before the
advent of the crowds of tourists, and the
inevitable modern 'hotels,' the manses were
often the only houses, other than those of
the lairds, where travellers could find decent
accommodation. Their hospitality was often
sought, and it became in the end proverbial.
Kilbride was an excellent example of this
type of manse. Not only did it receive
every summer a succession of guests who
made it their home for weeks at a time,

but every visitor of note was sure of a kindly welcome, even if he were unexpected. Astonishing is the capacity of these plain-looking Highland houses. When the company assembles at dinner it may seem impossible that they can all find sleeping quarters under the same roof. Yet they are all stowed away not uncomfortably, sleep well, and come down next morning with appetites prepared to do full justice to a Highland breakfast.

In those Highland parishes where Gaelic is still commonly spoken, two services are held in the churches on Sunday, the first in that language and the second, after a brief interval, in English. This practice was followed in Strath. In the days of the Celtic Church, a chapel dedicated to Christ stood in the middle of the parish and was known as Kilchrist. On the same site, the Protestant Church was afterwards erected, and continued to be used until towards the middle of last century. But, like the adjacent manse, it fell into disrepair and was ultimately allowed to become the roofless ruin which stands in the midst of the old grave-yard of Kilchrist. Instead of rebuilding it, the heritors, about the year 1840, resolved to erect a new church at Broadford, nearer to the chief centre of population. For two Sundays in succession the services are held at Broadford; on the third Sunday they take place at a little chapel in Strathaird, on the western side of the parish, for the benefit of a mixed crofter and fishing community.

At the Gaelic service in the Broadford church, a prominent feature used to be the row of picturesque red-cloaked or tartan-shawled old women, who, sitting in front immediately below the pulpit, followed the prayers and the sermon with the deepest attention, frequently uttering a running commentary of sighs and groans, while now and then one could even see tears coursing down the wrinkles into which age and peat-reek had shrivelled their cheeks.

The Sundays at Strathaird were peculiarly impressive. The house party from the manse —family, guests and servants—walked to the shore of the sea-inlet of Loch Slapin, embarked there in rowing boats, and pulled across the fjord and along the base of the cliffs on the opposite side. No finer landscape could be found even amidst the famous scenery of Skye,—the pink and russet-coloured cones and domes of the Red Hills, and the dark pinnacles and crags of Blaven behind us, and the blue islands that closed in the far distance in front.

During the long incumbency of the minister's father, no built place of worship existed in Strathaird. The little chapel of the early Celtic Church, of which the memory is preserved in the name Kilmaree, had long disappeared, and the clergyman used to preach from a recess in the basalt crags, with a grassy slope in front on which his congregation sat to hear him. My host, however, in the early years of his tenancy of the parish, had succeeded in getting a small church erected wherein his people could be sheltered in bad weather. I can recollect one of these Sundays when the weather was absolutely perfect—a cloudless blue sky, the sea smooth as a mirror, and the air suffused with the calm peacefulness which seems so appropriate to a Sabbath. We were a large but singularly quiet party, as we steered for the little bay of Kilmaree, each wrapped up in the thoughts which the day or the scene suggested. As we approached our landing place, we were startled by two gun-shots in rapid succession on the hillside above us. The sound would under any circumstances have intruded somewhat harshly into the quiet of the landscape. But it was

Sunday, and such a thing as shooting on the Lord's day had never been heard of in Strath. An Englishman had rented the ground for the season, and he and his wife were now out with their guns. The surprise and horror with which this conduct was viewed by the minister and his family soon found an echo through the length and breadth of the parish.

The sacramental season brought together to Kilbride some of the other clergymen of Skye, whom it was always a pleasure to meet. They were a race of earnest, hard-working, and intelligent men,[1] though, having remained in the Establishment, they would have been stigmatised by the seceding party as 'Moderates' who had clung to their loaves and fishes, in spite of the example of the Free Kirk. I remember being especially struck by Mr. Macrae of Glenelg and Mr. Martin of Snizort. With Mr. Macrae I had afterwards more intercourse. Over and above his ministerial duties, to which he conscientiously devoted himself, his great delight in life was to be on the sea. He had a little

---

[1] It will be remembered what a high opinion Johnson formed of the learning and breeding of the West Highland clergy. There is no reason to think they have deteriorated since his time, though possibly their learning would not now be singled out for special eulogium.

yacht or cutter, on which he lived as much
as he could, and which, as it passed up and
down the lochs and kyles, was as familiar as
Hutcheson's steamers. He was never happier
than when, with his two daughters, he could
entertain some friend on a cruise in these
waters, and tell what he knew about the ruins
and legends of the district—the Pictish towers,
the mouldering Barracks, the traditions of
1715 and 1745, the Spanish invasion, the
battle of Glen Shiel, the naval pursuit and
the battering down of Eilean Donan Castle.
Once when I was staying at Inverinate, the
minister landed there from his little vessel,
and hearing that I wished to examine a piece
of the Skye shore south of Kyle Rhea, was
delighted to offer to convey me there and
back next day. My host jocularly remarked
that the visit would be sooner made by land
and crossing the Kyle at the ferry, than by
trusting to the minister. The little cruise,
however, was arranged, according to Mr.
Macrae's desire, and he duly dropped anchor
in front of Inverinate next morning. We
started early, and, with a gentle south-easterly
breeze and unclouded sky, made good progress
down Loch Duich. But the wind soon fell,
and we crept more and more slowly past the

ruined Eilean Donan into Loch Alsh. There could not have been a more glorious day for a lazy excursion, or a nobler landscape to gaze upon, as hour slipped after hour. Behind us rose the great range of the Seven Sisters of Kintail, in front were the hills of Sleat with the Cuillins peering up behind them, all suffused with the varying tints of the atmosphere. It was a source of keen interest to watch how the hues of peak and crag which one had actually climbed, were transformed in this aerial alembic, and one felt the truth of Dyer's beautiful lines :

> Mark yon summits, soft and fair,
> Clad in colours of the air,
> Which to those who journey near,
> Barren, brown, and rough appear.

The worthy minister, in his capacity of experienced yachtsman, playfully indulged in the usual whistling incantations that are supposed by the nautical imagination to propitiate Æolus, but without success. The air became so nearly motionless as to be able to give only an occasional sleepy flap to the sail. But we continued to move almost imperceptibly towards our destination, borne onward by the last efforts of the ebbing tide. By the time we had reached the open part of

Loch Alsh, however, and had come well in sight of the coast I intended to traverse, the tide turned and began to flow. Gradually the yacht was turned round with her prow directed up the loch, and to our disgust we saw ourselves being gradually carried back again. Helpless on a perfectly smooth sea, and without a breath of wind, we had to resign ourselves to fate, and got back opposite to Inverinate just in time for dinner.

Another Highland minister of a very different type lived on the shores of Loch Striven —a long inlet of the sea which runs far up among the mountains of Cowal, and opens out into the Firth of Clyde opposite to Rothesay. He was a bachelor and somewhat of a recluse, with many eccentricities which formed the basis of sundry anecdotes among his colleagues. One of these reverend brethren told me that the erection of a volunteer battery on the shore of Bute, where it looks up Loch Striven, greatly perturbed the old minister, for the reverberation of the firing rolled loud and long among the mountains. One morning before he was awake, the chimney-sweeps, by arrangement with his housekeeper, came to clean the chimneys. Part of their apparatus consisted of a perforated iron ball through which a rope was passed, and which by its weight dragged the rope down to the fireplace. By some mistake this ball was dropped down the chimney of the minister's bedroom, where, striking the grate with a loud noise, it rebounded on the floor. The rattle awoke the reverend gentleman, who, on opening his eyes and seeing, as he thought, a cannon-ball dancing across the room, exclaimed, 'Really, this is beyond my patience; it is bad enough to be deaved with the firing, but to have the shot actually sent into my house is more than I can stand. I'll get up and write to the commanding officer.'

As he had a comfortable manse and a fair stipend, various efforts were made by the matrons of the neighbourhood to induce the minister to take a wife, and he used innocently to recount these interviews to his co-presbyters, who took care that they should not lose anything by repetition to the world outside. One of these interviews was thus related to me. A lady in his parish called on him, and after praising the manse and the garden and the glebe, expressed a fear that he must find it a great trouble to manage his house as well as his parish. He explained that he had an excellent housekeeper, who

E

took great care of him, and managed the household to his entire satisfaction. 'Ah, yes,' said the visitor, 'I'm sure Mrs. Campbell is very careful, but she canna be the same as a wife to you. You must often be very lonely here, all by yourself. But if you had a wife she would keep you from wearying, and would take all the management of the house off your hands, besides helping you with the work of the parish. Now Mr. —— there's my Isabella, if you would but take her for your wife, she would be a perfect Abishag to you.' This direct and powerful appeal, however, met with no better success than others that had gone before it. The incorrigible old divine lived, and, I believe, died in single blessedness.

In the Lowlands the younger ministers, educated in Edinburgh or Glasgow, and accustomed to the modernised service of the churches, and the more distinctive ecclesiastical garb of the officiating clergy, have lost the angularity of manner which marked older generations. I can remember, however, a number of parish ministers who belonged to an earlier and perhaps now extinct type. Though thoroughly earnest and devoted men, they would be regarded at the present day as

at least irreverent, and their sayings and doings would no doubt scandalise modern eyes
and ears. One of these clergymen had a
large Ayrshire parish. He was apt to forget
things, and on remembering them, to blurt
them out at the most inappropriate times.
On one occasion he had begun the benedic-
tion at the close of the service, when he suddenly stopped, exclaiming: 'We've forgot the
psalm,' which he thereupon proceeded to read
out. Another time, in the midst of one of
his extempore prayers, he was asking for a
blessing on the clergyman who was to address the people in the afternoon, when he
interrupted himself to interject: 'It's in the
laigh Kirk, ye ken.'

One evening the same clergyman was dining
with a pleasant party at a laird's house about
a mile from the village, when it flashed across
his mind that he ought to have been at that
moment performing a baptism in the house of
one of the villagers. Hastily asking to be
excused for a little, as he had forgotten an
engagement, and with the assurance that he
would soon be back, he started off. It was
past nine o'clock before he reached the village
and knocked at the door of his parishioner.
There was no answer for a time, and after a

second and more vigorous knock, the window overhead was opened, and a voice demanded who was there. 'It's me, Mrs. Maclellan. I'm very sorry, indeed, to have forgotten about the baptism. But it's not too late yet.' 'O minister, we're in bed, and a' the fowk are awa'. We canna hae the baptism noo.' 'Never mind the folk, Mrs. Maclellan; is the bairn here?' 'Ow ay, the bairn's here, sure eneuch.' 'Weel, that will do, and so you maun let me in, and we'll hae the baptism after all.' The husband had meanwhile pulled some clothes on, and with his wife came downstairs to let in their minister. The 'teathings,' which the good woman had prepared with great care for her little festival, had been carried back to the kitchen, whither the husband had gone for a lamp. The woman appeared with the child, and begged that they would come into her parlour. But the minister, assuring her that the room made no difference, proceeded with the ceremony in the kitchen. When the moment came for sprinkling the baby, he dipped his hand into the first basin he saw. 'O stop, stop Mr——, that's the water I washed up the tea-cups and saucers in.' 'It will do as well as any other,' he said, and continued his prayer to the end of the short service. As soon as it was over, he started back to the laird's, and rejoined the party after an absence of about an hour.

To this baptismal experience another may be added, where the rite was celebrated in the face of great natural obstacles. Dr. Hanna relates that a Highland minister once went to baptise a child in the house of one of his parishioners, near which ran a small burn or river. When he came to the stream it was so swollen with recent rains that he could not ford it in order to reach the house. In these circumstances he told the father, who was awaiting him on the opposite bank, to bring the child down to the burn-side. Furnished with a wooden scoop, the clergyman stood on the one side of the water, and the father, holding the infant as far out in his arms as he could, placed himself on the other. With the foaming torrent between the participants, the service went on, until the time came for sprinkling the babe, when the minister, dipping the scoop into the water, flung its contents across at the baby's face. His aim, however, was not good, for he failed more than once, calling out to the father after each new trial : 'Weel, has't gotten ony yet?' When he did succeed, the whole contents of

the scoop fell on the child's face, whereupon
the disgusted parent ejaculated, 'Ach, Got
pless me, sir, but ye've trownt ta child.' Dr.
Chalmers, in telling this story, used to express
his wonder as to what the great sticklers for
form and ceremony in the sacraments would
think of such a baptism by a burn-side, performed with a wooden scoop.[1]

A certain parish church in Carrick, like
many ecclesiastical edifices of the time in
Scotland, was not kept with scrupulous care.
The windows seemed never to be cleaned, or
indeed opened, for cobwebs hung across them,

And half-starv'd spiders prey'd on half-starv'd flies.

There was an air of dusty neglect about the
interior, and likewise a musty smell. One
Sunday an elderly clergyman from another
part of the country was preaching. In the
midst of his sermon a spider, suspended from
the roof at the end of its long thread, swung
to and fro in front of his face. It came against
his lips and was blown vigorously away.
Again it swung back to his mouth, when, with
an indignant motion of his hands, he broke
the thread and exclaimed, 'My friends, this

[1] *Life of Chalmers*, vol. iv., p. 450. The catastrophe of the
last ladleful is not given by Dr. Hanna.

is the dirtiest kirk I ever preached in. I'm like to be pusioned wi'' speeders.'

It is recorded of an old minister in the west of Ross-shire that he prayed for Queen Victoria, 'that God would bless her and that as now she had grown to be an old woman, He would be pleased to make her a new man.'

The same worthy divine is said to have once prayed 'that we may be saved from the horrors of war, as depicted in the pages of the *Illustrated London News* and the *Graphic*.'

One of the most serious functions which the Presbyterian clergymen of Scotland had formerly to discharge was that of publicly examining their congregation in their knowledge of the Christian faith. Provided with a list of the congregation, the officiating minister in the pulpit proceeded to call up the members to answer questions out of the Shorter Catechism, or such other interrogatories as it might seem desirable to ask. Nobody knew when his turn would come, or what questions would be put to him, so that it was a time of trial and trepidation for old and young. The custom appears to be now obsolete, but reminiscences of its operation are still preserved.

An elderly minister was asked to take the catechising of the congregation in a parish in the pastoral uplands of the South of Scotland. He was warned against the danger of putting questions to a certain shepherd, who had made himself master of more divinity than some of his clerical contemporaries could boast, and who enjoyed nothing better than, out of the question put to him, to engage in an argument with the minister on some of the deepest problems of theology. The day of the ordeal at last came, the old doctor ascended the pulpit, and after the preliminary service put on his spectacles and unfolded the roll of the congregation. To the utter amazement of everybody, he began with the theological shepherd, John Scott. Up started the man, a tall, gaunt, sunburnt figure, with his maud over his shoulder, his broad blue bonnet on the board in front of him, and such a look of grim determination on his face as showed how sure he felt of the issue of the logical encounter to which he believed he had been challenged from the pulpit. The minister, who had clearly made up his mind as to the line of examination to be followed with this pugnacious theologian, looked at him calmly for a few moments, and then in a gentle voice asked, 'Wha made you,

John?' The shepherd, prepared for questions on some of the most difficult points of our faith, was taken aback by being asked what every child in the parish could answer. He replied in a loud and astonished tone, 'Wha made *me*?' 'It was the Lord God that made you, John,' quietly interposed the minister. 'Wha redeemed you, John?' Anger now mingled with indignation as the man shouted, 'Wha redeemed *me*?' The old divine, still in the same mild way, reminded him 'It was the Lord Jesus Christ that redeemed you, John,' and then asked further, 'Wha sanctified you, John?' Scott, now thoroughly aroused, roared out, 'Wha sanctified ME?' The clergyman paused, looked at him calmly, and said, 'It was the Holy Ghost that sanctified you, John Scott, if, indeed, ye be sanctified. Sit ye doon, my man, and learn your questions better the next time you come to the catechising.' The shepherd was never able to hold his head up in the parish thereafter.

An old woman who had got sadly rusty in her Catechism was asked, 'What is a sacrament?' to which she gave the following rather mixed answer, 'A sacrament is—an act of saving grace, whereby—a sinner out of a true knowledge of his sins—doth rest in his grave till the resurrection.'

Dr. Hanna used to tell of a shoemaker who lamented to his minister that he was spiritually in a bad way because he was not very sure of his title to the kingdom of heaven, and that he was physically bad because 'that sweep, his landlord, had given him notice to quit and he would have nowhere to lay his head.' The minister could only advise him to lay his case before the Lord. A week later the minister returned and found the shoemaker busy and merry. 'That was gran' advice ye gied me, minister,' said the man, 'I laid my case before the Lord, as ye tell't me—an' noo the sweep's deid.'

In connection with the regular clergy, reference may be made to the free-lances who, as street-preachers, have long taken their place among the influences at work for rousing the lower classes in our large towns to a sense of their duties. These men have often displayed a single-hearted devotion and persistence, in spite of the most callous indifference or even active hostility on the part of their auditors. The very homeliness of their language, which repels most educated people, gives them a hold on those who come to listen

to them, while now and then their vehement
enthusiasm rises into true eloquence. The
most remarkable of these men I have ever
listened to was a noted character in Edinburgh
during the later years of the first half of last
century, named Bobbie Flockhart. He was
diminutive in stature, but for this disadvantage
he endeavoured to compensate by taking care
that

> The apparel on his back,
> Though coarse, was reverend, and though bare, was black.

Eccentric in manner and speech, he long
continued to be an indefatigable worker for
the good of his fellow townsmen. He used
to spend the forenoon and afternoon of every
Sunday in flitting from church to church,
listening to the sermons, of each of which
he remained to hear only a small portion.
Then in the evening, not only of Sundays but
of week days, he would hold forth from a chair
or barrel outside the west gate of St. Giles,
and gather round him a crowd of loafers
from the High Street, who, it is to be feared,
were attracted to him rather by the expectation
of some new drollery of language, than from
any interest in the substance of his discourses.
They would interrupt him now and then with
ribald remarks, but they often met with such

a rebuke as turned the laugh against them, and increased the popularity of the preacher. He was discoursing one evening on the wickedness of the town, especially of the district in which his audience lived, when in his enthusiasm he pointed up in the direction of the Castle, where stands the huge historic cannon, and exclaimed: 'O that I could load Mons Meg wi' Bibles, and fire it doon every close in the High Street!' On another occasion he was depicting to the people the terrors of the day of judgment. 'Ay,' said he, 'some of you that mock me the day will be comin' up to me then and sayin', "Bobbie, ye'll mind us, we aye cam' to hear ye." But I'll no' help ye. Maybe ye'll think to cling on to my coat-tails, but I'll cheat ye there, for I'll put on a jacket.' He was fond of similes that could bring home to the rough characters around him the truths he sought to impress on them. He was once denouncing the careless ingratitude of man for all the benefits conferred on him by Providence. 'My friends,' he said, 'look at the hens when they drink. There's not ane o' them but lifts its heid in thankfulness, even for the water that is sae common. O that we were a' hens.'

CHAPTER III.

THE sermon in Scottish Kirks. Intruding animals in country
churches. The 'collection.' Church psalmody. Precentors
and organs. Small congregations in the Highlands. Parish
visitation. Survival of the influence of clerical teaching.
Religious mania.

FROM the time of the Reformation onwards
the sermon has taken a foremost place in the
service of the Church of Scotland. There
was a time when a preacher would continue
his discourse for five or six hours, and when
sometimes a succession of preachers would give
sermon after sermon and keep the congregation continuously sitting for ten hours. These
days of perfervid oratory are past. But a
sermon of an hour's duration or even more
may still be heard, and, when the preacher
is eloquent, will be listened to with deep
interest. This part of the service maintains
its early prominence. It is from his capacity
to preach that a man's qualifications for the

ministry are mainly judged, not merely by the church which licences him, but by the congregation which chooses him as its pastor. The half-yearly celebration of the sacrament, which included a fast-day, services on two or three week days, and a long 'diet' on Sunday, was appropriately known as 'The Preachings.' The Fast-Day, when the shops were closed and there were at least two services in the churches, forenoon and afternoon, became in the end a kind of public holiday in the large towns. Attracted to the country, rather than to the sermons, the people used to escape from town, and railways carried an ever-increasing number of excursionists away from the services of the Church. The ecclesiastical authorities at last, some years ago, put a stop to this scandal, and the Fast-Day no longer ranks as one of the public holidays of the year.

Scottish sermons have always had a prevalent doctrinal character and a markedly logical treatment of their subject. It has never been the habit north of the Tweed to think that 'dulness is sacred in a sound divine.' The clergy have appealed as much to the head as to the heart. In bygone generations the doctrines evolved from the text were divided into numerous heads, and these into subordinate sections and subsections, so that the attention of those listeners who remained awake was kept up as at a kind of intellectual exercise. If anyone wishes to realise the extent to which this practice of subdivision could be carried by an eminent and successful preacher, let him turn to the posthumous sermons of Boston of Ettrick.[1] Thus, in a sermon on 'Fear and Hope, objects of the Divine Complacency,' from the text, Psalms cxlvii. 11, this famous divine, after an introduction in four sections, deduced six doctrines, each subdivided into from three to eight heads; but the last doctrine required another sermon, which contained 'a practical improvement of the whole,' arranged under 86 heads. A sermon on Matthew xi. 28 was subdivided into 76 heads. If it is not quite easy to follow the printed sermon through this maze of sub-division, it must have been much more difficult to do so in the spoken discourse. All the enthusiasm and fire of the preacher must have been needed to rivet the

---

[1] *Primitiæ et Ultima, or the Early Labours and Last Remains that will meet the public eye*, etc., etc., *of the late Rev. and learned Mr. Thomas Boston, minister of the Gospel at Ettrick, now first published from his MSS.* In three volumes. Edinburgh, 1800.

attention and affect the hearts of his congregation. It is still usual to treat the subject of a text under different heads, but happily their number has been reduced to more reasonable proportions.

It was not given to every occupant of a pulpit to rival the fecundity and ingenuity of Boston of Ettrick in the elucidation of his text. A subdivision of a simpler type was made by the worthy old Highland divine who preached from the verse, 'The devil, as a roaring lion, walketh about, seeking whom he may devour.' Following a Highland habit of inserting an unnecessary pronoun after the noun to which it refers, he began his discourse thus : 'Let us consider this passage, my brethren, under four heads. Firstly, who the Devil, he is ; secondly, what the Devil, he is like ; thirdly, what the Devil, he doth ; and fourthly, who the Devil, he devoureth.'

In many instances the sermons prepared during the first few years of a ministry served for all its subsequent continuance, with perhaps some modifications or additions suggested by the altered circumstances of the time. It used to be said of some clergymen that they kept their sermons in a barrel, which when emptied was refilled again with the old MSS. Dr.

Hanna, the biographer of Chalmers, used to tell of one such minister who had preached the same short round of sermons for so many years that at last the beadle was deputed by one or two members of the congregation to ask whether, if he could not prepare a new sermon, he would at least give them a fresh text. Next Sunday, to the astonishment of the audience, the minister gave out a text from which he had never before preached : 'Genesis, first chapter, first verse, and first clause of the verse.' Every Bible was opened at the place, and the listeners, nearly all of whom were ignorant of the suggested arrangement, leant back in their pews in eager anticipation of the new sermon. With great deliberation the preacher began : '"In the beginning God created the heavens and the earth." Who this Nicodemus was, my brethren, commentators are not agreed.' And the old story of Nicodemus was repeated, as it had been so often before.

Sometimes the manuscript of a sermon was by mistake left behind at the manse, and the minister or the beadle had to set off to procure it. On one of these occasions, the manse being at some little distance from the church, the minister, who had to go and find the

F

document himself, gave out the 119th Psalm, that the congregation might engage in singing during his absence. When he returned with his MS. he asked his man, who was waiting for him anxiously at the door, how the congregation was getting on. 'O sir,' said he, 'they've got to the end of the 84th verse, and they're jist cheepin' like mice.'

To interrupt the service by requesting the congregation to sing a psalm or hymn is an expedient which sometimes relieves a clergyman when, from faintness or other cause, he finds a difficulty in performing his duty in the pulpit. Some years ago a young minister had recourse to this mode of extrication. On the conclusion of the service, one or two of his friends came to him in the vestry to ascertain what had ailed him. He told them that he could with difficulty refrain from laughing, and his only resource was to leave the pulpit. 'Did you see,' he asked, 'a man with an extraordinarily red head sitting in the front of the gallery?' 'Yes, we noticed him, but he appeared to be a quiet attentive listener.' 'So he was, so he was; but did you see a small boy sitting behind him? That young rascal so fascinated me that, though I tried hard to look elsewhere, I could not keep my eyes from sometimes turning to watch him. He was holding up the forefinger of his left hand behind the red head, as if he were heating an iron bolt in a furnace, and he would then thump it on the desk in front of him, as if he were hammering the iron into shape. This went on until I had to leave the pulpit, and send the beadle up to the gallery to have the young sinner cautioned or removed.'

The English sermon in Highland churches was often a curious performance. As already mentioned, there were, and still generally are, two sermons—one in Gaelic as part of the earlier service, and one in English in the second part. Those of the congregation who thought they understood both languages might stay from the beginning to the end, but the purely Gaelic-speaking population generally thinned away after the Gaelic service. In some cases, the preacher's command of English being rather limited, his evident earnestness could hardly prevent a smile at his solecisms in grammar and the oddity of his expressions. Many years ago an acquaintance told me he had been yachting in Loch Eil, and on a Sunday of dreary rain and storm went ashore not far from the roots of Ben Nevis to attend the English service, when he heard the following passage from the lips of the preacher :

'Ah, my friends, what causes have we for gratitude ; O yes, for the deepest gratitude! Look at the place of our habitation. How grateful should we be that we do not leeve in the far north! O no ; amid the frost and the snaw, and the cauld and the weet, O no ; where there's a lang day tae half o' the year, O yes ; and a lang, lang nicht the tither, ah yes ; that we do not depend upon the *auroary boreawlis*, O no ; that we do not gang shivering about in skins, O no ; snoking amang the snaw like mowdiwarts, O no, no !

'And how grateful should we be too that we do not leeve in the far south, beneath the equawtor and a sun aye burnin', burnin'; where the sky's het, ah yes ; and the earth's het, and the water's het, and ye're burnt black as a smiddy, ah yes! where there's teegers, O yes ; and lions, O yes ; and crocodiles, O yes ; and fearsome beasts growlin' and girnin' at ye amang the woods ; where the very air is a fever, like the burnin' breath o' a fiery draigon. That we do not leeve in these places, O *no* ! NO !! NO !!!

'But that we leeve in this *blēssed* island o' ours, called Great Britain, O yes! yes! and in

that pairt o' it named Scotland, and in that
bit o' auld Scotland that looks up at Ben
Naivis, O *yes*! YES!! YES!!! where there's
neither frost nor cauld, nor wind nor weet,
nor hail, nor rain, nor teegers, nor lions, nor
burnin' suns, nor hurricanes, nor'——— At this
part of the discourse a fearful gust from Ben
Nevis aforesaid drove in the upper sash of the
window at the right hand of the pulpit, and
rudely interrupted the torrent of eloquence.[1]

When we remember the length and techni-
cality of the sermons, the bad ventilation of
the kirks, and the effects of six days of toil
on a large number of each congregation, we
can hardly wonder that somnolence should be
prevalent in Scotland. Many anecdotes on this
subject have long been in circulation. The
same tale may be recognized under various
guises, the preacher or sleeper being altered

---

[1] Many years ago I told this story to my friend Mr. Thomas
Constable (son of Scott's publisher), and a few days thereafter
received a note from him asking if I would write it down.
This I did, and he told me afterwards that for a time he carried
my MS. in his pocket and read from it to his friends, but that
the paper becoming tender with frequent use, he had the
manuscript thrown into type, struck off a number of copies,
and circulated them among his acquaintance. One of these
copies must have fallen into the hands of Mr. Mark Boyd,
who, in his *Social Gleanings*, London, 1875, p. 57, printed the
story as here given.

according to local circumstances. Perhaps no series illustrates better how such stories continue to float down through generation after generation, and are always reappearing as new, when they receive a fresh personal application. Sleeping in church is such a natural failing, and the reproof of it from the pulpit is so obvious a consequence, that even if no memory of the old incidents should survive, the recurrence of similar circumstances could hardly fail to give birth to similar anecdotes. For example, a story is at present in circulation to the effect that in a country church one Sunday the preacher after service walked through the kirkyard with one of the neighbouring farmers, and took occasion to remark to him, 'Wasn't it dreadful to hear the Laird of Todholes snoring so loud through the sermon?' 'Perfectly fearful,' was the answer, 'he waukened us a'.' Two or three generations ago a similar incident was said to have occurred at Govan, under the ministration of the well-known Mr. Thom, who in the midst of his sermon stopped and called out, 'Bailie Brown, ye mauna snore sae loud, for ye'll wauken the Provost.' But more than two centuries ago the following epigram appeared :—

Old South, a witty Churchman reckoned,
Was preaching once to Charles the Second,
But much too serious for a court,
Who at all preaching made a sport:
He soon perceived his audience nod,
Deaf to the zealous man of God.
The Doctor stopp'd; began to call,
'Pray wake the Earl of Lauderdale:
My Lord! why, 'tis a monstrous thing,
You snore so loud—you'll wake the King.'

Though this scene took place in the south of England, it is interesting to note that the snorer specially singled out for rebuke was a Scottish nobleman.

Now and then a reproof from the pulpit has drawn down on the minister a sarcastic reply from the unfortunate sleeper, as in the case of the somnolent farmer who was awakened by the minister calling on him to rouse himself by taking a pinch of snuff, and who blurted out 'Put the snuff in the sermon, sir,'—an advice which found not a little sympathy in the congregation.

In a parish church about the middle of Ayrshire the central passage leading from the entrance to the pulpit is paved with large stone-flags. On the right side a worthy matron had her family pew, wherein, overcome with drowsiness, she used to fall asleep, with her head resting on her large brass-clasped Bible. She was an admirable housekeeper and farmer, looking after all the details of management herself. In her dreams in church her thoughts would sometimes wander back to her domestic concerns and show that she was not 'mistress of herself, though china falls.' One Sunday, in the course of her slumbers, she succeeded in pushing her massive Bible over the edge of the pew. As it fell on the stone-floor, its brass mountings made a loud noise, at which she started up with the exclamation, 'Hoot, ye stupid jaud, there's anither bowl broken.'

The genial Principal of Glasgow University, in the course of a public speech a year or two ago, told a story of an opposite kind. An old couple in his country parish had taken with them to church their stirring little grandson, who behaved all through the service with preternatural gravity. So much was the preacher struck with the good conduct of so young a listener, that, meeting the grandfather at the close of the service, he congratulated him upon the remarkably quiet composure of the boy. 'Ay,' said the old man with a twinkle in his eye, 'Duncan's weel threetened afore he gangs in.'

When an afternoon service is held, the attendance is sometimes apt to be scanty. A minister who was annoyed at a lukewarmness of this kind on the part of his congregation, remonstrated with them on the subject. 'I canna tell,' he said, 'how it may look to the Almichtie that sae few o' ye come to the second diet o' worship, but I maun say that it's showin' unco little respect to mysel'.'

In summer weather, when the doors and windows of churches are sometimes kept open for air, occasional unwelcome intruders distract the people and disturb the preacher. Butterflies and small birds are the most frequent; dogs are not uncommon, and in some districts these calls are varied by the occasional appearance of a goat. A dog is amenable to the sight of the minister's man approaching with a stick, and bolts off without needing any audible word of command, but a goat is a much more refractory visitor. One of these creatures entered a country church one Sunday in the midst of the service and deliberately marched down the central passage. Of course every eye in the congregation was turned upon it, and the luckless preacher found much difficulty in proceeding with his discourse. The beadle at last sprang from his seat and proceeded to meet the intruder. He had no stick, however, and the goat showed fight by charging him with its horns and making him beat a retreat. A friendly umbrella was thereupon passed out to him from one of the pews, and he returned to the combat. By spreading his arms and wielding the umbrella, he prevented the animal from reaching the pulpit stairs and succeeded in turning it. But once or twice it wheeled round again, as if to renew the fight. He contrived, however, to press it onwards as far as the church porch, when, lifting up his foot and dealing the goat a kick which considerably quickened its retreat, he gave vent to his feelings of anger and indignation in an imprecation, distinctly audible through half the church, 'Out o' the house o' God, ye brute.'

A characteristic feature of many churches in Scotland is the 'collection,' that is, the gathering of the contributions of the congregation for the poor of the parish or other purpose. In the Highlands where there are services both in Gaelic and English, the performance is repeated at the end of each. One or more of the elders, attired in Sunday garb, and looking as sad and solemn as if they were at a funeral, take the 'ladle' or wooden box at the end of a pole, and push it into each pew. The alms as they are dropped into the receptacle make a noise so distinctly audible over the building that a practised ear can make a shrewd guess as to the value of the coin deposited. Nearly the whole contribution is in coppers, only the larger farmers and the laird's families furnishing anything of higher value. Hence such congregations have been profanely valued at threepence a dozen. An amusing incident in one of these collections took place at a parish church in the west of Cowal. A family whom I used to visit there had come to their seat in the gallery while the earlier service was still going on, and when the Gaelic ladle came round they put into it their contributions. After the ladle had traversed the church at the end of the second service and was being brought back to the foot of the pulpit, the minister, who noticed that it had not been taken up to the laird's seat, beckoned vigorously to the man who was approaching with the money and pointed to the gallery. In response he received only a knowing shake of the head from the collector, who at last, impatient at the ministerial gesticulations, exclaimed aloud, 'Na, na, sir, its a' richt, I wass takin' the laird's money at the Gaelic.' In this same kirk on another occasion, after the whole contributions of the congregation had been collected, the box came up to the gallery, but unluckily was carried violently against the corner of a pew, the bottom came out, and the accumulated coppers rattled noisily to the floor.

Another part of the church service which cannot but strike a stranger, especially in the Highlands, is the singing. In the more remote and primitive parishes the precentor, standing in a lower desk directly under the minister, reads out one, now more usually two lines of the psalm, and then strikes up the tune. At the end of the first two lines, he reads out the second two, which he proceeds to sing as before. The congregation usually joins heartily in the music, which is the only part of the service wherein it can actively participate.

It is not always easy to secure a precentor. He must, in the first place, be a man of tried good character, and in the second place, he must of course be able to distinguish the metres of the psalms, and have voice and ear enough to raise at least three or four psalm-tunes. His repertoire is seldom much more extensive. Occasionally he begins a tune that will not suit the metre of the psalm, or he loses himself altogether. A precentor in the north Highlands to whom this happened, suddenly stopped and exclaimed, 'Och, bless me, I'm aff the tune again.' Another more sedate worthy struck up the tune three times, but always lost it at the second line. He paused, looked round the congregation, and after solemnly saying 'Hoots, toots, toots,' went at it the fourth time successfully. When the precentor at Peebles had failed twice in his efforts, the old minister looked over the pulpit and said aloud to him, 'Archie, try it again, and if ye canna manage it, tak' anither tune.'

A precentor is naturally jealous of any more practised and clearer voice than his own, which, he rightly thinks, ought to predominate. In the little Free Church of Raasay Island, the precentor had it all his own way until the minister's sister came. She sat at the far end of the church, and, having some knowledge of music and a good voice, she made herself well heard as she sang in much quicker time than the slow drawl to which the people had been accustomed. Before the precentor had done a line she was ready to begin the next, and the half

of the congregation nearest to her followed
her excellent lead. This was too much for the
precentor. He raised his voice till it almost
cracked with the strain, and for a few notes
drowned the rival performer at the other end.
But he could not keep it up, and as his notes
dropped, the clear sweet voice of the lady
came out as before. Sitting about the middle
of the church, I was able to appreciate the
strange see-saw in the psalmody.

The most remarkable change which has
taken place within living memory in the services of the Scottish Church is unquestionably the introduction of instrumental music.
In most of the large congregations of the
chief towns, the precentor has given way to
an organ, which leads the choir, as the choir
leads the congregation. Had any one in the
earlier half of last century been audacious
enough to predict that in a couple of generations the 'kist o' whistles,' which had been
long banished as a sign and symbol of black
popery, would be reintroduced and welcomed
before the end of the century, he would have
been laughed to scorn, or branded as himself
a limb of the prelatic Satan. Of course, there
has been much searching of heart over this
innovation, and many have been the head-

shakings and even open denunciations of such manifest backsliding. But the cause of enlightenment has steadily gained ground in the Lowlands, and a few generations hence it may not improbably prevail even over the Highlands. Meanwhile in most Highland parishes, the first notes of an organ in the church would probably drive the majority of the congregation out of doors, and lead to years of angry controversy.

The horror of anything savouring of what is thought to be popery shows itself sometimes in determined opposition to even the most innocent and useful changes. Sir Lauder Brunton has told me that in a Roxburghshire parish with which he is well acquainted, the church being excessively cold in winter, a proposal was mooted to introduce a stove for the purpose of heating it. This innovation, however, met with a strong resistance, especially from one member of the congregation, who said that a stove had a pipe like an organ, and he would have nothing savouring of popery in the Kirk of Scotland. He actually delayed the reform for a time.

In the same county, where it had been the custom from time immemorial to winnow the corn with the help of the wind, a farmer, alive to the value of modern improvements, procured and began to use a machine which created an artificial and always available current of air. He was at once rebuked for an impious defiance of the ways of Providence.

A proposal to put a stove into a Fifeshire parish met with the opposition of one of the heritors, who, when the minister came to him for a subscription towards the warming of the kirk, indignantly refused, asking, 'D'ye think John Knox asked for a stove, even for the cauldest kirk he ever preached in? Na, na, sir, warm the folk wi' your preachin', and they'll never think about the cauld.'

At the time of the Disruption of the Church of Scotland in 1843 the congregations were apt to side with their minister, if he were an able and efficient pastor to whom they were attached. Thus in Skye, as I have above mentioned, so powerful was the influence of John Mackinnon among his people that he kept them with him in the pale of the Establishment. But in most Highland parishes the Free Church early took ground, and in a large number it has been so predominant that the congregation of the Parish Church sometimes consists of little more than the clergyman and his family. In such cases the position of the adherents of the 'Auld Kirk' may sometimes be rather trying. More especially is it felt by the 'minister's man,' who is sometimes placed in sad straits in his endeavour to put the best face on the situation and conceal the feebleness of his flock. Without knowing his official position, or to which of the churches he belonged, I once met one of these worthies in the west of Ross-shire, and, with a friend who accompanied me, had some talk with him about the parish.

'How does the Established Church get on here?' we asked.

'O fine, fine, sirs.'

'Has the minister been here a long time?'

'Ow ay, it'll be a long time noo, I'm sure.'

'And has he a large congregation?'

'Ow ay, it's a fery goot congregation, whatefer.'

'Is it as big as the Free Kirk?'

'Weel, I'll no say that it will be just as big as the Free Kirk.'

'How many do you think there may be in church on Sunday?'

'Weel, ye see, there'll be sometimes more and sometimes fewer.'

G

'But have you no idea how many they may be?'

'Weel, sir, I dinna think I wass ever counting them.'

'You go to the parish church yourself, I think?'

'O, to be sure, I do: where wad ye think I wad be goin' else?'

It was quite clear that our interlocutor must be a staunch adherent of the Auld Kirk, and probably had some scantiness of the congregation to conceal; but we had no idea then of what we learnt soon afterwards, that he was no less a personage than the 'minister's man,' and that, saving the family from the manse and an occasional stranger, he was himself the whole congregation.

It has been made a matter of reproach to the clergy of the Scottish Church that, though they spend more time over the preparation of their sermons and place these on a higher intellectual level than is common in the English communion, they fall short of their brethren south of the Tweed in the assiduity of their visitation of their people. Where a parish extends over an area of many square miles, it must obviously be difficult for the minister to move freely and constantly among his parishioners, so as to be in close touch with all of them in their mundane as well as their spiritual affairs. In such cases, he finds it necessary to arrange the times of his visits, which are thus apt to become somewhat formal ceremonies, announced beforehand, and prepared for by those to whom notice is given. An example of this kind is related of a minister who had recently been appointed to the parish of Lesmahagow, and who made known from the pulpit one Sunday that he would visit next day a certain hilly district of the parish. Accordingly, on Monday morning he set out, and, after a walk of some seven or eight miles, arrived at a farm-house, where he meant to begin. After knocking for some time and getting no reply, he hailed a boy outside, when the following conversation ensued :

'Is Mr. Smith at home?'

'Na.'

'Is Mrs. Smith here?'

'Na.'

'Are you their son?'

'Ay.'

'Well, I have walked a long way, and I would like to sit and rest for a little. May

I go in?' (answering the question by entering). 'And did your father and mother not expect me?'

'Na, they didna think ye wad begin up here; sae they're awa' doon to the roup o' Ritchie's farm.'

'Well, now, my man, are these all the books that your father has in the house?'

'Ay.'

'Now tell me which of them does he use oftenest?'

'That ane,' pointing to a large leather-covered family Bible.

'O, the Bible; that's right: I am pleased to know that; and when does he use it?'

'On Sabbath mornin's.'

'Only once a week! Well, how does he do? Does he read it aloud to you all?'

'Na, he shairps his raazors on't.'

I once had quarters at South Queensferry in a house through the centre of which ran the boundary between that burgh and the adjacent parish of Dalmeny. I asked my landlady how she arranged about the claims of the clergy. 'Well, ye see, I go to the Burgh Kirk, and my minister comes to see me frae time to time. And Mr Muir of Dalmeny, he visits me too, but I try to be quite fair to them both. The parlour here is in the burgh, so I take my ain minister in there, and, as the other half of the house is in Dalmeny, I put the other minister in the kitchen, which belongs to his parish.'

In the striking delineation which Wordsworth has given of the early surroundings of his 'Wanderer,' and the circumstances that moulded his character, special stress is laid on the clerical influence which from infancy had guarded this son of the Braes of Athol.

> The Scottish Church, both on himself and those
> With whom from childhood he grew up, had held
> The strong hand of her purity; and still
> Had watched him with an unrelenting eye.

It is to be feared, however, that the result of such continual guardianship is to be recognised rather in the theological bent of the people than in their moral behaviour. The high standard of conduct held up in the pulpit, and generally followed by the clergy themselves, has not prevented the statistics of drunkenness and illegitimacy from attaining an unenviable notoriety. Yet no one can turn over the pages of the records of kirk-sessions and presbyteries without obtaining a deep impression of the untiring earnestness and devotion with which the Church has struggled against these two great national sins. If in the heyday of her power she could not eradicate the evils, her task must now be tenfold more onerous, when the 'strong hand' can no longer reach large masses of the population, and when the 'unrelenting eye,' though as keenly watchful as ever, can only note the decadence which the hand is powerless to reclaim. Unhappily a spirit of heathen ignorance, or of pagan indifference, has largely replaced the unquestioning faith of an older time, especially among the artisans of the large towns and the miners in the great coal-fields. It is mainly in the country districts, where social changes advance more slowly, that the religious instruction given at school and in church still continues to colour the outlook of the people on life here and hereafter.

If indeed we could judge from expressions that have survived from older generations, we might infer that many of the articles of the Christian faith retain a firm hold on minds which, if questioned on the subject, would probably express doubt or denial of them, such as the doctrine of a material heaven and hell, of a system of future rewards and punishments, of a personal devil intent on man's ruin, and of the sinfulness of Sunday work.

The way in which the acceptance of a material heaven and hell shows itself in ordinary conversation, might be illustrated by many anecdotes. One or two examples may here suffice. About forty years ago a well-known wealthy iron-master gave a dinner-party at his country house. Among his guests was an old friend of mine, from whom he had purchased a portion of his estate. The conversation turned on the great changes that had taken place in the district within the memory of those present, —the dying out of old families and the incoming of new, the making of railways, the laying out of roads, the growth of villages, and so forth,— when my friend remarked, 'Ah, me! I dare say I would see just as much change again if I were to come down sixty years hence.' Whereupon the host instantly ejaculated from the other end of the room, 'What's that ye say? Come down! Tak' care ye haena to come up.'

Of similar character is another Ayrshire story which has been told of a man who built a large and ostentatious tomb for himself and family, of which he was so proud that he boasted to the gravedigger that it would last till the day of judgment, when they might have some trouble to get up out of it. As the man's reputation was none of the highest, the gravedigger replied, 'I'm thinkin' ye needna be wonderin' how ye're to come up, for if they knock the bottom out o't ye'll aiblins gang doun.'

A country doctor, who was attending a laird, had instructed the butler of the house in the art of taking and recording his master's temperature with a thermometer. On repairing to the house one morning he was met by the butler, to whom he said : 'Well, John, I hope the laird's temperature is not any higher to-day?' The man looked puzzled for a moment, and then replied : 'Weel, I was just wonderin' that mysell. Ye see he deed at twal' o'clock.'

A clergyman's son had taken to drink, and had given great trouble and pain to his worthy father. On one occasion, after a debauch of several days, he returned to the manse in the evening, and found that there had been a presbytery dinner in the house, and that the reverend fathers who had dined were now engaged over their toddy and talk in the study. He made for the room, and was immediately welcomed by his father, who tried to put the best face he could on the situation. He asked the young man where he had been. 'In hell,' was the answer. 'Ah, and what did you find there?' 'Much the same as I find here: I couldna see the fire for ministers.'

In a country parish in the West of Scotland the minister's man was a noted pessimist, whose only consolation to his friends in any calamity consisted in the remark, 'It micht hae been waur.' One morning he was met by the minister, who told him he had had such a terrible dream that he had not yet been able to shake off the effects of it. 'I dreamt I was in hell, and experienced the torments of the lost. I never suffered such agony in my life, and even now I shudder when I think of it.' The beadle's usual consolatory remark came out, 'It micht hae been waur.' 'O John, John, I tell you it was the greatest mental distress I ever suffered in my life. How could it have been worse?' 'It micht hae been true,' was the reply.

Cases of religious mania have been common enough in Scotland, where questions of theology have for centuries been keenly debated among all classes of the community. It has been said that 'the worst of madmen is a saint run mad.' Whether this dictum be true or not there would appear to have been always cases where brooding upon some one doctrine of the Christian faith has led to mental aberration more or less serious. An instance of this kind occurred in the north of Ayrshire, where a man, who had lost his wits over theological speculation, would sometimes accost a stranger on a quiet country road, and taking him by the button-hole would abruptly ask him, 'What do you think of effectual calling? Isn't it a damned shame? Good day to you.' And off the poor fellow marched, ready to propound the same or some similar problem to the next passenger he would meet.

A less pronounced case of the same tendency was that of a countryman who felt much aggrieved by the story of the fall of man as told in the Book of Genesis. 'And it comes specially hard on me,' he would complain, 'for I never could byde apples raw or cooked a' my days.'

CHAPTER IV.

ALTHOUGH ever since the Reformation the clergy have done their best to eradicate the pagan superstitions, which were alluded to in a previous chapter, traces of these superstitions have survived down to the present day in the Highlands. Even so late as the beginning of last century, people in the Lewis continued to make offerings of mead, ale, or gruel, to the God of the Sea. A man at midnight between Wednesday and Thursday walked waist-deep into the sea, poured out the offering and chanted the following prayer :

> O god of the sea
> Put weed in the drawing-wave
> To enrich the ground
> To shower on us food.

Those behind the offerer took up the chant and wafted it along the midnight air.[1]

An interesting account of the surviving Highland superstitions will be found in two recently published volumes by the late Rev. John Gregorson Campbell, parish minister in the island of Tiree, who devoted himself with unwearied enthusiasm to collect the fading customs and traditions of the Hebrides and the Western Highlands.[2] In my early wanderings over Skye I came upon many relics of the pagan period. At Kilbride, for example, one is reminded of a pre-Protestant or even a pre-Christian past by the tall rude standing stone known as the Clach na h-Annait, or stone of Annat, a name which, by some Gaelic scholars, is thought to be that of a pagan goddess, though by others it is regarded as a term of the early Celtic Church, applied to a chapel where the patron-saint was educated, or where his relics were kept. Near the obelisk is the Tobar na h-Annait, or Annat's well.

The fairies once formed an active and

---

[1] A. Carmichael, *Carmina Gadelica* (1900), vol. i. p. 163.

[2] *Superstitions of the Highlands and Islands of Scotland, collected entirely from oral sources*, 1900, and *Witchcraft and Second Sight in the Highlands and Islands of Scotland*, 1902.

important community among the population
of Strath. One of their chief abodes was
underneath a large green mound in the
middle of the valley, called after them Sithein
(Sheean). Such fairy dwellings were looked
upon with veneration ; and it was a popular
belief that the 'people of peace' who lived in
them liked to have them kept scrupulously
clean. Hence to remove the droppings of
any horses or cattle that had strayed upon
the rich green sward was believed to be a
grateful deed to these beings, who would
manifest their thankfulness by some significant
reward to the thoughtful cotter who took the
pains to do it. With the acknowledged example of the fairies before them, I never could
quite understand how the West Highlanders
could themselves live in such conditions of dirt
and untidiness as have been so long prevalent
among them.

The top of the Sithein of Strath is crowned
with a few gnarled, stunted, storm-blasted
black-thorns, like a group of shrivelled carlines
stretching out their arms towards the east.
These trees, or rather bushes, have undergone
no appreciable change since I first saw them
half a century ago, and I was told by the
minister that they had not altered at all in

his time, so that they must have stood, much
as they are now, for more than a hundred
years. If one first comes upon these weird
forms in the mist of a stormy evening, when
they seem to remain motionless, though the
wind howls down the valley of Strath Suardil,
one can easily realise how they might be connected in popular belief with the mysterious
beings of another world. The fairy cattle,
or red deer, live up in the corries of the Red
Hills. On the top of one of these eminences
a carline lies buried under a cairn and the
hill is named after her, Beinn na Cailleach.

Near the house of Kilbride, a spring or
well has been said, for more than two hundred
years, to contain a single live trout. It is
mentioned by Martin in his *Description of
the Western Islands of Scotland*, written at
the end of the seventeenth century, where he
states that the fish had been seen for many
years, and the natives, though they often caught
it in their wooden pails, were careful to preserve
it from being destroyed. The minister assured
me that there was still a trout in the well,
whether the same as that spoken of by Martin,
he could not affirm. I must confess that I
was never able to catch a sight of this
legendary fish.

As in Ireland, springs or wells in the Highlands, not improbably famous even in pagan times, have often been subsequently dedicated to Celtic saints, and have long been credited with medicinal or miraculous healing powers. There used to be a number of such wells in Skye, which were visited by the sick and the maimed, who went round them three times *deiseal*, that is, with the sun, or from east to west, and drank of the water or bathed the injured limb with it. On retiring they always left by the side of the spring, or on its overhanging tree, some little offering, were it only a torn bit of rag. On the mainland some of the holy wells, or saints' wells, are still objects of pilgrimage from a distance. Thus the well of St. Maree, or the Red Priest, on a little islet in Loch Maree, still attracts its patients, and the trees that overshadow it are hung with tags of rag and ribbon which they have placed there as votive offerings. This tribute of recognition doubtless dates back to pagan times. It was adopted by the Celtic and then by the Roman Catholic Church, and in spite of the denunciations of the reformers and their successors, it is rendered still by presbyterians, who give it from the mere force of custom. Some years ago, while boating

along the coast south of the Sutors of
Cromarty, I was struck with the strange
appearance of a tree that overhung the upper
part of the beach. From a distance it seemed
to be decked with blossoms or leaves of black,
white, red, and other colours. On landing I
found that these were bits of rag hung up
by the pilgrims who had come to drink of
the saint's well that gushed forth under the
shadow of the tree. In the same region
the well of Craiguck, parish of Avoch, has
long been a place of annual resort on the
first Sunday of May, old style. The water
used to be taken in a cup and spilt three
times on the ground before being tasted, and
thereafter a rag or ribbon was hung on the
bramble-bush above the spring.

In connection with this subject, it may
be mentioned here that some years before
his death, the late Mr. Patrick Dudgeon, of
Cargen in Kirkcudbright, told me that he had
cleared out one of these holy or pilgrim wells
on his property, which had fallen into disuse,
though still occasionally visited for curative
purposes. Among the stuff which had gathered
on the bottom of the pool, a large number of
copper coins was found, extending in date from
the reign of Victoria back to the times of the

Stuarts. The surfaces of the coins had in many cases been dissolved to such an extent as to reduce the metal to little more than the thinness of writing paper. Yet so persistent was the internal structure superinduced by the act of minting that, even in this attenuated condition, the obverse and reverse could still be deciphered.

Another superstitious belief of which I found lingering traces in Skye was that of the water-horse (*Each Uisge*) and the water-bull (*Tarbh Uisge*). These fabulous creatures were believed to inhabit some of the lakes in the lonely moorland of the south of Strath. I could not find anybody who had actually seen one, but the belief in their existence was by no means confined to 'the superstitious, idle-headed eld.' I was told that the water-horse had a special fondness for young women, and would seize them and carry them off into the lake, whence they were never more seen. No young woman in the parish would venture near one of these sheets of water, except in daylight, and not without fear and trembling even then.

Relics of old superstitions could be noticed, sometimes even among the details of domestic management in the houses of intelligent people.

H

At Kilbride they would not make butter at a certain state of the moon. In like manner they took care that the peats should only be cut when the moon was on the wane. Though the reason alleged was that the moon must influence the milk, just as much as it did the tides, there could be little doubt that the habit was a relic of the same pagan belief which survives in bowing to the new moon and turning a coin in her honour. The prejudice against the sow as an unclean animal survived in full vigour. Not only were no pigs kept at Kilbride, but, so far as I was aware, no ham, pork, or bacon ever formed part of the commissariat of the house.

While the reformed clergy endeavoured to uproot the ancient superstitions, they at the same time were engaged in rivetting upon the people other forms of superstition destined to exercise much more pernicious effects than those they replaced. One of these was their doctrine of the Devil and his doings, and another the enforcement of the views which they gradually adopted as to Sabbath observance.

Much has been written on the subject of the Devil and his influence in religion, mythology, superstition, and literature, as well as on topographical features. The subject is discussed from a historical point of view in the learned volumes of Professor Roskoff of Vienna; but there is probably still room for a dissertation on the part which the Devil has played in colouring the national imagination of Scotland. As is well known, all over the country instances may be found where remarkable natural features are assigned to his handiwork. Thus we have 'Devil's punchbowls' among the hills and 'Devil's cauldrons' in the river-channels. Perched boulders are known as 'Deil's putting stanes,' and natural heaps and hummocks of sand or gravel have been regarded as 'Deil's spadefuls.' Even among the smaller objects of nature a connection with the enemy of mankind has suggested itself to the popular mind. The common puff-ball is known as the 'Deil's snuff-box'; some of the broad-leaved water-plants have been named 'Deil's spoons'; the dragonfly is the 'Deil's darning-needle.' Then the unlucky number thirteen has been stigmatised as the 'Deil's dozen,' and a perverse unmanageable person as a 'Deil's buckie.'

In association with witches and warlocks Satan plays a leading part in the legends, myths, and superstitions of the country. The general popular estimation of him in Scotland has never been so admirably expressed in words as by Burns, more particularly in his *Address to the Deil*. But even in his day ocular proofs of the evil spirit's presence and activity were becoming scanty, and the poet had to rely partly on the testimony of his 'rev'rend grannie.' In the interval since that poem was written, now nearly a century and a quarter ago, the belief in a personal devil, ready to present himself as a hairy monster with a tail, cloven feet, and horns—'Auld Hornie, Satan, Nick, or Clootie'—has still further faded. The late Dr. Sloan of Ayr, however, told me that in the year 1835, after he came out from making the post-mortem examination of a poor miner who was taken out alive from a coal-pit near the village of Dailly, after having been shut up for three weeks without food, but who died three days after his rescue, he was accosted by some of the older miners with the question, 'Did ye fin' his feet?' The doctor had to confess that he had not specially looked at the man's feet, whereat the miners went off with a knowing expression on their faces, as much as to say, 'We thought you had not, for if you had, you would have found them to be cloven hoofs. We believe that the body was not that of our

John Brown, but the Devil himself, who had come for some bad purpose of his own.'

Although even the most superstitious cotter in the loneliest uplands of the country would hardly expect it to be possible now that the Devil should waylay him at night, relics of this belief may be found in the language of to-day, especially in the imprecations prompted by anger or revenge. Various versions have been given of an illustrative incident which I have been told really occurred at a slim wooden foot-bridge over the river Irvine in Ayrshire. An ill-tempered man was crossing the bridge, when a dog, coming the opposite way, brushed against his leg. 'Deil burst ye,' exclaimed he. Immediately behind him came a woman, and as they were nearly across the bridge a small boy, trying to press past the man on the narrow pathway, was greeted with the same angry imprecation. The little fellow drew back, but was encouraged by the voice of the woman behind, who called out to him, 'Never fear, my wee man, come on here outowre. The Deil canna harm ye eenoo, for he's thrang on the ither side o' the brig burstin' a dog.'

Occasionally the apparition of a dark hairy body crowned with a pair of horns has received a natural explanation, but not before revealing

the innate belief in the designs and power of
the Prince of Darkness.   There used to be a
goat in Greenock which occasionally escaped
from its enclosure, and prowled about the
streets in the dark.   On one of these occasions,
in the midst of its perambulations, it came to
an outside stair, which it thereupon ascended.
At the top of the short flight of steps stood
the closed door of a room wherein an elderly
couple were asleep in bed. Nannie, being of
an inquisitive turn, and having some experience
of gate-fastenings, easily succeeded in opening
the door and entering the room.   The fire still
gave a low ruddy light, and the goat at once
descried a tin pitcher, at the bottom of which
there remained some milk over from the frugal
supper of the little household.   The animal
had forced its nose so well down in order to
lap the last drops, that when it raised its head
it brought up the pitcher firmly clasped round
it, and the handle fell with a thump against
the metal. The crash awoke the old woman,
who in the dim light could see a pair of horns
and a hairy body.   Thinking it was the arch
enemy that had come for her, she called out
imploringly, 'O tak' John, tak' John; I'm no
ready yet.'

The adjective 'devilish' has in recent times

come to be used by many in the humbler walks
of life as almost synonymous with wonderful,
extraordinary, supernatural; as may be illustrated by the ejaculation of a Paisley workman,
who with a companion ascended to the top of
Goatfell in Arran. He had never conceived
anything so impressive as the panorama seen
from that summit, with its foreground of serrated crests and deep glens. After the first
silence of amazement, he exclaimed to his friend,
'Man, Tam, the works o' God's deevilish.'

It is an interesting study to trace among
the records of kirk-sessions and presbyteries
the gradual growth of strict Sabbath observance until it became a kind of fetish. The
first reformers enjoyed their relaxation on
Sunday, and for many years after the old
system had been displaced by the new, the
youth of the country continued to play their
pastimes after church hours. Markets were still
held on Sunday, and in many places plays
were performed, especially that of *Robin Hood*.
But after the establishment of the reformed
religion in 1560 these amusements and employments came to be frowned upon more and
more by the clergy, who by persistent efforts
succeeded in securing a succession of Acts
of Parliament which made Sabbath-breaking

an offence punishable by a civil magistrate.
Delinquents were everywhere brought up
before kirk-sessions and subjected to church
discipline, while, if they proved impenitent
sinners, they might be handed over to the civil
power for more condign treatment. Nevertheless, in spite of the stringency of these
regulations, the ecclesiastical authorities had to
undertake a long struggle before they finally
uprooted the effects of the usage of many
centuries, and succeeded in impressing on the
mind of the general community the belief that
what they called 'violating the Sabbath-day'
was an act of moral turpitude that could only
be expiated by exemplary punishment and
public confession of penitence. Under the
head of this violation were included some of
the most natural and innocent habits. Men
were warned that not only must they refrain
from all ordinary week-day work, but that they
must not take a walk on Sunday, either in
town or country, save to and from church.
They must not sit at their doors, but remain
within. They were expected to maintain a
solemn demeanour; laughing, whistling, or any
other sign of gaiety or frivolity being rigidly
proscribed. They might not bathe, or swim,
or shave. They were forbidden to visit

each other, to water their gardens, to ride on horseback, or to travel in any other fashion. They must attend each church service; if they failed to appear, they were searched out by church officers deputed for the purpose, and were subject to ecclesiastical censure. In short, the first day of the week was one on which all mirth was expelled from the face and all joy from the heart, and when a funereal gloom settled down upon everybody.

Sabbath-breaking, as defined by this inquisitorial code of observance, was exalted into a crime more heinous even than theft. Thus, an entry in the Register of the Presbytery of Dingwall, of date 30th July, 1650, records that the case of Alexander M'Gorrie and his wife, within the parish of Kilmorack, had been referred to the Presbytery for censure, the charge being 'profanation of the Sabbath by stealling imediatelie efter the receaueing of the sacrament.'

The diligence with which the ecclesiastical authorities pursued their quest after Sabbath-breakers is well illustrated by the Register of the Kirk-Session of St. Andrews. During the latter half of the sixteenth century infinite trouble appears to have been taken to establish what the Session was pleased to term 'the cumlye ordour of this citie.' The fleshers (butchers) proved especially incorrigible. Though they had been often cited and admonished, they had 'nocht obeyit the sam, bot contemptuusly refusit to obey.' At last these recalcitrant parishioners were made the subject of a stringent decree whereby, if they did not thereafter keep holy the Sabbath day, they, their wives, children, and servants would be debarred from all benefit of the Kirk, and might further be excommunicated. Nevertheless, even the vision of these dire pains and penalties did not prevent an occasional transgression. Some years later one of the fleshers was summoned for putting out skins upon the causeway on Sunday—a practice which had formerly been general in his craft. He admitted the accusation, but stated that the fault had been committed, without his knowledge, by his servant. He was required to dismiss that servant, and to undertake that none of his servants in future should do the same, otherwise he would have to pay the penalty himself. There is an interesting entry in the Register, showing how far back the attractions of golf can be seen to have led men to neglect their duties. On the 19th

December, 1599, it is recorded that the brethren 'understanding perfytlie that divers personis of thair number the tyme of sessioun passis to the fieldis, to the goufe and uthir exercise, and hes no regard for keiping of the sessioun, for remeid quhairof it is ordinit that quhatsumevir person or personis of the session that heireftir beis fund playand, or passis to play at the goufe or uthir pastymes the tyme of sessioun, sall pay ten s. for the first fault, for the secund fault xxs., for the third fault public repentance, and the fourt fault deprivation fra their offices.'

It is curious to note that rigid enforcement of Sabbath observance was not effected on the north side of the Highlands for somewhere about a century and a half after it had been secured in the Lowlands on the south side. The proximity of the wilder Celtic population, on the one hand, and the existence of a considerable leaven of Episcopalian Protestantism in the community, on the other, probably had a large share in retarding the progress of the movement. The northern clergy themselves were not averse to sharing in the innocent amusements of their people. Marriages and funerals continued to be performed on Sunday, and to be accompanied, even in the case of the lyke-wakes, with festivities that sometimes reached a scandalous excess. Against these customs, which had come down from Catholic times, the kirk-sessions and presbyteries waged incessant war, but probably not until the extinction of the rebellion of 1745 and the abolition of the heritable jurisdictions, with the consequent freer commingling of the north with the south of Scotland, did the Sabbatarian spirit which had become rampant in the Lowlands reach the intensity with which it has maintained its sway in the north for the last three or four generations.

It has been suggested that this increasing strictness of observance arose from the desire of the clergy to obtain a greater hold on the minds and consciences of the people. According to this view they are believed to have found that the restoration of the Jewish Sabbath, with its prohibitions and injunctions, would serve their purpose, and 'being precluded by various circumstances of their situation from having recourse to the expedients of the Catholic priests to gain possession of the minds of the votaries, they have exerted all their power by its means to attain this object.' It has been further asserted that 'these are the reasons why we hear more of the heinous crime of Sabbath-breaking than of all other vices together.'[1]

Obviously it was not in human nature to keep always within the strict letter of such an artificial code of conduct. Joyousness of heart, so long as it was unquenched, could not be restrained from smiles and laughter, or from showing itself in song. The temptation to the young and happy to escape from imprisonment within the four walls of a house into the country, amongst birds and flowers and trees, must have been often wholly irresistible. Lapses from the strict rules of conduct laid down for observance were inevitable; and since, as Butler observed nearly two centuries and a half ago,

> In Gospel-walking times
> The slightest sins are greatest crimes,

such lapses, when repeated, tended to harden the mind in transgression. Sabbath-breaking being held up as so heinous a sin, the transition came to be imperceptibly made to the breaking of the moral laws, which according to the current dogmatic teaching did not seem to be more imperatively binding. 'Hence it is,' as has been pointed out, 'we continually find culprits at the gallows charging the sin

[1] *Horae Sabbaticae*, by Godfrey Higgins, 1833, p. 2.

of Sabbath-breaking, as they call it, with the
origin of their abandoned course of life; and
there can be no doubt that they are correct
in so doing.'[1]

This excessive zeal for a strict observance
of Sunday has been regarded as a special
characteristic of Calvinistic communities. But
it does not seem to have reached anywhere
else the height of intolerance which it maintained, and to a great extent still maintains,
in Scotland. Doubtless the prevalent Sabba-
tarianism was in Sidney Smith's mind when
he called Scotland 'that garret of the earth
—that knuckle-end of England—that land of
Calvin, oat-cakes, and sulphur.' And it may
have been Byron's recollections of sanctimonious Sundays in Scotland, as well as in
England, that inspired his exclamation:

> 'Whet not your scythe, Suppressors of our vice!
> Reforming Saints! too delicately nice!
> By whose decrees, our sinful souls to save,
> No Sunday tankards foam, no barbers shave;
> And beer undrawn, and beards unmown, display
> Your holy reverence for the Sabbath-day.'[2]

An octogenarian friend has told me that he
believes he was the first man in Edinburgh to

[1] Higgins, *Horae Sabbaticae*, p. 53.
[2] *English Bards and Scotch Reviewers*, l. 632.

make a practice of taking a Sunday walk.   He remembers that on some of these occasions he was accompanied by a well-known professor in the University, who besought him not to get back to the town until the church-goers had safely returned to their houses from afternoon service, as he was afraid of the public odium he might draw down not only on himself, but on the University.   I myself recollect when it was a common practice to pull down the window blinds on Sunday, in order that the eyes of the inmates might be hindered from beholding vanity, and that their minds might be kept from wandering away from the solemn thoughts that should engage them.   There was one lady who carried her sanctimonious scruples so far that she always rose a little earlier than usual on Sunday morning, and took care, as her first duty, to carry a merry-hearted and loud-throated canary down to the cellar that its carol might not disturb the quiet and solemnity of the day.   It was considered sinful to use any implement of ordinary week-day work.   Hence though a servant might perhaps scrape away with her fingers the earth from the roots of potatoes in the garden, if these were unexpectedly wanted for the

Sunday dinner, on no account could a spade or graip be used to dig them up expeditiously. In the same spirit, a lad might be employed for half an hour on a Sunday morning in laboriously carrying armfuls of turnips or other vegetables for feeding the cattle, but he could not be allowed to use a wheelbarrow with which he could have done the whole work in a few minutes. As it was a heinous offence to write letters on Sunday, people used to sit up till midnight; what would have been a sin before the clock struck twelve, became quite legitimate thereafter.[1]

Happily this rigidity is gradually being relaxed, except perhaps in parts of the Highlands. How it looks to an observer from outside may be illustrated from some of my own personal experiences.

In the summer of the year 1860, I found that the strict maintenance of the Highland view of Sabbath observance might have had serious consequences for myself. In company with my old chief, Sir Roderick Murchison, I had walked on a Saturday from the head of Loch Torridon, through the

---

[1] Thus Mrs. Grant of Laggan tells us that she sat up on Sunday night, 17th October, 1794, that she might write a letter to a friend 'without infringing on a better day.'—*Letters from the Mountains*, 5th edit., vol. iii., p. 14.

wild defile of Glen Torridon, to Loch Maree.
Along the mountain slopes that sweep upwards
from the southern side of that valley, I
noticed so many features of interest, some of
which, if further and more closely examined,
might help to clear up problems of Highland
geology for the solution of which we were
seeking, that I felt I must ascend these
mountains and look at their crests and corries.
But we were pressed for time, and although
next day was Sunday I determined to devote
it to the quest. The morning broke auspi-
ciously, and ushered in one of the most superb
days which I have ever been fortunate enough
to meet with in the West Highlands. As it
was desirable to save time and fatigue by
driving some six miles to the point of the
road nearest to the ground to be traversed,
a request was made for a dog-cart. But the
answer came, that it was the Sabbath, and
nobody would drive a 'machine' on the Lord's
Day. There was no objection, however, to
allow the use of a dog-cart, nor to charge for the
same in the bill (for Highland innkeepers, like
Dryden's Shimei, 'never break the Sabbath
but for gain'); we must, however, do the driving ourselves. It was accordingly arranged
that Sir Roderick's valet should drive me to

I

the place and return with the vehicle, leaving me to make my tramp and find my way back to the inn on foot. The fresh buoyant air of the mountains; the depth of the glens with their piles of old moraines; the ruggedness and dislocation of the cliffs and slopes; the utter solitude of the scene, broken only now and then by the bound of a group of red deer, startled from a favourite corrie, or by the whirr of the snowy ptarmigan; the ever-widening panorama of mountain-summit, gorge, glen, and lake, as each peak was gained in succession; and then from the highest crest of all, the vista of the blue Atlantic, with the faint far hills of the Outer Hebrides and the nearer and darker spires of Skye—all this, added to the absorbing interest of the geology, filled up a day to the brim with that deep pleasure of which the memory becomes a life-long possession. The sun had sunk beneath the western hills before I began to retrace my steps, and night came down when there still lay some miles of trackless mountain, glen, river, and bog between me and the inn where my old chief was expecting me at dinner. Fortunately, in the end the moon rose, and I arrived at the end of the journey somewhere near midnight.

The delay in my return gave Murchison not a little uneasiness. As hour after hour passed, he grew so impatient that he began to insist on some of the people of the inn turning out with lanterns as a search party. His remonstrances, however, were met with a sullen indifference, very unlike the usual attentiveness of the household. 'It was the Sabbath day,' they said, 'the gentleman shouldn't have gone out to walk on the Lord's Day.' In short, the gentleman, had he been lost, would have deserved his fate, and would have furnished to the pulpits of the district a new and pregnant illustration of the danger of Sabbath-breaking!

Some fifteen years later, being in the east of Sutherland, I greatly desired to visit the two remarkable cones of Ben Griam, which, rising far over out of the desolate moorland, form such a prominent feature in the landscape of that region. Had they stood within easy reach of the little inn where I was staying, I would have walked over to them in order to spend a quiet Sunday in examining them and in meditation over the marvellous story of past time which they reveal. But the distance being much more than a Sabbath day's journey, I applied to my host for a dog-cart to take me by road to the nearest point from which I could strike across the moor on foot. He confessed that none of his servants would drive me, and that he did not wish to shock the prejudices of his neighbours in the parish, but that if I would wait until the people were in the kirk, he would drive me himself. As we passed along the lonely road he gave me his history, which had no ordinary interest. Born in the district, he had gone south early in life, and eventually became an engine-driver on one of the main railways. He was next attracted, by the offer of better pay and prospects, to enter the service of the Chemin de Fer du Nord and drove the first train between Paris and Calais. He continued in the service of that railway for many years, made his home in France, and finally retired with a pension from the French Government. As he had no longer any daily occupation, a longing for the old country came on him and grew so strong that he in the end broke up his home in France and took the inn where I found him. But he soon discovered that his long stay in a freer theological atmosphere than that of Calvinistic Sutherland had taught him to look on life from a very different point of view from that still maintained by his fellow-countrymen. He found them, he said, narrow-minded, prejudiced, and bigoted, disposed to look askance on him and what they thought his laxity of belief, and to show in many little spiteful ways the antagonism between them. The old home was no longer the place that had dwelt all these long years treasured in his memory, and he seemed disposed to regret that he had ever come back to it. That Sunday was a day of sunshine, of white floating clouds, and of blue distances stretching away from the purple moors to the sea on the one side and to the inland mountains on the other—a day to be alone with Nature and one's own thoughts. My reverie on Ben Griam, which led me far into the backward of time, was touched now and then with thoughts of the strange fetichism of to-day that has turned the Sunday from a day of joyfulness to one of gloom.

That this relentless intolerance of any inno-cent and instructive employments, other than that of church-going, still persists in certain quarters with undiminished rigour was brought painfully to my notice only six years ago in Skye. A reading party of bright young men from one of the English Universities had settled down for steady work and recreation at a well-known hotel, and the landlady, anxious to obtain for them more space and quiet than they could find under her own roof, arranged for the use of a large room in a house which had been temporarily taken by a Free Church clergyman who had been displaced during the progress of the controversy respecting the union of his church with the United Presbyterians. On the first Sunday, the young men spent the morning partly in reading and partly in examining under the microscope some of the natural history specimens they had been collecting during the week. The sight of these instruments, opened on the Lord's Day, was too much for the minister's wife. Next morning my hostess received a letter from her requesting that the young men might be removed, bag and baggage, as she could not submit to such profanation under her roof. She concluded by beseeching that the innkeeper's children might be sent to her as a consolation, 'that she might hear their innocent prattle.' The landlady showed me this letter, but was anxious that, at least while they were her guests, the students should know nothing about it, as she would not like them to think that this intolerance was a fair sample of Highland opinion.

I have sometimes been astonished to see how this superstitious veneration for the Sabbath has blinded intelligent men and women, otherwise liberal and enlightened in their views, to the real meaning and use of the day. Having been taught from their youth to deem certain things unlawful and reprehensible if done on that day, they studiously refrain from these, but at the same time they unconsciously allow themselves to say and do other things which on due reflection they would admit to be no better than those which they condemn, if not indeed much worse. I once spent a Sunday in a Highland Free Kirk manse, and in the afternoon was entertained by the minister's wife, who was as kindly in disposition as she was narrow in her views. We discussed the whole parish. Some Roman Catholics had come to the district, which filled her mind with dismay. She was grieved, too, that a well-known dignitary of the Church of England had called the day before on her husband, a broad-minded and accomplished scholar, and had carried him off to examine some ecclesiastical ruins in the neighbourhood. She gave me an account of various marriages which were in contemplation, and of the changes that were imminent in the tenancy of the farms. At last I asked her to excuse me as I had some letters to write which I was anxious should go by the early post in the morning. 'What?' she exclaimed in surprise, 'Do you mean to say that you write letters on the Sabbath?' I could not resist the temptation to assure her that I thought writing to my friends and relatives on that day was at least as allowable as to spend the afternoon over parish gossip.

A story is told of a young clergyman on the mainland who had not been long placed in his charge when rumours began to circulate about his orthodoxy. Some of his friends hearing these reports set themselves to enquire into the grounds for them. But they could only elicit vague hints and suggestions. At last they came upon an old woman who declared roundly that the minister was 'no soun'.' 'Not sound! what makes you think that?' 'Weel then,' she answered, 'I maun tell ye. I wass seein' him wi' my ain een, standin' at his window on the Lord's Day, dandlin' his bairn.'

An incident which illustrates the strictness of Sabbath observance in the North Highlands has been told me by a friend. During one of her tours in the Highlands Queen Victoria visited Ross-shire. When spending a Sunday at Loch Maree, the Royal party, tempted by the beauty of the day, made an expedition by boat to one of the islands of the loch. This 'worldly acting' upon the Lord's day caused a great scandal in the neighbourhood, and eventually the Free Church Presbytery took up the matter and addressed a letter to the Queen 'dealing with' her for her conduct. Our good Queen was naturally much disquieted that she had unwittingly offended any section of her faithful subjects, and consulted one of her chaplains, a distinguished minister of the Church of Scotland, who was then at Balmoral, as to what she ought to do. He counselled her not to take any notice of the letter, and allayed her anxiety by recounting to her the following incident illustrative of the attitude of mind of the Highlanders towards all departures, however trivial, from their notions of strict Sabbath observance. The story greatly amused the Queen, and at her request it had to be repeated to other members of the royal household.

A Highland minister, after the services of the Sunday were over, was noticed sauntering by himself in meditative mood along the hillside above the manse. Next day he was waited on by one of the ruling elders, who came to point out the sin of which he had been guilty, and the evil effect which his lapse from right ways could not fail to have in the parish. The clergyman took the rebuke in good part, but tried to show the remonstrant that the action of which he complained was innocent and lawful, and he was about to cite the famous example of a Sabbath walk, with the plucking of the ears of corn, as set forth in the Gospels, when he was interrupted with the remark: 'Ou ay, sir, I ken weel what you mean to say; but, for my pairt, I hae nefer thocht the better o' them for breakin' the Sawbbath.'

A member of the Geological Survey was, not many years ago, storm-stayed in a muirland tract of South Ayrshire upon a Saturday, and gladly accepted the hospitality of a farmer for the night. Next morning he asked the servant if she thought her master could oblige him with the loan of a razor. In due time the razor arrived, but was found to be so wofully blunt that the maid had to be summoned again to see if a strop was available. She soon came back with this message, 'Please, the maister says this is the Sawbbath, and ye're jist to put pith to the razor. Ye canna get the strop.'

The late Lord Playfair, when he was Professor of Chemistry in the University of Edinburgh, told me that, passing his nursery-door one Sunday, he overheard the nurse stilling a child in this fashion: 'Whisht, whisht, my bonnie lamb; it's the Sawbbath, or I wud whustle ye a sang, but I'll sing ye a paraphrase.'

The sacredness of the Sabbath, by a natural transition, came to be also attributed to the Fast Day, which heralded the half-yearly Communion-Sunday. A Fife shepherd, who was in the Grassmarket of Edinburgh on a week-day, found that his dog had strayed to some distance, and was making off in a wrong direction. He begged an acquaintance whom he had met to whistle for the animal. ' Whustle on your ain dowg,' was the indignant reply. ' Na, na, man,' said the perturbed drover. ' I canna dae that, for you see it's our Fast Day in Kirkcaldy.'

Nobody has satirised the Scottish perversion of the day of rest with more effective sarcasm than Lord Neaves in his *Lyric for Saturday Night*:

> We zealots made up of stiff clay,
>   The sour-looking children of sorrow,
> While not over-jolly to-day,
>   Resolve to be wretched to-morrow.

We can't for a certainty tell
　　What mirth may molest us on Monday;
But at least to begin the week well,
　　Let us all be unhappy on Sunday.

What though a good precept we strain
　　Till hateful and hurtful we make it!
What though, in thus pulling the rein,
　　We may draw it so tight as to break it!
Abroad we forbid folks to roam,
　　For fear they get social or frisky;
But of course they can sit still at home,
　　And get dismally drunk upon whisky.

A habit which has been followed for generations to the sound of the 'drum ecclesiastic' is not easily thrown off. The Sabbath look of funereal sadness may still be seen on many a sturdy Presbyterian face. But happily the gloomy intolerance is passing away. In no respect is the freer air of the modern spirit more marked than in the relaxation of the old discipline in regard to the keeping of the Sabbath in lowland Scotland. A country walk on that day is no longer always proclaimed to be a violation of one of the ten commandments, innocent laughter is not everywhere denounced as a sin, nor does it appear that the growth of Sunday cheerfulness leads to any depravation of character, or to a less keen feeling for whatsoever is of good report. There is now, however, a tendency for the pendulum to swing perhaps too far on the other side. Welcome though the disappearance of the old gloom may be, there would be a questionable gain if what should be a day of quiet rest and refreshment were turned into one of frivolous gaiety and dissipation.

In other directions a relaxation of the old rigour in regard to the innocent enjoyments of life is to be welcomed. But these various signs of greater charity and enlightenment have made much less rapid progress in the Highlands and Islands. In these regions the influence of the protestant clergy, as it was longer in bringing the people into subjection, still maintains much of the vehemence which has elsewhere died down. The intolerance appears to be decidedly more marked in the Free Church communion than in that of the Establishment. One of the latest examples of it which has come under my own observation was that of a lady who went to a dance. For this enormity she was reprimanded by the Free Church minister to whose congregation she belonged. Things at last became so unpleasant that she left his ministrations and went to the parish kirk.

CHAPTER V.

THE natural unreclaimed Scot is apt to be litigious. He likes to have a 'ganging plea,' although the matter in dispute may not be worth contention. He does not care to be beaten by a neighbour, even in a trifle, and will willingly spend and be spent to secure what in the end is but a barren victory. This liking for law can be traced far back in history. We see it in full force during the lifetime of Sir David Lyndsay, who satirised it and the ecclesiastical courts that encouraged it. He recounts how when the pauper's mare was drowned by his neighbour, the poor man at once ran off to the consistory to lodge his complaint, and there he 'happinit amang a greidie menzie':

> Thay gave me first ane thing thay call *citandum*;
> Within aucht days, I gat bot *lybellandum*;

Within ane moneth, I gat ad *opponendum* ;
In half ane yeir, I gat *interloquendum*.
But, or thay cam half gate to *concludendum*,
The fiend ane plack was left for to defend him.
For sentence silver, thay cryit at the last.
Of *pronunciandum*, thay made me wonder faine ;
But, I gat never my gude gray mear againe.[1]

The same national tendency has survived
down to our own times. It is excellently
pourtrayed by Scott in several of the Waverley Novels. Dandie Dinmont, for instance,
having won the 'grand plea about the
grazing of the Langtae-head,' was keen to
have another legal tussle with his neighbour,
Jock o' Dawston Cleuch, about a wretched
bit of land that might 'feed a hog or aiblins
twa in a good year'; not that he valued
the land, but he wanted 'justice,' and could
ill bear to be overridden, even in regard to
what was in itself quite worthless. The
phraseology of the law courts came glibly to
the tongues of men who, like Bartoline
Saddletree, picked it up from attendance in
the Parliament House, but had only an imperfect notion of what it meant. In some
cases, such as that of Poor Peter Peebles,
loss of wits and fortune, together with a

[1] *Satyre of the Three Estaitis*, Part ii.

parrot-like facility in repeating law terms, was all the outcome of years of litigation.

Burns, too, has admirably indicated the litigious quarrels of his countrymen and a thoroughly national mode of composing them when the disputants can be induced to adopt it.

> When neebors anger at a plea,
> An' just as wud as wud can be,
> How easy can the barley-brie
>   Cement the quarrel!
> It's aye the cheapest lawyer's fee,
>   To taste the barrel.

From the number of writers, solicitors, and advocates who still every year enter the legal profession, one may infer that this national peculiarity shows no marked sign of abatement. The institution of local courts of first instance, all over the country, has enabled the Scot to indulge in the luxury of law, without the trouble and expense of going up to Edinburgh. He can bring his case before the Sheriff-Substitute, and appeal from his decision to that of the Sheriff-Principal. If an adverse judgment from both of these officials has not damped his enthusiasm or emptied his pocket, he has still the Court of Session in the Scottish capital to fall back on, and can there appeal to the Inner House; and, finally, if any fighting power should still be left in him, he may carry his case to the House of Lords. It is obvious that the legal system of the country has been admirably arranged for the gratification of his litigious propensities.

That admirable story-teller, Sir Daniel Macnee, President of the Royal Scottish Academy, used to delight his friends with dramatic pictures of his experiences of law-courts and other scenes of Scottish life. It is matter for infinite regret that his stories were never written down. I used frequently to be privileged to hear him, and may try to give from recollection a mere outline of one of his favourite narratives which had reference to legal matters. He had been engaged as a juryman in a trial, and after a long day in court had finished his duties and come back rather tired to his hotel. He there met an old acquaintance, a Western laird, who spoke with a strong Highland accent, and with whom he had the following conversation:

'Ah, Mr. Macnee (it was before the painter received his knighthood), I'm glad to see you again. But you look very weary; are you well enough?'

K

'Oh yes, thank you, I am quite well, but somewhat tired after a long day in the jury-court.'

'A juryman! Mr. Macnee, were you a juryman? Well now, I hope you had some personal satisfaction out of the case.'

'I really don't know what you mean. I had the satisfaction of serving my turn and doing my duty; and I hope I am not likely to be called again for some time to come.'

'Of course, of course, you would be doing your duty, whatever. But did you have no *personal* satisfaction in your verdict?'

'I am entirely at a loss to understand what you can mean. I gave the verdict which seemed to me just, and according to the evidence.'

'No doubt, no doubt, Mr. Macnee, you would indeed do that. But I'll explain by giving you an account of a case that once happened to myself,' and he proceeded to recount a narrative worthy of the days 'when wretches hung that jurymen might dine.' 'Well, you see, there was a man in the village near my place and his house was broken into and a lot of valuable things were stolen from it. The police were on the spot next morn-

ing, but for a time they could get no clue at
all. They found in the end that the last man
seen at the house was a baker in the village,
and their suspicions began to fall on him.
Well this baker was a notorious radical, and
he was corrupting the village with his radical
notions and theories And I had determined,
if I could manage it anyhow, to get him away.
So I was not sorry to hear that the police
were looking up the baker and his doings.
At last, as they could get nobody else to
suspect, they arrested him, and after a while
a day was appointed for his trial. A jury was
summoned, and I was one of the jury; and
being the chief man in the place, I was chosen
as foreman. Well, the case went to trial, and
we heard all the evidence the police could
scrape together, and the jury retired to consider
their verdict. When we were all met, I said
to them, "Well, gentlemen, what do you think
of the case?" And they answered to a man,
"O the baker's as innocent as any of us." So
I looked amazed and said, "What's that you
say, gentlemen? Innocent! I really am
astonished to hear you say that. Just let us
go over the evidence." So I went over all
the facts and inferences, bit by bit, and showed
how they all made for the prisoner's guilt.

I argued down every objection, and when they were all silenced and convinced, we marched back into the court with a unanimous verdict of "guilty as libelled." You should have seen the face of the judge, but still more, you should have seen the face of the baker. But *there* was the verdict, and so the judge passed sentence of imprisonment on the baker, and we have never seen him more in the village. Now, Mr. Macnee, that's what I mean by *personal satisfaction* !'

The Scottish judges of the type of Hermand, Braxfield, Eskgrove and others, so vividly pictured by Lord Cockburn, and of whom so many anecdotes have been recorded, have long passed away. One of the latest of them was Patrick (or as he was familiarly called, Peter) Robertson, of whose wit and humour many reminiscences have been preserved. He was noted for his obesity which occasioned the soubriquet applied to him by Scott. According to the well-known story, Robertson, while still an advocate, was one day the centre of a group in the Parliament House which he was amusing with his drollery when Scott was seen approaching. 'Hush, boys,' said he, 'here comes old Peveril—I see his peak,' alluding to the novelist's remarkably

high skull. Scott, coming up in the midst of
the general laugh which followed, asked Lock-
hart what was the joke. When Robertson's
personal remark was repeated to him, Scott,
with a look at the advocate's rotund figure,
retorted with another personality, quietly
remarking, 'Ay, ay, my man, as weel Peveril
o' the Peak ony day as Peter o' the Paunch.'

In his younger days Robertson was travelling for a stage or two on the coach from
Inverness to Perth, when a number of ministers
were his fellow-passengers, bound for the
General Assembly at Edinburgh. He engaged
in conversation with them, and led them to
believe that he was also a clergyman from
the extreme north of Scotland. When they
reached the point at which he meant to quit
the coach there was a halt for breakfast, and
Robertson was asked to say grace. He began
with a word or two of Gaelic, but as his
acquaintance with that language was but
slender, he poured forth a torrent of gibberish
pronounced through his nose with an occasional Gaelic word interjected. The ministers
listened with praiseworthy decorum, uncertain
what particular dialect of Gaelic it might be,
for it was one with which none of them had
any acquaintance. But while Robertson still

continued his nasal monologue the coachman's horn blew, and the clerical guests had to hurry breakfastless back to their seats.

In the early years of last century Gaelic was frequently heard in the Court of Session, as Highland witnesses were often ignorant of English, and their evidence had to be translated by interpreters kept for the purpose. Sometimes the ignorance of English was more assumed than real. There is a story told of Lord Cullen, long remembered for his brilliant feats of mimicry, who had a case in court where a Highland witness was evidently 'hedging' and prevaricating. The judge at last lost his patience and asked the Gaelic expert, 'Mr. Interpreter, will you inquire of the witness whether he saw the thing or did not see it, if his language is capable of so fine a distinction.'

Another witness got the better of his cross-questioner in a simple way. The question in dispute turned upon the identity of a particular box, and this witness was called to prove that the nails in the box had been made by him. The advocate for the other side ridiculed the idea that any man could recognise his own made nails, and badgered the man into desperation. The poor fellow at last leant across the witness-box and asked his tormentor if he would allow him to look at a sheet of paper lying in front of the counsel, who had been making some jottings on it. Having got the paper into his hands, the man turned to the advocate and asked, 'Is that your hand o' vrite?' 'Yes, it is,' was the reply. 'But hoo can you prove it's yours? Could you swear to it anywhere?' 'Of course I could.' 'Weel, then, if you can swear to your hand o' vrite, hoo the deevil should I no' swear to my ain nails?'

One of the last of the old race of Scottish judges was Lord Neaves, an excellent lawyer and accomplished scholar, with so much humour, wit and bonhommie that he generally became the centre of any company where he might be. One of his favourite diversions was to write songs, which he sang at convivial gatherings, such as the Royal Society Club in Edinburgh. Many of these appeared first in print among the pages of *Blackwood's Magazine*, to which he was for many years a valued contributor, and he collected them into a little volume entitled *Songs and Verses, Social and Scientific, by an Old Contributor to 'Maga.'* Some of these were inimitably clever, and as sung or chanted by him in his cracked, unmusical voice, with appropriate gesticulations and modulations, they were irresistibly droll. Some of the scientific ditties, dashed off in the intervals of work in court, and sung the same evening at the club, were brimful of fun and wit, hitting off points in theory or in dispute with great acumen. Among these may be mentioned 'The Origin of Species,' a versified account of Darwin's views; 'Stuart Mill on Mind and Matter'; and 'The Origin of Language.' Some of the social ditties were likewise delightful, such as 'I'm very fond of water,' 'The Permissive Bill,' 'Let us all be unhappy on Sunday' (which has already been cited), and the 'Sheriff's life at sea.' A verse of one or two of these may be quoted here.

> Pray what is this Permissive Bill
>   That some folks rave about?
> I can't with all my pains and skill
>   Its meaning quite make out.
>
> 'O! it's a little simple Bill
>   That seeks to pass *incog.*
> To *permit* ME—to *prevent* YOU—
>   From having a glass of grog!'

When appointed Sheriff of Orkney and Shetland, Neaves had at stated times to pro-

ceed by steamboat from Granton to these
northern isles, and in one of the songs above
enumerated he gives a humorous account of
his experiences, which shows that he was
not always a good sailor.

> The zephyr soon becomes a gale,
>   And the straining vessel groans, boys;
> And the Sheriff's face grows deadly pale
>   As he thinks of Davy Jones, boys.
>   Thinking here,
>   Sinking there,
>   Wearily, drearily,
>   Shakingly, quakingly;
>   Not from fear or sickness free
>   Is the Sheriff now at sea, my boys.

The late Lord Rutherford Clark was an
admirable example of the cultured lawyer,
quiet and restrained in manner, with a keen
sense of humour, and a singular power of witty
criticism. One evening at the house of the
late Professor Sellar, he came up to me before
dinner with a grave face, and remarked:
'There is a geological problem that puzzles me
a good deal; perhaps you can throw some
light on it. How does it come about that all
the Scottish hills with which I am acquainted
are so much higher and steeper than they
used to be thirty years ago?' Towards the end
of his life I met him on the shore at Cannes.

Being a keen golfer he had brought his clubs with him to the Mediterranean, and enjoyed a daily game there. But the disease which carried him off had already fastened its grip upon him, and I saw him no more.

An advocate at the Scottish bar whom I remember was a somewhat pompous orator, and went by the name of Demosthenes. He had written a book on *Bills*, and in the course of pleading one day in Court he had occasion to refer to his work. In a loud voice he called out to the attendant; 'Bring me myself on Bills.'

Some of the Writers to the Signet and Solicitors of the old school still survived in my younger days. One of these characters had some odd peculiarities. He paid his clerks more liberal salaries than were common with other lawyers, but he insisted on unremitting attention to duty. He used to carry a thermometer in his pocket, and from time to time would go downstairs to the room in which the clerks worked. If he found one of them off his stool, he would clap the thermometer upon it, and should the mercury not rise a certain number of degrees, he inflicted a money fine on the unfortunate occupant. But for the large salaries, he could not have retained the men in his service, or gratified his propensity for fines. Another venerable Writer to the Signet had a good library, and on his shelves a fine series of the Scottish philosophers. He insisted that if at any time a clerk should finish his task before another piece of work was ready for him, he must come into the library and take a book, so as not to be a moment idle. One of the staff selected Hume's *Essays*, but every time he put the book away in his desk for further perusal, he found next morning that it had been removed and replaced on the shelves. The old gentleman was an ardent Free Churchman, and excluded Hume from the authors that his clerks might read.

CHAPTER VI.

AMONG the professions that of medicine has long held a high place in Scotland. Its reputation at home and abroad has been maintained for a century and a half by a brilliant succession of teachers and practitioners. The schools of medicine in Edinburgh and Glasgow continue to attract students from all quarters of the British Islands, and from our colonies. Every year hundreds of medical graduates are sent out from the Universities, and they are now to be found at work in almost every corner of the wide globe.

At the beginning of the eighteenth century one of the noted medical characters in Edin-

burgh was the surgeon eulogised by Byron
in the couplet:

> Oh! for an hour of him who knew no feud,
> The octogenarian chief, the kind old Sandy Wood.

He was greatly admired for his medical skill,
and beloved for his kindly nature. His popularity saved him once from instant death.
During a riot, the mob, mistaking him for
the provost, were preparing to pitch him over
the North Bridge, when he shouted out to
them, 'I'm lang Sandy Wood; tak' me to a
lamp and ye'll see.' He used to take a
constitutional walk to Restalrig in the evenings, and frequently met a tailor carrying a
bundle, whom he invariably saluted with,
'Weel, Tam, are ye gaun hame wi' your
wark?' The tailor rather resented this monotonous enquiry, and one day he had his
revenge. Noticing the tall figure of the well-
known surgeon walking at the end of a funeral
procession, he instantly made up to him to
ask, 'Weel, doctor, are ye gaun hame wi'
your wark?'

Rather later came the times of Burke and
Hare, with the terrors of the resurrectionists.
A prominent individual in Edinburgh at that
time was Robert Knox the anatomist, to whose
dissecting room the bodies of the victims

murdered in the West Port were sold. He was for many years a successful lecturer, but afterwards got into difficulties, when he tried to retrieve his position by announcing courses of lectures, or a single lecture on a sensational subject. When one of the teachers in the medical school, who had introduced the practice of illustrating his lectures with models, was discoursing on the anatomy of the ear, Knox posted up a notice that on a certain day he too would give a lecture on the human ear, illustrated with the modern methods of demonstration. When the day came, the lecture-room was crowded with students on the outlook for amusement. The lecturer began his demonstration by holding up an ear, which he had obtained from a human subject, and pointing out the leading features in its structure. At a particular part of his lecture he gave a signal, and the door behind him was opened by two men who carried in a monstrous and grotesquely shaped model of an ear. It was set down on the table, and in a little while Knox, holding up the ear he had already exhibited, said, ' This, gentlemen, is the human ear according to God Almighty, and that (pointing to the huge model), and that is the human ear according to Dr. ———,'

There was once a good deal of rivalry between the medical staff of the Universities and the extra-mural schools of medicine. On one occasion, a University professor, wishing to make fun at the expense of a distinguished member of the non-university school, told a story of a man who consulted a famous surgeon as to constant pains in the head. The surgeon pronounced that the complaint could be completely cured by the removal of the brain and the excision of some diseased parts. The man consented to the operation, and was told to come back in ten days, when the renovated brain would be ready for him. The ten days elapsed, however, and gradually grew into three weeks without the patient having returned. At the end of that time the surgeon met him on the street, and anxiously enquired why he had never re-appeared. The man answered that, since the operation, he had obtained a government appointment, and thought that as he was getting on very well without the brain, he had better remain as he was. A titter of course went through the audience, in the midst of which the extramural lecturer, against whom the tale was pointed, rose and calmly said, 'May I enquire of the speaker whether the crown appoint-

ment in question was a University professor-
ship?' The laugh was thus most effectively
turned the other way.

A medical professor having been appointed
Physician to Queen Victoria, the announcement
of this honour was written up on the black-
board of his class-room just before the hour
of lecture. A wag among the students, seeing
this notice, wrote in large letters underneath
it—'God save the Queen!'

It is not unusual for medical men to have
two practices, one in this country, and one
abroad. A man may attend a circle of patients
during the summer in London, at Harrogate
or in the north of Scotland, and another
circle during the winter on the Riviera, in
Italy or in Egypt. One able physician, for
example, had an excellent practice for half
of the year at Nairn and for the other half
in Rome. He was on a friendly footing with
Sir William Gull, whose patients, worn out with
the distractions of London, were sent up to
him to be looked after in the salubrious
climate of the Moray Firth. A lady resident
of Nairn, who believed herself to be far from
well, and to be suffering from some complaint
which the local doctor did not understand,
insisted upon going to London and consulting

Sir William Gull.   That eminent physician diagnosed her case and prescribed ; 'What you chiefly require, madam,' he said, 'is to live for a time in a dry bracing climate. There is one place which I am sure would suit you admirably, and that is Nairn in the north of Scotland.'

One of the difficulties of life among the smaller islands of the Hebrides has long been the inadequacy of medical attendance. A stranger who first enters the region, and realises from some painful experience what are the conditions of the people in this respect, may be forgiven if at first he may be inclined to think that the authorities, whose duty it should be to provide such attendance, share the opinion of Churchill that—

> The surest road to health, say what they will,
> Is never to suppose we shall be ill.
> Most of those evils we poor mortals know
> From doctors and imagination flow.

It must be remembered, however, that many of the islands are too small, and many of the districts too thinly inhabited to provide work for a resident practitioner, even if the funds for his salary were readily procurable. All that has hitherto been attempted is to place a doctor in some central position whence,

L

commanding as wide an area as he can be supposed able to undertake, he may be ready to proceed to any case where his services may be required. But the distances are sometimes considerable, and the weather often stormy, so that for days at a time no boat can pass from one island to another. Even under the most favourable skies, it often happens that when a message arrives, urgently requesting the attendance of the medical man, he is found to be engaged with another serious case in an island some leagues distant, from which he may not be expected to return for some days. An instance which happened a few years ago in the little island of Canna will illustrate this feature of social life in the Inner Hebrides.

One of the workmen engaged in building a dry-stone dyke met with a serious accident. The materials he had to use consisted of large rounded boulders and blocks of basalt, which required some little care to adjust in order that the structure might remain firm. When the wall had been raised to its full height, a portion of it gave way, and some large masses of heavy basalt fell on the workman, smashing one of his legs. His companions on extricating him from the ruins, saw the serious nature of the injuries. But there was no doctor on the island, nor anywhere nearer than at Arisaig, a distance of some twenty-five miles across an open sea. No time was lost in getting the poor man carried into a boat, which two of his comrades navigated to the mainland. On arriving there, however, they found that the doctor had gone away inland and would not be back for a day or two. As there was no time to lose, the boatmen at once set out for Tobermory in Mull, where the next medical man was to be obtained. They had to traverse a tract of sea which is often rough. Even in calm weather more or less commotion may always be looked for in the water round the Point of Ardnamurchan— the 'headland of great waves.' It was some thirty-six hours after the accident before the poor sufferer was at last placed in medical hands. The first thing to be done was, of course, to amputate the mangled leg. The patient stood the operation well, and in two or three weeks was sufficiently recovered to be able to be taken back to Canna. His two faithful comrades, who had waited on with him at Tobermory, had him carried down to the pier, where their boat was ready for him. When he came there he looked all round him with some anxiety, and at last exclaimed, 'But where's my leg?' 'Your leg! in the kirkyard, to be sure.' 'But I maun hae my leg.' 'But I tell ye, ye canna hae your leg, its been buryit this fortnicht in the graveyard.' 'Weel' said the lameter, steadying his back against a wall, 'I'll no stir a fit till I get my leg. D'ye think I'm to gang tramp-tramping aboot at the Last Day lookin' for my leg.' Finding persuasion useless, the unhappy boatmen had to interview the minister and the procurator-fiscal, and obtain authority to dig up the leg. When the lost limb came up once more to the light of day, it was in such a state of decomposition that the men refused to have it in the boat with them. Eventually a compromise was effected. A second boat was hired to convey the leg, and with a length of ten yards of rope between them, was towed at the stern of the first. In this way the procession reached Canna.

Throughout the Highlands the desire to be buried among one's own kith and kin remains wide-spread and deep-seated. And it would also appear that a Highlander cannot bear that the parts of his body should be interred in different places. The Canna dyke-

be paid for the general advancement. Yet
we pay it with a certain measure of regret.
There was a marked originality and individuality among the Professors of the older type,
which gave a distinctive character to the
colleges where they taught, and in some
degree also to their teaching.

About the middle of last century the Professor of Mathematics in the University of
St. Andrews was an able mathematician and
a singularly picturesque teacher. He spoke
not only with a Scottish accent, but used many
old Scottish words, if they were effective in
making his meaning clear. If, for instance,
he noticed an inattentive student, looking anywhere but at the black-board on which he was
demonstrating some proposition, he would stop
and request the lad to ' e'e the buird ' (look
at the board). He lectured in a dress suit,
and as he always wiped his chalky fingers on
his waistcoat, his appearance was somewhat
brindled by the end of the hour. One of his
old students gave me the following recollection
of an incident that took place in the class-
room. A certain student named Lumsden was
one day conspicuous for his inattention. The
professor at last stopped his lecture, and
addressed the delinquent thus : ' Mr. Lums*deil,*

will you come forrit here and sit down on that
bench there in front o' me. I have three
reasons for moving you. In the first place,
you'll be nearer my een; in the second place,
you'll be nearer my foot; and in the third
place, you'll be nearer the door.'

Among the Glasgow professors towards the
middle of the century, one with a marked
individuality was Allan Maconochie, afterwards
Maconochie Welwood. Coming of a race of
lawyers, for he was the son of one Scottish
judge and the grandson of another, he took
naturally to the bar, and became Professor of
Law in 1842. Being prompt and decisive in
his business habits, he soon acquired a considerable practice as referee and arbiter in
disputed cases among the mercantile community of Glasgow, and thus saved the
disputants the long delays and heavy expenses
of the Court of Session. He gave himself
up with much energy to the work of his chair,
and to college business during the session,
but as soon as the winter term was over,
he used to depart at once for the Pyrenees,
where he possessed a chateau, and where he
would spend most of his time until he had to
resume his professional labours in this country.
During these years of residence abroad, he

acquired facility in speaking Spanish, and he would make long solitary excursions, mingling freely among the people.

In the year 1854 his father, Lord Meadowbank, succeeded to the Fife estates of Garvock and Pitliver, and then took the surname of Welwood. About the same time the reform of the Scottish universities began to be mooted, and as the professor looked forward with much dislike to some of the proposed innovations in the constitution and arrangements of these institutions, he resigned his chair and established himself as a country gentleman at Pitliver, near Dunfermline. Having lost his first wife, he had lately married Lady Margaret Dalrymple, daughter of the Earl of Stair. I was a frequent guest at Pitliver, and much enjoyed his racy reminiscences of Glasgow and of his experiences in Spain. One of these last which he told me seems worthy of now being put on record as an instance of the courage and boldness of a peaceable Scottish professor.

During the 'forties' of last century, Spain was convulsed with revolution. Maconochie had a strong desire to travel through some of the disturbed districts and see the state of the country for himself. He accordingly arranged to make a long detour and cross

the frontier to a French town, where his wife
was to await his coming. Disguising himself
as a miner, he procured a bag, a pick, and
a few pieces of rough stone. His money he
carried with him in gold, which he enclosed
in lumps of plaster of Paris, coloured and
dirtied to look like bits of natural rock. Thus
accoutred he set out on his journey, and passed
through the districts where the insurrection
was hottest. At night he would come into
a village inn, filled with insurgents, and throwing his bag into a corner would retire to see
after his horse. Coming back to the chamber
where the warriors were assembled, he sometimes found them examining the contents of
his bag and holding some of his specimens
in their hands, with an exclamation about their
weight—' Plomo, plomo '; they were sure the
stones must be bits of lead-ore. He would
then join in the talk, and so disarm all
suspicion of his nationality that he had no
difficulty in gathering from them all the information he wanted, while they on their side
took him for a Castilian miner prospecting
through the country for metals.

In this way he travelled through all the
tract he wished to see, and had come at last
to the Spanish town nearest to the frontier

place where he was to meet his wife. He now discarded his disguise, and attired himself in ordinary costume. The horse that had carried him was a sorry nag which he had chosen to be in harmony with the general outfit of his supposed occupation. He now made himself known to the mayor of the town and asked his assistance to procure a good horse. It so happened that a fine animal, which had belonged to a government official recently deceased, was for sale, but the price asked for it was beyond the means of those who would fain have bought it. The professor, however, had money enough with him to acquire the horse, and to fit himself for the rest of his journey. A guide was procured to conduct him through the mountains, and he was advised to go armed and to be constantly on his guard. In particular, he was warned on no account to stop at the top of the last pass, whence the road descended in sharp zig-zags into the plain of France. All went well until he came to that very place, when his guide said they must halt a little. This he refused to do, but insisted on his companion riding on in front of him. They had not gone far down when voices from above called on them loudly to stop. The guide turned round, put his horse across the narrow road, and on Maconochie trying to brush past him drew out a pistol from his belt. The professor, suspecting some action of this kind, was on the alert, with his hand already on his own pistol, which he at once discharged at the breast of the guide, who rolled off his horse into the bushes below. Realising now the plot against him, and that there were accomplices above, he put spurs to his horse, and dashed down the road. So steep was the descent, and so shaded with trees and bushes, that he could only be seen at the bends, at each of which a shower of bullets whizzed past him. He succeeded in keeping ahead of his assailants, who continued to pursue and fire at him until they were almost within gun-shot of the French sentries.

As soon as he arrived at the town, he sought the commandant and told his story. The officer, on learning where he had got his horse, told him that he owed his life to the animal, not merely for its speed. It appeared that the insurgents knew the horse well, and desired to procure it for one of their leaders. When they heard that it had been sold, they had evidently planned to possess themselves of it, and had arranged the ambush to which the professor of law had nearly fallen a victim. But it was the horse they wanted, not its rider. Had mere robbery been their object, they could easily have shot the horse, and whether or not they put a bullet through him also, they would have stripped him of all his possessions. But they purposely fired high for fear of wounding or killing the animal, which they had expected to be able to present to their leader.

Robert Chambers used wittily to classify mankind in two divisions—those who had been 'under Pillans,' and those who had not. I am glad to be able to range myself in the first class. Pillans was Professor of Latin (or Humanity as the subject used to be termed in Scotland) in the University of Edinburgh. Perhaps his name was most widely known from its having been unwarrantably pilloried by Byron in his *English Bards and Scotch Reviewers*. He was a born educationist, far in advance of his time in certain departments of teaching, more particularly in his recognition of the place that should be assigned to geography in the educational system of the country. When I sat in his class-room he had reached his seventy-seventh year, and was no longer as able as he had once been to control a large gathering of lads fresh from school. But even then no one who was willing to learn could fail to find much that was suggestive in his prelections. As he sat in his chair behind his desk, his small stature was not observable. One only saw the round bald head, the rubicund cheeks, the mild blue eyes, the hands wielding a huge reading glass (for he would never consent to wear spectacles) and the shoulders wrapped round in his velvet-collared black gown. He was a scholar of the antique type, more intent on the subject, spirit, and style of his Latin favourites, than on grammatical niceties or various readings. How he loved his Horace, and how he took to his heart any student in whom he could detect the rudiments of the same affection! Having gained his friendship in this way, I saw a good deal of him in later years. He kept up the pleasant old custom of asking his students to breakfast with him. In later years I met some of his early friends at that meal, among them, Leonard Horner. I remember one morning having a talk with him about English literature, when he said, ' I have been all my life fond of poetry, and I find great solace in it still. But I must go back several generations for what really interests and pleases me. There is Tennyson, and another writer, Browning, that I hear people raving about. I have tried to read them, but I confess that I cannot understand much of them, and they give me no real pleasure. When I want to enjoy English verse, I go back to the masterpieces of Dryden and Pope.'

Pillans was one of the early pioneers in the organisation of infant-schools. He energetically combated the system of teaching by rote, and of compelling young children to burden their memories with genealogies and dates. He once remarked to me, 'I was in an infant-school lately, and you won't guess what question I heard put to a class of little tots, not more than four or five years old—"How long did Jeroboam reign over Israel?"'

The most perfervidly Scottish professor of my time was undoubtedly John Stuart Blackie, who taught a multifarious range of subjects, including some Greek, of which he was Professor. Although those of his students who really wanted to increase their knowledge of Greek would fain have been spared some of his disquisitions on the current politics or problems of the day, they could not but recognise his boundless enthusiasm, his cheery good nature, and his high ideals of life and conduct. In my time he wore a brown wig, which was so manifestly artificial that we used sometimes to imagine that it was coming off, and speculated on what the professor would be like without it. But in later years he allowed his own white hair to grow long, and with his clean-shaven face, his broad soft felt hat, and his brown plaid over his shoulders, he became by far the most picturesque figure in the Edinburgh of his time. He had been so much in Germany, and was so well versed in German life and literature, that he seemed naturally to assume the manner of a German professor. There was, indeed, a good deal of external resemblance between him and the late venerable historian Mommsen. But Blackie was distinguished from his more typical continental brethren by the boisterous exuberance of his spirits. Even in the class-room this feature could not be wholly repressed, but it reached its climax among friends at a dinner table, more especially at such gatherings as those of the Royal Society Club. After eloquent talk he would eventually be unable to remain seated, but would start up and march round the room, gesticulating and singing a verse of some Scottish song, or one of his own patriotic ditties.

Besides the genial Blackie, the Senate of

Edinburgh University, when I was a member
of it, contained some other less vociferous but
extremely clubbable professors. Two of them
deserve special mention here—Christison and
Maclagan. Sir Robert Christison was excellent company, with his ample fund of reminiscence and anecdote. At the club-dinners Sir
Douglas Maclagan never failed to regale us
with one of his inimitable songs. He had a
good voice, and sang with much expression
and humour. His ' Battle of Glen Tilt ' was a
source of endless pleasure to his friends, and
he entered so thoroughly into the spirit of it
that one could almost see the scene between
the duke and his gillies on the one side, and
the botany professor and his students on the
other. Some of the touches in that ditty are
full of sly fun, such, for example, as the description of the botanising :

> Some folk 'll tak' a heap o' fash
>   For unco little en', man ;
> An' meikle time an' meikle cash
>   For nocht ava' they 'll spen', man.
> Thae chaps had come a hunder' mile
> For what was hardly worth their while ;
>   'Twas a' to poo
>   Some gerse that grew
>   On Ben M'Dhu
>   That ne'er a coo
> Would care to pit her mouth till.

M

On rare occasions Christison and Maclagan sang a humorous duet in the most dolorous tones, acting the character of two distressed seamen begging on the street. It was comical beyond description.

Another of the luminaries in the Edinburgh University was Lyon Playfair, professor of chemistry, who, after quitting his chair and entering parliament, devoted himself mainly to politics, and was finally raised to the peerage. He too was a true Scot, though most of his life was passed in England. He enjoyed and could tell a good story, and relished it none the less if it bore against himself. In his later years he used to pay a yearly visit to America, and from one of these journeys he brought back the account of an experience he had met with among the Rocky Mountains of Canada, and which he would tell with great vivacity. He had halted at some station on the Canadian Pacific Railway, and in the course of a stroll had made his way to the foot of a heap of material that had been tumbled down from the mouth of a mine. He was poking out some of the pieces of stone with his stick, when a voice saluted him from the top of the bank, and the following conversation ensued:

'Hey! what are ye daein' there?'

'I am looking at some of these bits of stone.'

'But there's nae allooance here.'

'Is there not? I think you must be a Scotsman like me.'

'Ay! man, and are ye frae Scotland? And what's your name?'

'My name is Playfair.'

'Maybe ye'll be Lyon.'

'Yes, that's my name. How do you come to know it?'

'Od, man, your name has travelt far faurer nor thae wee legs 'll ever carry yoursell.'

When at the time of the Disruption the theological chairs were resigned by the professors who seceded to the Free Church, the classes of the new College which that church established in Edinburgh were held in a house next door to a well-known dentist. Dr. Chalmers was one of those who had left the University, and he had an enthusiastic body of students in the new rooms. The applause with which they greeted the Professor's bursts of eloquence proved, however, rather trying to the dentist and his patients, for the house partitions were none of the thickest. The story is told that a polite note was sent to

Dr. Chalmers, asking whether it would be possible for him to moderate the noise made by his pupils. Next day the doctor, before beginning his lecture, explained the circumstances to his class, and begged them to remain quiet, 'for,' he added, 'you must bear in mind that our neighbour is very much in the mouth of the public.'

The late Professor Tait, so widely known and so affectionately remembered, used to cite one of the answers he received in a class-examination. The question asked was, 'Define transparency, translucency and opacity,' and the following was the answer. 'I am sorry that I cannot give the precise definition of these terms. But I think I understand their meaning, and I will illustrate it by an example. The windows of this class-room were originally transparent; they are at present translucent, but if not soon cleaned, they will become opaque.' The professor, in repeating this reply, laughingly said that he had allowed the man full marks for it.

The Scottish schoolmaster of the old type is probably as extinct as the parish school system under which he flourished. What with revised codes, inspectors, examinations, grants in aid, Board of Education and other machinery, the educational arrangements of Scotland have during the last half-century been transformed to a remarkable degree. There can be no doubt that on the whole, and especially in recent years, the changes have been in the right direction. Nevertheless, we may regret the disappearance of some of the characteristic features of the old régime. The parish schools served to commingle the different classes of the community, and there was a freedom left to the teachers which gave them scope in their methods and range of subjects, and enabled them to send up to the university numbers of clever and well-trained scholars. Untrammelled by the fear of any school-board or Education Department, the 'dominie' was left to develop his own individuality, which, though it sometimes took the form of eccentricity, was in most cases the natural outgrowth of a cultivated mind, and was a distinct benefit to his pupils. In the delightful *Memories Grave and Gay* of Dr. Kerr, who has spent his active life in practically furthering the cause of education in the country, an interesting account is given of the process of transformation, together with many anecdotes of his experience of country schools and country schoolmasters.

To his ample stores those interested in the subject should turn.

In the early days of examinations an inspector came to a school, and in the course of the reading stopped to ask the class the meaning of the word curfew in Gray's line:

> The curfew tolls the knell of parting day.

There was complete silence in the room. He tried to coax the boys on to an answer, but without effect; until the teacher, losing patience with them, exclaimed in vexation, 'Stupit fules! d'ye no ken what's a *whaup*?' whaup being *Scottice* for *curlew*.

A clerical friend of mine was, many years ago, visiting a parish school in Argyleshire where Gaelic was taught as well as English. He spoke to them in Gaelic, and asked them to spell one of the words he had used. They looked in blank amazement at him, and gave no reply. At last the master, turning round deprecatingly to the clergyman, said, 'Oich, sir, there's surely no spellin' in Gaelic.'

A story is told in the north of Scotland of a certain school in which a boy was reading in presence of an examiner, and on pronouncing the word *bull* as it is ordinarily sounded, was abruptly corrected by the schoolmaster.

'John, I've told you before, that word is called *bull*' (pronouncing it like *skull*).

'Excuse me, sir,' said the examiner, 'I think you will find that the boy has pronounced it correctly.'

'O no, sir, we always call it *bull* in this parish.'

'But you must pardon me if I say that the boy's pronunciation is the usual one. Have you a pronouncing dictionary?'

'Dictionary! O yes. Charlie, rin round to the house and fetch me the big dictionary. Meantime, John, go on wi' the reading.' So John went on with 'bull,' and Charlie brought the dictionary, which the master turned up in triumph, 'There, sir, is the word with the mark above the *u*, and there are the words that it's to be sounded like—put, push, pull (pronouncing these all like but, brush, dull). And now, John, you will go on wi' *bull*.'

The questions put by the examiners are not always judicious. The man who asked 'If Alfred the Great were alive now, what part of our political system would he be likely to take most interest in?' need not have been surprised to receive the answer, 'Please sir, if Alfred the Great were alive now, I think he'd be so old he wouldn't take interest in anything.'

The difference between the pronunciation of Latin on the two sides of the Tweed used to give rise to curious confusion, whether we 'gave up Cicero to C or K.' I remember a boy who had previously attended a grammar school in Yorkshire and had come to the Edinburgh High School, being called on to read the introductory lines of the first book of Ovid's *Metamorphoses*. He began pronouncing in the English way, 'Ante mare et tellus.' 'What, what do you say?' interrupted Dr. Boyd, 'Aunty Mary,' forsooth! 'I suppose we shall have Uncle Robert next.'

CHAPTER VII.

OLD and new type of landed proprietors in Scotland. Highland Chiefs—Second Marquess of Breadalbane; late Duke of Argyll. Ayrshire Lairds—T. F. Kennedy of Dunure; 'Sliddery Braes'; Smith of Auchengree. Fingask and Charles Martin. New lairds of wealth.

THE most outstanding change in regard to landed proprietorship during the last half century has been in Scotland, as elsewhere in Britain, the successive extinction or displacement of families that long held their estates, and 'proud of pedigree, but poor of purse,' have had to make way for rich merchants, bankers, brewers, iron-masters, and manufacturers. Of the great landowners the most striking personality in my time was undoubtedly the second Marquess of Breadalbane. Tall and broad, with a head like that of Jupiter Tonans, having the most commanding presence combined with the most winning graciousness of manner, he was the incarnation of what one

imagined that a great Highland chief should
be. When in 1860 at the head of his Highland
Volunteers, all in kilts of the clan tartan, he
marched to the great review held by Queen
Victoria in Edinburgh, one's thoughts travelled
back to the days of Prince Charlie, for since
that time there had been no such mustering of
warlike men straight from the Highland glens,
and no such chieftain in command of them.
When in the autumn he established himself at
the Black Mount, and filled his hospitable
house with guests, he would start off for a day's
deer-stalking, mounted on the box of a large
drag, with the reins and whip in his hands,
his friends seated around him and his gillies
behind. No one of the party was a keener
or more successful sportsman than he. A
liberal and enlightened landlord, he had done
much to improve his vast estates, and was
beloved by his tenantry and people. He never
could understand why the Scottish mountains
should not supply abundance of metallic ores,
and afford a source of wealth to the country.
For years he employed a German expert to
prospect all over his property, and he continued
to work his mines at Tyndrum even at a loss.
Among his acquirements he had gained some
knowledge of mineralogy. Sir Roderick Mur-

chison, when visiting him in 1860, after a tour
through the western Highlands, remarked to
him at dinner that one great difference between
the oldest rocks of the north-western and those
of the Central Highlands lay in the presence
of abundant hornblende in the former and its
absence from the latter. 'Stop a bit, Sir
Roderick,' interrupted the Marquess, 'You come
with me to-morrow, and I'll show you plenty
of hornblende.' Next day a walk was taken
across a tract of moor near the Black Mount,
Sir Roderick accompanying some ladies, while
the chief marched on in front. At last when
the rock in question was reached, the Marquess
shouted out in triumph, 'Here's hornblende
for you.' And he was right, as Murchison, with
a queer non-plussed look on his face, had to
admit. Nevertheless the geologist's generalisa-
tion, though not universally applicable, had in
it a certain element of truth.

Another distinguished Highland chief of last
century was the late Duke of Argyll. Gifted
with great acuteness and versatility of intellect,
he directed his thoughts to a wide range of
subjects, and having a remarkable command of
forcible language, he was able to present these
thoughts in such a form as to compel attention
to his reasonings and conclusions. As orator,

statesman, historian, poet, naturalist, geologist, agriculturist, chief of a great Highland clan, and landed proprietor, he was undoubtedly one of the living forces of his country during his active career. Moreover, he never failed to show that, like the long line of his illustrious ancestors, he was an ardent and patriotic Scot. In the midst of his conversation he would every now and then throw in a Scottish word or phrase, as more tersely expressive of his meaning than anything he could find in English. He knew the West of Scotland better than most of his countrymen, for not only was he born and bred there, and passed most of his life in the midst of his ancestral possessions, but for many years he kept a yacht on which he peered into every bay and creek among the Western Isles. He had considerable artistic power, and was never happier than when sketching some scene that delighted him. After a great speech, or during the intervals in the preparation of one of his published volumes, he found rest and solace in working up his sketches, of which he left a large collection.

Though cast in a smaller bodily mould than his burly kinsman of Breadalbane, he carried himself with a singular dignity of bearing. His

finely formed, expressive face and his abundant
golden hair made him a conspicuous figure in
any assembly. But he was perhaps best
seen under his own roof at Inveraray enter-
taining the landed gentry of Argyleshire, when
met for the transaction of county business—
including many of the Campbell clan who
counted the Mac Callum More as their chief,
and from some of whom he could claim feudal
service. One of them in particular used to
be prominent from the massive silver chain
which he wore with a key hung at the end
of it. His castle was now a ruin, but, in
accordance with ancient usage, he was bound
to present the key of it when he came to see
his chief. The Duke moved about among the
guests as the grand seigneur, entering into ani-
mated talk, now about land and rent, or improvements in the county, or some recently opened
tumulus, dredgings in Loch Fyne, the political
situation of the country, or the probability of
getting fossils out of his schists and limestones.
He was keenly desirous to preserve every
relic of antiquity on his property, and had
made a kind of museum in the central hall
of the castle in which he kept the smaller
objects that had been picked up. Among
these he was especially proud of an old knife

with what he believed to be Rob Roy's initials on it that had been found near the place where that Highland freebooter lived, when he placed himself for a time under the shelter of the Argyll of his day.

Perhaps no county in Scotland could furnish an ampler list of landed proprietors than Ayrshire, both of the old stock and of the new comers. The former included both titled possessors of large estates and smaller lairds who could trace their genealogy back to a remote ancestry. One of the best examples of these landed gentry whom I have known was the Right Honourable Thomas Francis Kennedy of Dunure. Educated in Edinburgh under Pillans and Dugald Stewart, he was associated from his youth with the brilliant literary coterie which then flourished in that city, and delighted to recount his reminiscences of the men and the clubs of the time. As he was born near Ayr, and had passed much of his life in Ayrshire, where he possessed considerable estates, he retained a lively recollection of the state of the south-west of Scotland in the closing years of the eighteenth and the early part of the nineteenth century. I have heard him tell of the hardships of the peasantry and small farmers in his boyhood, how in severe

winters they were compelled to bleed their
cattle and mix the blood with oatmeal to keep
themselves in life. He used to describe the
cuisine of his early days, and the contrast
between it and modern cookery. One of the
dishes, rather a favourite in Carrick, was roast
Solan goose from Ailsa Craig. But his account
of it was not itself appetising, for he told how
they had to bury the bird for some time in the
garden, and when it came to be cooked, all the
windows in the house had to be kept open, to
let out the 'ancient and fish-like smell.' White
and black puddings, now almost entirely
banished, still maintained their place, together
with 'crappit heads,' 'singed sheep's head,'
and sundry other national dishes which have
long been banished from the tables of polite
society. He used sometimes to revive a few
of these dishes, and I thought them excellent,
but he never, so far as I experienced, tried the
Solan goose again.

He was a gentleman of the antique cast,
courteous and stately in his manners, proud of
his descent and of his ancestral possessions,
and tenacious of his rights, which he was sometimes thought to insist upon rather more than
he need have done. When I came to know
him about the year 1863 he had retired from

public life, and devoted himself to the care of his property. He looked carefully after his breeds of cattle, and was keenly alive to new inventions for the improvement of agriculture, which he was always ready to test on his own land. Part of one of the smallest coalfields in Scotland underlay his estate of Dalquharran, and he worked the mineral according to the best known methods.

Yet he had been an active politician in his time. He was for sixteen years in Parliament, as member for the Ayr Burghs. In association with Cockburn, Jeffrey, Horner, Murray, Graham, and others, he took a leading part in the preparations for the Scottish Reform Bill. On retiring from Parliament, he obtained an official appointment in Ireland, where he spent some years, until in 1850 he received a commissionership in the Office of Woods and Forests. Owing to some dispute in the staff, he retired from this appointment in 1854, and thereafter lived entirely at his Ayrshire home, save that for some twenty years he continued to come up for the season to London. The Government of the day would not grant him a pension, a decision for which he believed that Gladstone was mainly responsible. His friend Lord Murray thought him so badly used that he settled a pension of £1200 a year upon him, which he enjoyed up to the time of his death. Though no longer actively interfering in politics, he continued to take the keenest interest in the events of the time, kept himself in touch with his old Whig friends in and out of Parliament, and gave free vent to his disapproval when he had to criticise their policy.

His wife, a daughter of Sir Samuel Romilly, was a singularly gentle and gracious old lady. They had been married twenty years before a son, their only child, was born to them. Kennedy used to remark on the curious coincidence that he himself was also an only child, born after twenty years of wedlock. The inhabited Dalquharran Castle is a large modern mansion, built in a massive but rather tasteless style, a strange contrast to the older castle which it replaced, and which now stands as a picturesque ivy-clad ruin a short distance off, near the river. The laird remembered when this ruin still had its roof on, and was partly habitable.

Another Ayrshire laird had a row of fine silver firs in the avenue to his romantically-placed old castle. As several of these trees had been struck by lightning during a series of

years, his wife asked me one day if I thought
it possible that the lightning was attracted
by a seam of ironstone in the ground beneath.
She hoped it was not, for if her husband suspected such a thing, she knew he would have
lawn, avenue, trees, and everything else dug
up in order to get at it. I was able to assure
her that there was no ironstone there, and
that the attraction was in the trees themselves.

In the same county I was acquainted about
forty years ago with a bachelor laird who
possessed a fine estate, on which he lived with
two maiden sisters. He had a large collection
of minerals, and more particularly of gems,
many of which were mounted as rings. When
low-spirited, he would array himself in his
dressing-gown, retire to his library, cover his
fingers with rings, and lay himself out on a
sofa to gaze at and admire them. He dabbled
a little also in water-colours, and it used to
be said of him that 'he painted a picture
every day, and on Sundays he painted a
church.'

One of the oddest specimens of a laird I
ever personally knew was the owner of a
small estate to the north of Kilmarnock, where
he lived with two unmarried sisters. He had

nicknames for everybody and everything. His mansion-house, owing to the steepness of the approach to it, he always called 'Sliddery Braes.' His sisters, he used to speak of, the one as the 'Mutiny at the Nore,' the other as the 'Battle of the Baltic,' because they were born in the years when these two events occurred. He used to take whims, pursue them with great earnestness for a time, and then change to something else. Many of these occupations had a theological cast. At one time he devoted himself to a serious study of the Book of Revelations, and in order to get the better at its meaning, he took to the Greek original. He found that Dr. Sloan of Ayr had a more modern lexicon than that at Sliddery Braes, so he would come down day after day, and work with this volume in the doctor's consulting room. His presence there, however, becoming troublesome, the book was sent upstairs to the drawing-room, and instructions were given to the servant to take the laird there the next time he came. On entering that room one day, he found the doctor's sister sitting at the window, engaged in some needle-work. With apologies for his interruption, he begged her not to allow him to disturb her, for he would be engrossed in his study of the chapter on which he was then engaged. After some time he turned to Miss Sloan and said, 'I've been investigating the account given in Revelation of the White Horse, and I think I now understand about it. The animal must have been a large beast, for standing in the street there, its back would be up on a level with the window you're sitting at.' And he proceeded to describe in the most whimsical way the look and qualities of this wonderful horse. His narrative was so comical, that the poor lady could hardly repress her laughter. At last he noticed that his discourse had not in the least solemnised her, and he thereupon started up remarking, 'Ah, Miss Sloan, you may laugh, but it's no laughing to some of them; good day.' So ended his Greek studies.

His eccentricities at last became so great, that Dr. Sloan thought it right to send a letter to the elder sister, pointing out the desirability of having her brother watched, and provided with an attendant, for his own sake as well as for that of others, since the doctor did not think it was safe to allow him to go about alone. The lady thoughtlessly left this letter inside her blotting-book, where it was soon afterwards found by the laird himself. He immediately sat down and wrote a long letter to Dr. Sloan, beginning, 'I am not mad, most noble Festus,' and maintaining that he knew what he was about, and could manage himself and his affairs without the help or interference of anybody. The doctor told me that for a long time afterwards he himself went about in some fear of his life, for he never could be sure what revenge 'Sliddery Braes' might be prompted to take.

But the laird had really no homicidal mania. He grew, however, queerer every year. One of his last crazes was to hunt up all the graves of the persecuting lairds of covenanting times. On one occasion he set out on horseback for Dunscore, to see where the notorious Grierson of Lag, 'damned to everlasting fame,' was buried. As he made his way through the lonely uplands of Dumfriesshire, and was nearing his destination, he overtook a pedlar with his pack, and asked him to mount on the horse behind him. When at last he reached the grave-yard, tying the horse to the gate, he insisted on his companion accompanying him to look for the tombstone of the persecutor, and on finding it, proceeded to read out and sing a Psalm, in which his companion was also instructed to join. At the end of this performance, the laird turned suddenly round, looked the pedlar sternly in the face and exclaimed, 'Now, sir, d'ye ken whaur ye are? Ye're sitting on the grave o' a man that's been in hell mair than a hundred years. It's a long time, sir, a long time.' The poor pedlar, now convinced that he was in the hands of a madman, made his escape from the place, and left the laird to complete his devotions and execrations.

About the same time that this whim possessed him, he determined to see the portrait of a certain member of the Cassilis family who had likewise distinguished himself for his zeal against the Covenanters. But the difficulty was how to get access to the picture, which formed part of the collection at Culzean Castle, the seat of the Marquess of Ailsa, and was hung in a room reserved for private use. Watching for an opportunity when the family was from home, he succeeded in prevailing upon the housekeeper to open this room for him and let him see the portrait in question. He used to describe his experience thus: 'I stood looking at the picture for a while; it was really a good-looking face, not what I thought a persecuting laird would be like. But at last I saw the truth in his eyes, for as I watched them, I could see that they had the true twinkle of damnation.'

Another crack-brained laird in the same county has left inscribed on a stone monument upon his property a record of his eccentricity. I came upon it standing by itself near an oak tree at Todhills in the parish of Dalry.   On the west side of the stone the following inscription has been cut;

'There is an oak tree a little from this, planted in the year 1761, it has 20 feet of ground round it for to grow upon, and all within that ground reserved from all succeeding proprietors for the space of 500 years from the above date by me, ANDREW SMITH, who is the ofspring of many Andrew Smiths who lived in Auchengree for unknown generations.'

On the south side the stone bears the subjoined lines :

My Trustees
ROBERT GLASGOW
Esq of
Montgreenan
WILLIAM COCHRAN
Esq of
Ladyland
I stand here to herd this tree
And if you please to read a wee
In seventeen hundred and sixty one
It was planted then at three feet long
I'll tell more if you would ken

It was planted at the byre end
I'll tell you more you'll think a wonder
It's alloud to stand for years five hundred
It has twelve yards a cross and round about
It belongs to no man till that time is out
But to ANDREW SMITH tho he were dead
He raised it out of the seed
So cut it neither Top nor Tail
Least that the same you do bewail
Cut it neither Tail nor Top
Least that some evil you oertak

Erected
By
ANDREW SMITH
of Todhills Octr 1817

When in the year 1867 the British Association met in Dundee, some of the members were entertained at Fingask—that charming old Scottish chateau, with its treasures of family and Jacobite antiquities. Among the visitors was Professor Charles Martin of Montpellier, who so delighted the Misses Murray Thriepland with his enthusiasm for Scotland and everything Scottish, that they bade him kneel, and taking a sword that had belonged to Prince Charlie, laid it on his shoulder and, as if the blade still possessed a royal virtue, dubbed him knight. Some years afterwards I chanced to meet him on a river steamer upon the Tiber, bound for Ostia with a party from the University of Rome. He was delighted to be addressed as 'Sir Charles Martin,' and recalled with evident enthusiasm the charms of Fingask and of the distinguished ladies who so hospitably entertained him there.

The new lairds include many excellent and cultivated men well worthy to take their place among the older families. Their command of wealth enables them to improve their estates, and to beautify their houses in a way which was impossible for the impoverished owners whom they have replaced; their taste has created centres of art and culture, and their public spirit and philanthropy are to be seen in the churches, schools, and village-reading rooms which they have erected, and in the good roads which they have made where none existed before. On the other hand, among their number are some of whom the less said the better, and who make their way chiefly in those circles of society wherein 'a man of wealth is dubbed a man of worth.'

Many incidents have been put in circulation regarding the race of coal and iron-masters who, starting as working miners, have made large fortunes in the west of Scotland. A good number of these tales are probably entirely mythical, others, though founded on

some original basis of fact, have been so
improved in the course of narration, that they
must be looked upon as mainly fabulous.   Yet
the alterations have generally kept to the spirit
of the story, and represent the current estimate
of the character and habits of the individual
round whom the legend has gathered.   According to one of these tales a wealthy iron-master
called on a country squire and was ushered
into the library.   He had never seen such a
room before, and was much impressed with
the handsome cases and the array of well-
bound volumes that filled their shelves.   The
next time he went to Glasgow he made a point
of calling at a well-known bookseller's, when
the following conversation is reported to have
taken place.

'I want you to get me a leebrary.'

'Very well, Mr. —— I'll be very pleased to
supply you with books.   Can you give me
any list of such books as you would like?'

'Ye ken mair aboot buiks than I do, so you
can choose them yoursell.'

'Then you leave the selection entirely to
me.   Would you like them bound in Russia
or Morocco?'

'Russia or Morocco! can ye no get them
bund in Glasco'.'

One of these men went to see Egypt, and took with him as a kind of guide and companion, an artist of some note. When they came to the Great Pyramid, the magnate stood looking at it for a time, and in turning away remarked to his friend, ' Man, whatna rowth o' mason-wark not to be fetchin' in ony rent!'

On the same occasion the iron-master, now getting tired of sight-seeing, was with some difficulty persuaded to cross over and see the Red Sea. He made no observation at the time, nor on the way back, but after getting to bed he found vent for his ill humour. Opening the mosquito curtains, he blurted out to the artist, who occupied another bed in the same room, ' D'ye ca' yon the Red Sea? It's as blue as ony sea I ever saw in my life. Gude nicht.'

It is told of a Paisley manufacturer that at the time of one of the meetings of the British Association at Glasgow, he entertained a large company of the members, a number of whom invited him to visit them when he came to London. He had noticed that his guests had various initials printed after their names on the programmes of the association—F.R.S., F.C.S., D.C.L., LL.D., etc., and, thinking that this was customary in good society, he

selected three letters to affix to his own name
on his visiting cards. In due time he made
his appearance in the south; and presented
his cards. Some of his southern acquaintances
ventured to ask what the letters after his
name were intended to signify. 'O,' said he,
'I saw it was the richt thing to hae the letters, and as I didna very weel ken what a'
you fowk's letters mean, I thocht I wud put
just L.F.P.; that means, Lately frae Paisley.'

CHAPTER VIII.

THE vicissitudes of agriculture have told on
the farmers and farm-labourers of Scotland,
as they have done everywhere else in the
British Islands. To a large extent the small
farms have been swallowed up in enlarged
holdings. It is much less common now than
it used to be to find one of them worked by
a single family, where the husband, wife, sons
and daughters all take their respective shares
of the labour. The extensive adoption of
agricultural machinery, and the replacement
of corn crops by pasture have reduced the

number of labourers needed in a farm, while the attractions of town life have still further tended to deplete the rural population. These important changes could not take place without affecting the position and characteristics of the farming class. It is for the most part only in the remoter districts of the country that one can now meet here and there with a specimen of the type that was prevalent a generation or two ago.

Forty years since there lived at Priestlaw, in the heart of the Lammermuir Hills, a family of farmers, Darling by name, who were perhaps the most excellent examples of that type I have ever encountered. The farm had been tenanted by their forebears for several generations, and the occupants were now two brothers and a sister, all unmarried. Active, intelligent, kindly and honourable, they were universally respected and esteemed throughout Lammermuir far and near. One of the brothers was once riding home from a fair when he was attacked by one of the navvies who were engaged in draining a neighbouring farm. The ruffian had pinned the old man to the grassy bank by the side of the road, and was dealing him some heavy blows, when a group of farmers returning from the same fair came in sight and rushed forward to save life. When they saw who the victim proved to be, their indignation rose to such a height that, but for the intervention of the policeman who happened to come up with another large contingent of pedestrians, they would have executed summary justice themselves. Some of the party conveyed the injured farmer to Priestlaw, while the great majority of the company marched their prisoner off to Haddington, a distance of some twelve miles, and never relaxed their hold of him until they saw him locked up within the police-cell.

The brothers were delightful men to converse with. The sister, besides the family charm, had a keen interest in natural history, and in all the legends and traditions of the hills. I had come to the district to carry on the Geological Survey there, and on making Miss Darling's acquaintance, found from her that when a girl she had accompanied Sir James Hall and Professor Playfair in their excursions up the Fassney Water. She had seen no geologist since then, she said, some sixty years before, and she would fain hear something of what was thought and said about the history of the earth now. We exchanged wallets, I giving her such information as I had been able to gather regarding the rocks around her home, and she, on the other hand, retailing to me a most interesting series of traditions that clung to particular spots visible to us as we sat in her garden, looking over to the Whitadder and across into the heathy uplands. One of her tales has always seemed to me to carry a strong appeal in favour of the trustworthiness of persistent local tradition. Ever since the time of the Battle of Dunbar, she said, it had been handed down that Cromwell, finding his way barred by Leslie and the Covenanters, sought to discover some route through the hills practicable for his army, and sent out scouts for that purpose. Two of these men, disguised as peasants, had made their way down the valley of the Whitadder, as far as the mouth of a little dell or cleugh, when a gust of wind from the hollow blew their cloaks aside, and showed their military garb to some of Leslie's emissaries who were on the outlook. They were promptly shot and buried, and tradition had always pointed to a low mound with some gorse bushes, as marking the site of their grave. Miss Darling sought and received permission from the proprietor who, I think, was the Marquess of Tweeddale, to open a trench at the place with the view of seeing whether any corroboration of the tradition could be obtained. To her great delight she found, among some decayed bones, a few buttons and a coin or two of the reign of Charles I.

It was arranged that after I had taken a few weeks of holiday, I should return to Priestlaw, where she was to have a collection of stones brought up from the river, that I might discourse to her from them, while she on her part promised to continue her stories and legends. But when I came back to the Lammermuirs, Miss Darling and one of her brothers had been already laid in their graves. The farm-house of Priestlaw stands not far from one of the old tracks or drove-roads through the hills, which, though now comparatively little used, serves as the chief thoroughfare for pedestrians from East Lothian into the Merse of Berwickshire. It appeared that one day a tramp had halted at the door of Priestlaw, from which, as was widely known, no needy beggar was ever turned away empty. The man looked ill, and when Miss Darling saw him she would not let him trudge any further on his way, but had a shake-down of straw made for him in one of the outhouses. She would not allow any of her servants to attend on him, lest he should have some infectious complaint, but took charge of him herself. It proved to be a case of scarlet-fever. The man ultimately recovered, but she and one of her brothers caught the infection and died. With this most excellent woman, I fear, much of the unwritten history of Lammermuir perished. She had from girl-hood collected and treasured in a tenacious memory every tradition of the district. She had watched every excavation, whether for drain-ing or building, and had gathered every relic of antiquity on which she could lay hands. The past was a living reality to her, and she found a keen pleasure in recounting it to any one of like tastes and sympathies. Of her, unhappily, it may be truly said that she is among those 'which have no memorial, who are perished as though they had never been, and are become as though they had never been born. But these were merciful men, whose righteousness hath not been forgotten.'

Among the Scottish farmers, though the general type is actively intelligent and pro-gressive, examples may be found, in the re-moter upland districts, of men—

Who scorn a lad should teach his father skill,
And having once been wrong, will be so still,

Thus a small farmer in Cunningham in descanting upon the changes he had himself witnessed in the agriculture and general conditions of his own neighbourhood had ruefully to make the confession—'When I was young I used to think my faither hadna muckle sense, but my sons look on mysel' as a born eediot.'[1]

A sheep farmer in the Cheviot hills had been told that it was useful to have a barometer in the house, for it would let him know when the weather would be good or bad. He was accordingly persuaded to procure a mercurial instrument with a large round dial, which he hung up in his lobby, and duly consulted every day without much edification. At last there came a spell of rainy weather, while the barometer marked 'set fair.' The rain continued to fall heavily, and still the hand on the dial made no sign of truth. At last he took the instrument from its nail, and marched with it to the bottom of the garden where a burn,

---

[1] This story is sometimes said to have been told by the Rev. Dr. Guthrie. It is also reported as having had its origin in a smiddy at Auchtermuchty, in Fife. The idea is probably as old as the human race. The Ayrshire farmer's expression of it however was a good deal more graphic than Pope's

We think our fathers fools, so wise we grow,
Our wiser sons, no doubt, will think us so,

swollen with the drainage of the higher slopes, was rushing along, brown and muddy.   He then thrust the glass into the water, exclaiming, 'Will you believe your ain een noo, then?'

Another farmer who had also procured a barometer had greater faith in its predictions. The ploughing on his farm had been stopped on account of the rain, but he noticed at last that the glass had begun to rise, whereupon he sent his daughter to get the ploughing begun again.   'Ye're to gang on wi' the plooin' noo, John, for faither says the glass is risin'.'   'Deil may care, the rain's aye fa'in,' was the gruff response.

The hill farmer has been the subject of a good many stories not much to the credit of his intelligence.   One of these men, whose holding was on the hills to the north of Strathmore, had laid in at Perth his stock of matches for the winter.   On his wife opening the first box she found that she could not get the matches to strike upon it.   The husband also tried unsuccessfully.   The next time he had to revisit Perth he took the pile of match-boxes with him, and going to the shopkeeper from whom he had bought them, threw them indignantly down on the counter, with the ejaculation, 'They wunna licht.'

'Wunna licht,' exclaimed the shopkeeper in amazement, as he opened a box. Taking out a match, he drew it smartly across the side of his trousers and brought it up, alight. He repeated the same action with a second, and a third, each of which burst into flame as before. 'What do you mean,' asked the aggrieved shopkeeper, 'by sayin' that thae matches wunna licht?'

'Ay,' answered the farmer, 'and div *you* think I can come doon a' the way to Perth, to hae a rub o' your breeks every time I want a licht?'

Hall Pringle was in my boyhood the tenant of a farm near Largo in Fife, and belonged to an antique type of farmer. He still wore knee-breeches, and when dressed for church, or for a visit to Edinburgh, used to mount a blue tail-coat with brass or gilt buttons, a broad-brimmed beaver-hat and a formidable walking-stick. He was tall and broad-shouldered, walked with a swinging pace, and when he appeared on the pavement of Princes Street, he cleared a way for himself and attracted universal attention. He was a great friend of John Goodsir, the anatomist, for they were both Largo men, and when in Edinburgh he usually stayed with the professor, who in return used from time to time to pay him visits at Hatton. On the occasion of one of these visits, Pringle was full of indignation over the post-mistress of the village, who he maintained was in the habit of opening his letters. He declared to Goodsir that he would not rest until he got her removed from her situation. The professor wagered him a new coat that he would fail in his endeavour. The task proved more difficult than he supposed, but in the end, with the assistance of the post-office officials at head quarters, he succeeded in gathering such unquestionable proofs of the delinquencies of the post-mistress, that she was dismissed. In due time the bet, with the existence of which the village was well acquainted, was paid, and the new coat duly arrived at Hatton. On the first Sunday thereafter Hall came to church wearing the garment, and as he passed the pew of the post-mistress, he was observed to give the tails of his coat a triumphant flourish.

I was once seated on the top of a stage-coach in the Lothians with a Peeblesshire farmer next to me, who had a sarcastic remark to make upon most of the farms as we passed along. I remember one place in particular where the owner had built a new house, and had taken infinite pains to lay out his garden, which he had stocked well with fruit-trees, herbaceous plants, and annuals. I had often admired the taste with which the whole had been planned and carried out, and turned to my neighbour to ask if he had not a good word to say for at least that little property. 'Ou ay,' was his remark, 'its a bonny bit place. The only thing it wants is soil.'

The farm-servant changes more slowly than his master. When resident in Ayrshire I frequently entered into talk with the 'hinds,' as they are called, and found among them some intelligent men. The young women who attend to the cows are often admirable specimens of their sex, comely, well-grown, and strong, with a frankness and good humour delightful to meet with. I was once walking up a hilly road on the south side of the valley of the Girvan water, and overtook one of these girls, who was trundling a heavy wheelbarrow in which lay a large cheese and other supplies for the farm. She had already come a distance of some miles, and was evidently a little tired with her exertions. I volunteered to take the wheelbarrow for a little—an offer which she willingly accepted, and she walked alongside, giving me an account of her farm, her master, his family, the farm-servants, the cows, the dairy, and so forth. I soon found that to arms unaccustomed to the task it was much harder to push a heavy wheelbarrow up a hill than might have been supposed. The girl's bare arms were muscular, and seemed fit for any amount of hard work. As we drew near her farm we could see the master and some of the servants at work in the field below the road, which now wound round the side of the hill. She named each of them, and laughed aloud when she saw them looking up at our little cavalcade, evidently puzzled to make out who the stranger could be that Jean had got hold of. 'O, look at Tam Glen,' she burst forth. 'See how he's glowerin'!' I presumed that Tam had a special interest in her, so not to give him cause for jealousy, I dropped the wheelbarrow at the corner of the steading and went on my way, with the good wishes of the milk-maid, who assured me that if ever I passed that way she would see that I got a good big glass of milk.

It is interesting to hear these young women calling to their cows 'proo, proo, proochiemoo,' a cry which the animals understand and obey. The words are said to be a corruption of *approchez moi*, and to date from the time, three hundred years ago, when French ways and French servants were widely in vogue throughout Scotland.

A farm-servant in service among the hills above Dingwall changed to another farm a long distance off. He was found there by some acquaintances, who enquired why he left his former situation.

'Well, you see,' said he, 'I wass not very fond of sāalt.'

'Sāalt! But what had sāalt to do wi' your shifting?'

'Well, I'll tell you all aboot it. The maister wass a very prudent man, and when a cow died he wad be sāaltin' the beast, and we wad be eatin' her. Then by and by there wass a great mortāality among the cocks and hens, and they died faster than we could be eatin' them; and the master, he sāalted the cocks and the hens, and we wad be eatin' them too. Well, ye see, it wass comin' on for Martinmas, and the weather wass mortial cowld, and at last the ould man, the maister's faither, he died. The maister, he cam' to me the next mornin', and said he, "Donald, I see we're rinnin short o' sāalt, so I'm thinkin' you'll need to be goin' doon to Dingwall for some more." Well, you see, I went down to Dingwall, whatefer, but I wass never going back to Auchengreean at all, at all.'[1]

Occasionally a farm labourer becomes a dexterous poacher, and shows by the ingenuity of his methods how well he would have succeeded had fortune opened a way for him in an honest calling that would have given scope for his abilities. The experienced poacher is not infrequently a successful competitor in games where skill as well as strength is required. In curling, for instance, which, even more than golf, brings together men of all ranks in the social scale, the Sheriff may sometimes be seen playing in the same game with men on whom he has had to pass sentence. There is a story of one of these associations, wherein a notorious poacher, who had often been imprisoned, shouted out to the Sheriff who had tried him, ' Now, Shirra, drive the stane in ; gie her sax months ' ; six months' imprisonment being an extreme display of the Sheriff's legal power with which the speaker had made practical acquaintance.

A former minister of the parish of Kirkmichael, in Ayrshire, was resting in his study one Saturday afternoon after having finished

[1] Another version of this story changes the father into the grandmother !

the preparation of his sermon for next day, when he was startled with sounds of violent quarrelling in his own house. He jumped up from his easy chair, opened the door, and heard the angry voice of his own 'man' shouting in the kitchen, 'Na, noo ye limmer, tho' I chase ye to Jericho I'll catch ye.' The minister rushed off to save life, burst into the kitchen, and found there, to his great surprise, nobody but the man himself who worked on the glebe, and who was now seated at a table taking his supper. 'John, John, what's the meaning o' this? What were ye swearing at? Wha were ye fechtin' wi'?' '*Me*, minister,' said the astonished John, 'I'm no fechtin', I'm no swearin' at onybody, I'm only suppin' thae cauld sowens oot o' a pewter plate wi' this thick horn-spoon, and they're gey an' fickle to catch.'

Let me now turn to some recollections of farm and crofter-life in the Highlands, as they presented themselves to me in the year 1854 and thence onwards. The house which for some happy weeks in that year, and at intervals for forty years afterwards, became my home in Skye, was Kilbride, to which I have already made reference as the residence of my friend the minister of Strath. Besides his ministerial duties, Mr. Mackinnon had a large farm, most of which was rough pasture for sheep and cattle, but with some arable land in the valley bottom, where crops of oats and potatoes were grown.

Farming in the neighbourhood of a deer forest entailed in those days some serious trials, besides what arose from scanty soil, tempestuous seasons, uncertain crops, and late harvests. And with these trials I soon came actively to sympathise at Kilbride. The farm lay at the west end of the valley of Strath, immediately at the foot of the range of the Red Hills. These heights formed part of Lord Macdonald's deer-forest, and though the deer were not numerous, the fields of oats or green crops at Kilbride and the neighbouring hamlet of Torrin offered a tempting pasturage to them, as a change from their sterile granite corries above. Barbed wire, or indeed wire of any kind, had not made its way to these parts, as a help towards the enclosing of land. The fields were only fenced in with low dry-stone dykes, which offered no protection against inroads even from stray sheep. Hence it was needful to watch all night and to make noise enough to frighten away the deer. I can remember sometimes awaking before daylight, and hearing the thumping of trays, blowing of horns, and shouting of the watchmen. And yet with all this labour and some occasional depredation and loss, when the deer contrived to elude detection, one seldom heard any complaints, and I never in those days knew of a deer being shot or injured either by the farm-servants or by the crofters around.

Another source of vexation in the farming operations at Kilbride arose from a very different cause. Although the arable fields were more or less enclosed, it had not been found possible to enclose the farm as a whole, much of the ground being rough hill-pasture. Sheep and cattle were thus liable to stray elsewhere unless watched. Through the lower ground, where, the herbage being best, the animals chiefly grazed, ran the only road from Strathaird to the east coast. To prevent the flocks from escaping along this thoroughfare into other pastures, a rude fence had been constructed there for some distance on either side of the road, across which a gate had been placed. Except the scattered crofters, who gave no trouble, as they performed their journey on foot and willingly closed the gate when they had passed through, Kilbride had

no near neighbours. On the west side, however, some six miles off, there lived an
eccentric and somewhat quarrelsome laird.
He received inebriates in his remote dwelling
with a view to their cure by distance from
temptation. If all tales we heard were true,
he was by no means a teetotaller himself. It
was even reported that he allowed strong
drink to be placed on the dinner-table, and
partook of it himself, but required his patients
to pass the bottle round without helping
themselves. We did not wonder that under
such a régime some of them, like Lucio,
'had as lief have the foppery of freedom as
the morality of imprisonment,' and that we
now and then met those who had escaped,
and who were walking all the way to Broadford, some nine miles off, and back again in
order that they might once more have a glass
or two of whisky.

Between the laird and the Kilbride family
there was no love lost. As the public road
passed through the heart of the minister's
farm, it was necessary to have a gate across
it at the farm boundary-wall, otherwise the
cattle and sheep would have escaped. But
this gate was a dire offence to the laird.
For a while, every time he drove that way,

he would lift the gate off its hinges and
fling it into the loch at Kilchrist. At last
the consequences of this conduct became too
serious to be tolerated, and the minister was
preparing to take legal steps to protect himself, when two of his giant sons quietly
resolved to take the law into their own
hands. Ascertaining when the laird would
pass along the road, they concealed themselves among some copse on the hillside
immediately above the gate, and waited for
their man. In due time he arrived, and
finding the gate closed as usual, he jumped
from his dogcart, wrenched it off its fasten-
ings, and threw it, with an angry imprecation,
into the lake. In an instant he was seized
by the two young men, and, after receiving a
sound horse-whipping, was sent on his journey.
As the result of this escapade, the assaulters
were summoned before the Sheriff and fined,
but they let it be widely known that they would
willingly pay the fine ten times over for the
pleasure of thrashing the laird once more, if
he ever ventured to remove the gate again.
He never did remove it, but he always left
it wide open thereafter, and some lad had to
be employed to see that it was duly shut
after he had passed.

At the head of the sea-inlet of Loch Slapin lies an alluvial plain, through which a broad stream brings down the drainage of the valley of Strath More. On this plain the water has gathered into a lake—a favourite haunt of sea-trout, which the minister had the right of dragging with the net. The days set apart for this employment were red-letter days at Kilbride. We sometimes hauled ashore large numbers of fine fish, which in various forms—fresh, dried, and pickled—supplied the commissariat for some time thereafter.

During my earlier visits to Skye I saw much of the crofters. On distant excursions I used to find quarters for the night in their cottages, being franked on to them by some minister or other friend who knew them well. In those days the political agitator had not appeared on the scene, and though the people had grievances, they had never taken steps to agitate or to oppose themselves to their landlords or the law. On the whole, they seemed to me a peaceable and contented population, where they had no factors or trustees to raise their rents or to turn them out of their holdings. In a later chapter, which will contain some reminiscences of my wanderings as a geologist among the Western

Isles, I shall give some particulars of my intercourse with the crofters of Skye.

One of the most vivid recollections which I retain of Kilbride is that of the eviction or clearance of the crofts of Suishnish. The corner of Strath between the two sea-inlets of Loch Slapin and Loch Eishort had been for ages occupied by a community that cultivated the lower ground where their huts formed a kind of scattered village. The land belonged to the wide domain of Lord Macdonald, whose affairs were in such a state that he had to place himself in the hands of trustees. These men had little local knowledge of the estate, and though they doubtless administered it to the best of their ability, their main object was to make as much money as possible out of the rents, so as on the one hand, to satisfy the creditors, and on the other, to hasten the time when the proprietor might be able to resume possession. The interests of the crofters formed a very secondary consideration. With these aims, the trustees determined to clear out the whole population of Suishnish and convert the ground into one large sheep-farm, to be placed in the hands of a responsible grazier, if possible, from the south country.

P

I had heard some rumours of these intentions, but did not realise that they were in process of being carried into effect, until one afternoon, as I was returning from my ramble, a strange wailing sound reached my ears at intervals on the breeze from the west. On gaining the top of one of the hills on the south side of the valley, I could see a long and motley procession winding along the road that led north from Suishnish. It halted at the point of the road opposite Kilbride, and there the lamentation became loud and long. As I drew nearer, I could see that the minister with his wife and daughters had come out to meet the people and bid them all farewell. It was a miscellaneous gathering of at least three generations of crofters. There were old men and women, too feeble to walk, who were placed in carts; the younger members of the community on foot were carrying their bundles of clothes and household effects, while the children, with looks of alarm, walked alongside. There was a pause in the notes of woe as the last words were exchanged with the family of Kilbride. Everyone was in tears; each wished to clasp the hands that had so often befriended them, and it seemed as if they could not tear themselves away. When they set forth once more, a cry of grief went up to heaven, the long plaintive wail, like a funeral coronach, was resumed, and after the last of the emigrants had disappeared behind the hill, the sound seemed to re-echo through the whole wide valley of Strath in one prolonged note of desolation. The people were on their way to be shipped to Canada. I have often wandered since then over the solitary ground of Suishnish. Not a soul is to be seen there now, but the greener patches of field and the crumbling walls mark where an active and happy community once lived.

Another island that formerly possessed a considerable crofter population is Raasay. When I paid it my first visit from Kilbride, the crofters had only recently been removed; many of their cottages still retained their roofs, and in one of these deserted homes I found on a shelf a copy of the Bible wanting the boards and some of the outer pages. When I revisited the place a few years ago, only ruined walls and stripes of brighter herbage showed where the crofts had been. In diminution of population, the island has changed much from what it was when Johnson was charmed with the society and hospitality of the Macleods. The old house, indeed, in which he was entertained still stands, but so built round with ampler additions as to be almost concealed behind the wings and frontage of a large modern mansion. The natural features of the island, however, must be pretty much as he saw them. The Dun Can, one of the most wonderful monuments of geological denudation in the Inner Hebrides, rises as a truncated cone, the flat top of which forms the summit of the island. This conspicuous landmark is the last fragment left of the sheets of lava which stretched eastwards from Skye across Raasay towards the mainland. Besides its geological importance, it has long had for me a sentimental interest, for at a picnic on the top my old friends, John Mackinnon of Kilbride and his future wife, became engaged to each other.

One of the characteristics of this island is to be found in the holes, tunnels, and perforations which in the course of ages have been made by rain-water descending through the calcareous sandstone that forms the higher part of the eastern cliffs. These holes open on the moor above, and as they are apt to be concealed by bracken and heather, they form dangerous pitfalls for sheep. In former days, when numerous crofts stretched along the eastern slopes and there was some traffic across the middle of the island, even an occasional crofter would be lost if benighted, or during the thick fog that sometimes settles on these heights. It is told that a woman, on her way back from the store on the west side of the island, fell into one of these chasms in the dark. Bruised, but not seriously injured, she succeeded in slowly descending between the rough walls, and was found late on the second day crawling along the track below the cliff, not far from her own cottage, with her clothes torn into tatters. All over the west Highlands the tradition is current that such subterranean tunnels have been traversed by dogs, which on emerging at the further end have appeared without any hair, their exertions in squeezing themselves through the long narrow passages having rubbed them bare.

One of the hamlets on the east side of Raasay, built beneath the cliff and at the top of the steep declivity that descends from the base of the precipice to the edge of the sea, was known by a Gaelic name meaning 'Tethertown,' because to prevent them rolling down the slope into the sea, the small children had ropes tied round their waists and were tethered to pegs firmly driven into the ground.

Up till towards the close of the eighteenth century it was the general practice in the Highlands to move the cattle and sheep in the summer up to the hills, where the pasture was held in common. One of the great events of the year was this migration to the 'shielings,' where for some happy and busy weeks the women and children made butter and cheese, and their flocks gained strength and flesh in the fresh open air and on the sweet young herbage. But the rapid development of sheep-rearing in large farms drove the communities away from their summer retreats, and began that impoverishment of the Highlanders which has continued ever since. Many a time, in my wanderings among the mountains, have I come upon the traces of these shielings—patches of greener verdure, with ruined walls or heaps of stones, overgrown with nettles and other plants indicative of human occupation, but all now solitary and silent.

At the mouth of Loch Scavaig lies a small flat island of red sandstone named Soay, which when I first came to the district was chiefly noted for possessing the fattest boy in the West Highlands. The soil of this island is thin and poor, the climate rather moist, and

the situation, facing the Atlantic, cuts the
island off from constant communication with
Skye. The crofters had their little bits of
land, and some of them possessed also frail
boats, with which they ferried themselves over
the sound to the Skye shore, and added to
their slender fare by a little fishing. But one
family owned the fat boy, and the brilliant
idea occurred to his parents to take him to
Glasgow, and earn an honest penny by ex-
hibiting him to the public. They left the
island for this purpose, with bright visions of
success. But they had no Barnum to take
charge of them, nor do they seem to have
fallen into the hands of any other showman
experienced in

> All our antic sights and pageantry,
> Which English idiots run in crowds to see.

Had large posters been widely placarded announcing that the veritable fat boy of Pick-
wickian fame could be seen in all his rotundity
for the modest charge of sixpence, enough
money might have been made, not only to
keep the family for the rest of their lives,
but perhaps to buy up the whole island, and
establish a dynasty of Kings of Soay. But
the young prodigy and his disappointed

parents had sorrowfully to return wiser and poorer to their northern home.

The first visit to Glasgow is a memorable event in the lives of those West Highlanders who have never seen more people together than at a fair or a sacrament, or more houses than make one of their little clachans. Donald's astonishment at the crowded streets, the interminable array of high houses, and the bustle and swirl of city-life, has been chronicled in many ludicrous anecdotes. One of these may be quoted as illustrative of one aspect of commercial dealing. Many years ago a newly-arrived Highlander was being shown the sights of Glasgow by a fellow-countryman who had now got used to them. As they crossed a street, they saw in the distance a dense crowd of people, and the newcomer naturally asked what it meant. He was told that there was a man being hanged. He then enquired what they were hanging him for, and was told it was for sheep-stealing. He looked aghast at this news, and at last exclaimed: ' Ochan, ochan ; hanging a man for stealing sheeps ! Could he no' ha' bocht them and no' peyed for them ? '

The best opportunity of seeing the whole crofter population of a district is furnished by the summer fairs or markets. In Strath, this important gathering is held on an open moor not far from Broadford. Everybody who has anything to sell or to buy makes a point of attending it, from far and near, accompanied by a still larger number of idlers, intent only on fun and whisky. Old and young, men, women, and children, horses and cattle, sheep and dogs, find their way to the 'stance.' Whether or not much business profitable to the crofters was done, the fair to the outside spectator used always to be eminently amusing and picturesque.

The quantity of whisky consumed on these occasions must have been enormous. There was likewise a kind of epidemic of bargaining. I remember the case of a woman who brought a small terrier dog for sale, which she had named Idir—a Gaelic word, equivalent to our expression 'At all.' Having sold her dog she passed on complaining, 'Cha 'n 'eil margadh IDIR, IDIR' (This is no market, at all, at all), sounding out the last word so loudly as to reach the ears of the dog, which, when it came to her, she caught up in her arms and sold again in a more distant part of the fair. Another occasion which brought the scattered crofter communities of Strath together was the half-yearly celebration of the communion in Broadford Church. Not only the people of the parish, but numbers of others from adjacent parishes, tramped many a long mile to attend the services.

One cannot live much in the Highlands without meeting with instances of that inveterate laziness already alluded to, more especially on the part of the men. They have a certain code of work for women, and another for themselves, and that of the women is generally the heavier of the two. This national characteristic has been often noticed. Writing as far back as 1787, Mrs. Grant, of Laggan, gave what is not improbably its true explanation. After alluding to the Highlanders as formerly fighters, hunters, loungers in the sun, fond of music and poetry, she continues thus : 'Haughtily indolent, they thought no rural employment compatible with their dignity, unless, indeed, the plough.' Hence they left all the domestic and family concerns to their women, who worked the farms, attended to the cattle and other cognate labours. 'The men are now civilised in comparison to what they were, yet the custom of leaving the weight of everything on the more helpless sex still continues. The men think they preserve dignity by this mode of management; the women find a degree of power or consequence in having such an extensive department, which they would not willingly exchange for inglorious ease.'[1]

More than a hundred years have passed since these words were written, yet the usages Mrs. Grant described may still be seen in operation. A few years ago, in boating along the north shore of Loch Carron, on a warm day, I passed a field where the women were hard at harvesting work, while the men were leaning against a wall, with tobacco-pipes in their mouths and their hands in their pockets. I remarked to my two boatmen that these hulking fellows should be ashamed of themselves, to let the women do that heavy work under the hot sun, while they looked on in idleness. The answer was characteristic and not unexpected: 'Ye surely wadna hae men doin' women's wark, wad ye, sir?'

This habit of allowing the women to do menial drudgery, so characteristic of uncivilised races, seems hard to throw off, though probably it is now undergoing amelioration. Burt, writing in the earlier part of the eighteenth century, gives an amusing instance of how

[1] *Letters from the Mountains*, 5th edition, vol. ii., p. 124

the treatment of women in the Highlands
appeared to a foreigner. 'A French officer
coming hither to raise some recruits for the
Dutch service, met a Highlandman with a
good pair of brogues on his feet, and his wife
marching bare-foot after him. This indignity
to the sex raised the Frenchman's anger to
such a degree, that he leaped from his horse
and obliged the fellow to take off the shoes,
and the woman to put them on.' In com-
menting on this incident, the editor of the
fifth edition of Burt's volumes records an
instance in which 'a stout fellow of the very
lowest class in Ardgour, took his wife and
daughter, with wicker baskets on their backs,
to a dunghill, filled their baskets with manure,
and sent them to spread it with their hands
on the croft; then, with his greatcoat on,
he laid himself down on the lee side of the
heap, to bask and chew tobacco till they
returned for another load. A stranger, who
merely looked at the outside of things, would
hardly believe that this man was a kind and
tender husband and father, as he really was.
The maxim that such work (which must be
done by some one) *spoils the men*, has been so
long received as unquestionable by the women,
that it makes a part of their nature; and a

wife would despise her husband, and expect the
contempt of her neighbours on her husband's
account, if he were so forgetful of himself, as
to attempt to do such a thing, unless her situation at the time did not admit of her doing it.'[1]

Manufactures have never flourished in the
Highlands. Yet the region has many advan-
tages for the establishment of industries, especially abundant water-power and the existence
of numerous inlets and natural harbours to
and from which commodities could easily be
shipped. Whisky-making, indeed, has long
flourished, the traditions of the 'sma' still' no
doubt making it natural to take service in a
large distillery. Mrs. Grant of Laggan maintained that 'nature never meant Donald for
a manufacturer; born to cultivate or defend
his native soil, he droops and degenerates in
any mechanical calling. He feels it as losing
his caste; and when he begins to be a weaver,
he ceases to be a Highlander. Fixing a mountaineer on a loom too much resembles yoking
a deer in a plough, and will not in the end
suit much better.'[2] The indignant imprecation

---

[1] Burt's *Letters*, 5th edition (1818), vol. ii., pp. 46, 47.

[2] *Essays on the Superstitions of the Highlanders of Scotland*
(1811), vol. ii., p. 143. Writing some thirty years earlier she
expressed herself to the same effect in her *Letters from the
Mountains*, vol. ii., p. 103.

which Scott puts into the mouth of Rob Roy,
when honest Bailie Nicol Jarvie proposes to
make the Highlander's sons weavers, repre-
sents the ingrained national repugnance to
mechanical crafts. In recent years a few industries have been introduced on a small scale
into some of the little Highland towns, such
as Inverness, Oban, and Campbeltown. These
innovations, however, make slow progress.
Possibly the utilisation of the Falls of Foyers
by a Sassenach company of manufacturers
may prove to be the forerunner of other
similar invasions. But if the future of the
Highlands be left to Donald himself, the
lovers of the unspoilt charms of the mountains
may console themselves with the belief that
these charms will remain much as they still
are for many a long day to come.

CHAPTER IX.

IN continuation of the Highland reminiscences contained in the last chapter, reference may here be made to some further characteristics of the Western Isles, and to a few of the more marked changes which, during the last half century, have affected the Highlands as a whole.

Fifty years ago Highland ferries were much more used than at the present day, when railways and steamers have so greatly reduced the number of stage-coaches and post-horses. These little pieces of navigation across rivers, estuaries, and sea-lochs, afforded ample scope for certain Celtic idiosyncrasies. The ferryman could, as occasion served, contract his knowledge of English, and on one pretext or another contrive to exact more than the legal or reasonable fare, remaining imperturbably insensible to the complaints and remonstrances of the passengers. An illustrative story is told by Dr. Norman Macleod in his charming *Reminiscences of a Highland Parish*. A Highland friend of his who had been so long absent in India that he had lost the accent, but not the language of his native region, had reached one of these ferries on his way home, and asked one of the boatmen in English what the charge was. The question being repeated in Gaelic by the man to his elder comrade, the answer came back at once in the same language, ' Ask the Sassenach ten shillings.' ' He says,' explained the interpreter to the supposed Englishmen, ' he is sorry he cannot do it under twenty shillings, and that's cheap.' No reply was made to this extortion at the moment, but as the boat sailed across, the gentleman spoke to the men in good Gaelic. Whereupon, instead of taking shame to himself for his attempted cheat, the spokesman turned the tables on the traveller: ' I am

ashamed of you,' he said, 'I am, indeed, for
I see you are ashamed of your country ; och,
och, to pretend to me that you were an
Englishman! You deserve to pay *forty* shillings—but the ferry, is only five!'

On another occasion, when a sea-loch had
to be crossed where strong currents swung the
ferry-boat round and some manoeuvring with
the oars was required, the chief ferryman kept
saying, 'Furich, Donald,' to the one assistant,
and 'Furich, Angus,' to the other. At the
other side of the loch the passenger paid the
fare and then said to the ferryman, 'Now, I'll
give you another shilling if you will tell me
what you mean by "Furich, furich," which I
have heard you say so often in the passage
across. It must surely have many different
meanings.' The coin was duly pocketed and
the Highlander thus deliberately explained :
'Ah, it's ta English of ta Gaelic "furich" 'at
you wass wantin' to know. Well, I'll tell you ;
it's meanin' "Wait," "Stop" ; och ay, it means
"Howld on," "Niver do the day what you can
by any possibeelity put off till to-morrow."'

I was once crossing in an open rowing boat
from Skye to Raasay, propelled by two men,
a younger Highlander, who sat nearest to me,
and an elderly man on the bench beyond.

The latter was dressed in a kilt, and with his unkempt locks and rugged features, made a singularly picturesque figure.　My neighbour caught my eye now and then fixed on his comrade, and at last he broke silence with a question :

'You're looking at Sandy, sir, I see?'

'Yes, he is well worth looking at.　He must be an old man, though he seems to pull his oar well still.'

'Ay, I'm sure, he's an auld man noo.　But ye wass hearin' o' Sandy afore?'

'No, I don't think I have ever seen or heard of him before.　What about him?'

'D'ye mean, sir, railly noo, that you never heard tell o' Sandy o' the Braes?'

'No, really, I never did.　What is he famous for?'

'Ochan! Ochan! wass ye never kennin' aboot his medal?'

'Medal! no, so he is an old soldier is he? What battle was he at?'

'Sodger! He's never been at ony battles, for he wass never oot o' Skye and the islands.'

'But how did he come to get a medal, then?'

'Just to think that ye wass never hearin' o' that! Weel, ye see, there's some Society in Embro, I wass thinkin' they call it the "Heeland

Society," and they gied Sandy a medal, for he wass never wearin' onythin' but a kilt all his days.'

Besides the ferrymen, the drivers of the old Highland coaches included some quaint characters, who have disappeared with the vehicles which they drove, and occasionally capsized. Half a century ago the coach that ran between Lochgoilhead and St. Catherine's through the pass known as 'Hell's Glen' was driven by a facetious fellow, one of whose delights was to make fun at the expense of his English passengers. One day when he had brought the coach to the top of the pass and halted the horses, he got down, remarking to an English lady who sat on the box seat beside him, and on whom the brunt of his sarcasms had fallen, that if now this place had been in England, he would doubtless have to search a long time before he could find a bit of old leather to stick into the drag for the run down hill. Looking under a stone he pulled out an old shoe, which of course he had placed there on a previous journey, and which he now held up as a proof of the great superiority of Scotland. Some weeks afterwards, a barrel arrived addressed to him. As he was not accustomed to such presents, he opened it with not a little excitement. Pulling out some straw he saw a large paper parcel inside, and after removing a succession of coverings, came at last upon a small packet carefully sealed. He felt sure it must be something of great value from the pains that had been taken to protect it. So he opened it with trembling hands and found that it contained—a pair of old shoes, with the compliments of the lady whom he had made his butt.

Among the Western Isles two of small size have attained a distinguished celebrity—Staffa and Iona. Three times a week in the summer season, a large and miscellaneous crowd is disembarked upon each of them from Macbrayne's steamboat, which, starting from Oban in the morning, makes the round of Mull, and returns in the evening. If any one desires that the spell of these two islets should fall fully upon him, let him avoid that way of seeing them. They should each be visited in quietude, and with ample time to enjoy them. There is a ferry from the Mull shore to Iona, and in the Sound a stout boat or smack may usually be obtained for the voyage to Staffa.

I once spent a delightful week in Iona, where a comfortable inn serves as excellent headquarters for the stay. There was a copy there of Reeve's edition of Adamnan's *Life of Saint Columba.* Reading the volume where it was written, and amidst the very localities which it describes, and where the saint lived and died, one gets so thoroughly into the spirit of the place, the present seems to fade so far away, and the past to shine out again so clearly, that as one traces the faint lines of the old monastic enclosure, the mill-stream and the tracks which the monks must have followed in their errands over the island, one would hardly be surprised to meet the famous white horse and even the gentle Columba himself. But, apart from its overpowering historic interest, Iona has the charm of most exquisite beauty and variety in its topography. Its western coast, rugged and irregular, has been cut into bays, clefts, and headlands by the full surge of the open Atlantic. Its eastern side is flanked by the broad, smooth, calm Sound, which, where it catches the reflection of a cloudless sky, rivals the Mediterranean in the depth of its blue; while towards the north, where the water shallows over acres of white shell-sand, it glistens with the green of an emerald. Then, as if to form a fitting background to this blaze of colour, the granite of the opposite shores of Mull glows with a warm pink hue as if it were ever catching the reflection of a gorgeous sunset. For wealth and variety of tints, I know of no spot of the same size to equal this isle of the saints.

If Iona seems to be profaned by a crowd of gaping tourists (I always crossed to the west side of the island on steamboat days), Staffa, on other grounds, no less requires solitude and leisure. The famous cave is undoubtedly the most striking, but there are other caverns well worthy of examination. The whole coast of the island indeed is full of interest, from the point of view both of scenery and of geology. It combines on a small scale the general type of the cliffs of Mull and Skye, with this advantage that, as the rocks shelve down into deep water, they can be approached quite closely. My first visit was made in a smack, which I found anchored at Bunessan, in Mull, and from which I got a boat and a couple of men, who pulled me slowly round the whole of the shore, stopping at every point which interested either myself or my crew. My eyes were intent on the forms and structure of the cliffs; theirs were directed to the ledges where they saw any

young cormorants crowded. They scrambled
up the slippery faces of rock, and seizing
the birds, which were not yet able to fly,
pitched them into the bottom of the boat.
These captures, however, were not made
without some loss of blood to the huntsmen,
for the birds, though they had not gained
the use of their wings, knew how to wield
their beaks with good effect. I was told that
young cormorants make excellent hare-soup,
and for this use the men took them. A less
legitimate cause of stoppage was found in the
desire to pull up the lobster creels, of which
we saw the corks floating on the surface of
the water. Several pots were examined, and
I am sorry to say that, in spite of a mild
protest on my part against this act of piracy
on the open sea, some of the best of their
contents were abstracted. The boatmen could
not understand why I should decline to share
in the spoil. Two or three years ago I
landed on Staffa with the captain and officers
and a few of the crew of the Admiralty surveying vessel, 'Research.' Some forty years had
intervened between the two landings. I found
the place to be no longer in its primitive
state of wild nature. Ropes and railings and
steps had been placed for the comfort and

convenience of the summer crowd—a laudable object, no doubt, but I prefer to remember these cliffs when they showed no trace of the presence of the nineteenth century tourist.

From the west side of Skye the chain of the Outer Hebrides can be seen in one long line of blue hills rising out of the sea at a distance of some five and twenty miles. The outlines of these hills had long been familiar to me before I had an opportunity of actually visiting them. In later years, thanks to the hospitality of my friend Mr. Henry Evans, of Ascog, I have made many delightful cruises among them in his steam yacht 'Aster,' of 250 tons, and have been enabled to sail

Round the moist marge of each cold Hebrid isle.

One of his favourite anchorages has been Loch Roag, on the west side of Lewis, where the typical scenery of these islands is well displayed—a hummocky surface of rounded rocky knolls, separated by innumerable lakelets and boggy or peaty hollows, or green crofter-holdings, the land projecting seawards in many little promontories, and the sea sprinkled with islets. On one of the cruises, we landed and examined with some care the famous stones of Callernish—the most numerous group of stand-

ing stones in the British Islands. Seen from the
sea on a grey misty day, they look like a company of stoled carlines met in council. On a
near view, they are found to be disposed in
the figure of a cross and circle, the longer
limb of the cross being directed about ten
degrees east of north. The monoliths consist
of between 40 and 50 slabs of flaggy gneiss,
the largest being 17 to 18 feet in height.
It was interesting to observe that after the
purpose for which they were erected had perhaps been forgotten, boggy vegetation began to
spread over the ground and form a layer of
peat, which, in the course of centuries, increased
to a depth of six feet or more; the lower portions of the upright monoliths were thus buried
in the peat. The late proprietor had this vegetable growth removed, so as to lay bare the
original surface of the ground; but the upper
limit of the turbary could still be traced in
the bleached aspect of that lower part of the
stones which had been covered by the peat,
the organic acids of the decaying vegetation
having removed much of the colouring material
of the gneiss. How long this accumulation
of peat took to form must be matter for
conjecture.

Loch Roag makes a convenient starting point

for St. Kilda, to which I have several times crossed in the 'Aster.' From the higher eminences around this loch the top of St. Kilda may be seen in clear weather, the distance being not more than about 50 miles. But it is the open Atlantic which lies between, and the anchorage of St. Kilda is not good, there being only one available bay, from which, however, a vessel had better at once depart if the wind should shift into the south-east. On one of our visits we were fortunate in finding the weather calm and sunny, so that it was possible to pull in an open boat round the base of the cliffs. And such cliffs and crests! It is as if a part of the mountain group of Skye had been set down in mid-ocean—the same purple-black rocks as in the Cuillin Hills, split into similar clefts, and shooting up into the same type of buttresses, recesses, obelisks, and pinnacles, and in the lofty hill of Conacher, the conical forms and pale tints of the Red Hills. But it is the bird life which most fascinates a visitor. In the nesting season, the air is alive with wings and with all the varied cries of northern sea-fowl, while every ledge and cornice of the precipices has its feathered occupants. Each species keeps to its own part of the cliff. The puffins swarm in the crannies below, while higher up come the guillemots, razor-bills, and kittiwakes. The gannets breed on the smaller islets of the group. We could watch the sure-footed natives making their way along ledges which, seen from below, seemed impracticable even to goats. These men, however, from early boyhood

> Along th' Atlantic rock, undreading, climb,
> And of its eggs despoil the solan's nest.

In ascending one of the crags on the west side of St. Kilda I was fortunate enough to come, unperceived, within a few yards of some fulmars, and had a good look at these most characteristic birds of this island. They yield a strongly odoriferous musky oil, of which the natives make much use, and of which every one of them smells. In passing between the main island and Boreray, we sailed under a vast circle of those majestic birds, the gannets, wheeling and diving into the sea all around us. After swallowing their catch they bent their wings upward to rejoin the circle, and make a fresh swoop into the deep. While watching this magnificent meteor-like bird-play, we were surprised by the appearance of three whales, parents and son, which slowly made their way underneath the swarm of gannets. It seemed as if the backs of these huge animals could hardly escape being transfixed by some of the crowd of descending bills, but we could trace their leisurely and unmolested course by the columns of spray which they blew out into the air every time they came up to breathe.

One of the most curious sea-inlets in the Outer Hebrides is the passage known as the Sound of Harris—a tortuous channel between the Long Island and North Uist, strewn with islets and rocks, and giving a passage to powerful tides. The navigation of this Sound is extremely intricate, and needs good weather and daylight. On one of my cruises to St. Kilda the open sea had been rather rough, but once inside the archipelago, the water became rapidly smooth, showing only the swirl and foam of the tidal currents that sweep to and fro between the Minch and the Atlantic. At the eastern end of the Sound stands the nearly perfect ancient church of Rodil—an interesting relic of the ecclesiastical architecture which followed that of the Celtic church.

As one moves about among the Western Highlands and Isles, now so peaceful, and in many places so sparsely peopled, it is difficult to realise the conditions of life there two or three centuries ago, when the population was

not only more numerous, but was subdivided
into clans, often at feud with each other.   Of
these unhappy times many strikingly picturesque memorials remain in the castles perched
on crags and knolls all along the shores.   Most
of these buildings were obviously meant mainly
for defence, but some suggest that the chiefs
who erected them sought convenient places
from which to attack their neighbours, or to
sally forth against passing vessels.   Each of
them, strongly constructed of local stone, and
of lime which must often have been brought
from a distance, might have seemed designed
to be

> A forted residence 'gainst the tooth of time
> And razure of oblivion.

But almost without exception they are now in
ruins.   The tourist who would try to picture to
himself what these fortalices meant, should sail
through the Sound of Mull and note the succession of them on either side, from Duart at
the one end to Mingarry at the other.   Dun-
vegan, in Skye, the ancient stronghold of the
Macleods, which still remains in good preservation and inhabited, affords an idea of the aspect
of the more important of these strengths in old
times.   But many of them were little more
than square keeps, strong enough, however, to

withstand sudden assault, and even to endure a siege, as long as provisions held out.

Other memorials of ancient strife and bloodshed, less conspicuous than the castles, but even more impressive, may here and there be found, which bring the brutal realities of savagedom vividly before the eyes. Within my own recollection, Professor Macpherson, then proprietor of Eigg, gathered together the skulls and scattered bones in the cave on that island where some 200 Macdonalds, men, women, and children, were smothered alive by an invading band of Macleods, who kindled brushwood against the cave-mouth. For nearly three hundred years these ghastly relics of humanity had lain unburied where the victims fell, and might be kicked and crushed by the careless feet of any inquisitive visitor. Even now, although every care has been taken to remove them, stray vestiges of the massacre may perchance still be found on the rough dank floor of the dark cavern. From the mouldering straw and heath I picked up, many years ago, the finger-bone of a child.

The tragic fate of the Macdonalds of Eigg is a well-known event. But here and there one comes upon relics of unchronicled slaughters. The most impressive of these which I have ever met with is to be found on the west side of Jura. In a cruise round this island in the 'Aster' with Mr. Evans, we were accompanied by Miss Campbell of Jura, who, in the course of a talk about clan-battles in the Highlands, referred to the last raid that had been made on Jura, where, according to tradition, a party of Macleans had landed and were opposed by Campbells. She added that the skeleton of one of the Macleans who was slain lies on the moor still. On my expressing some incredulity as to this last statement, she assured me that it was true, and that I might verify it with my own eyes. So the yacht was turned into a little indentation of the coast, at the head of which stood a shepherd's cottage. We landed from the long boat, and the shepherd, recognising the party, came down to meet us. Miss Campbell asked him where the skeleton was, and he pointed to an overhanging piece of rock about a hundred yards from where we were standing. On reaching this spot, we found a few rough stones lying at the foot of the low crag. These the man, stooping down, gently removed, and below them lay the bleached bones. We took up the skull, which was well formed and must have belonged to a full-grown man. A piece of bone about the size of half-a-crown had, evidently by the sweep of a claymore, been sliced off the top of the skull, leaving a clean, smooth cut. This wound, however, had not been considered enough, for the head had been cleft by a subsequent stroke of the weapon, and there was the gash in the bone, as sharply defined as on the day the deed was done. We gently replaced the bones, with the stones above them, and there they remain as a memorial of 'battles long ago.' [1]

The west side of Jura is pierced by many caves, which were worn by the sea at a remote period when the land stood somewhat lower than it does now. At the far end of one of these caves a human skull is said to lie. This grim relic has more than once been removed

[1] There were probably many descents and slaughters in these islands of which no historic record remains. It is known, however, that in 1585 a party of Macdonalds from Skye was forced by stress of weather to take refuge in the part of Jura belonging to Maclean of Dowart. Two gentlemen of the Macdonald clan, independently driven at the same time into a neighbouring inlet, remained concealed from their kinsmen and secretly carried off by night a number of Maclean's cattle, which they took with them to sea, intending that the blame should fall on their chief. The Macleans, on discovering the robbery, attacked the Macdonalds who remained, and slew sixty of them, the chief escaping only because he had slept that night on board his galley.

and buried, but always in some mysterious manner finds its way back again. Nothing appears to be known of its history, and nobody likes to say much about it. If it exists at all, its return to its cavern may be due to a superstitious feeling on the part of the natives, some one of whom secretly transfers it back to what is regarded as its rightful resting-place. These Jura caves are the scenes of certain weird legends where a black dog, a phantom hand, and a company of ghostly women perform some wonderful feats.[1]

When I first visited the island in 1860, the proprietor of Jura was a keen deerstalker, and used to live for a day or two at a time in one of these caves, when his sport took him over to that side of the island. On one occasion a party of ladies from an English yacht, then at anchor in the inlet, had landed, and in passing the mouth of the cave had noticed the laird inside, whom they took to be a hermit, retired from the vanities of this world. Pitying his forlorn condition and the necessarily scanty supply of food which he could scrape together in so wild a place, they, on their return to the yacht, very kindly made up a basket of

[1] See J. G. Campbell's *Superstitions of the Highlands an Islands of Scotland* (1900), pp. 112, 114, 121.

R

provisions and sent it ashore for his sustenance. Next morning, before the anchor was weighed, a boat came alongside with a gamekeeper, who had brought a haunch of venison for the owners of the yacht, with the thanks and compliments of Campbell, of Jura.

I cannot pass from the subject of these Western Isles and the adjacent part of the mainland without a reference to their indescribable charm, and an expression of my own profound indebtedness to them for many of the happiest hours of my life. To appreciate that charm one must live for a while amidst the scenery, and learn to know its infinite diversity of aspect under the changing moods of the sky. The tourist who is conveyed through this scenery in the swift steamer on a grey, rainy day, naturally inveighs against the climate, and carries away with him only a recollection of dank fog through which the blurred bases of the nearer hills could now and then be seen. Nor, even if he is favoured with the finest weather when, under a cloudless heaven, every island may stand out sharply in the clear air, and every mountain, corrie, and glen on the mainland may be traced from the edge of the crisp blue sea up to the far crests and peaks, can he realise on such a day how different these same scenes appear when the atmospheric vapour begins to show its kaleidoscopic transformations. Having sailed along a good part of the coast of Europe, including Norway and the Aegean Sea, I am convinced, that for variety of form, the west coast of Scotland is unsurpassed on the Continent, while for manifold range and brilliance of colour it has no equal. One who has passed a long enough time amidst this scenery, more especially if he has made his home upon the water, sailing across firth and sound, threading the narrows of the kyles, and passing from island to island, can watch how the very forms of the hills seem to vary from hour to hour as the atmospheric conditions change. Features that were unobserved in the full blaze of sunlight come out one by one, pencilled into prominence by the radiant glow of their colour, as the cloud-shadows fall behind them. In the early morning, when the sun climbs above the Inverness-shire and Argyleshire mountains and the mists ascend in white wreaths from the valleys, there is presented to the eye a vast and varied panorama, comprising the highest and most broken ground in the British Isles, rising straight out of the Atlantic. In the evening, when the sun sets behind the islands, and the hills, transfigured by the mingled magic of sunlight, vapour, rain and cloud, glow with such luminous hues as almost to be lost in the glories of the heaven, one feels that surely 'earth has not anything to show more fair.'

Wandering through these scenes, one's mind comes to be filled with a succession of vivid pictures printed so indelibly on the memory that, even after long years,

> In vacant or in pensive mood,
> They flash upon that inward eye
> Which is the bliss of solitude.

Among these mental impressions some stand out with especial prominence in my own memory. Such is a sunset seen from the top of the lighthouse on Cape Wrath when, above the far ocean-horizon, there rose a mass of cloud, piled up into the semblance of mountains and valleys, with sleeping lakes and bosky woods, castle-crowned crags and one fair city with its streets and stately buildings, its steeples and spires. The late Professor Renard of Ghent, had accompanied me to that far north-western headland, and we amused ourselves naming the various parts of the topography of this gorgeous aerial Atlantis. Another memorable sunset was seen from the

Observatory on the top of Ben Nevis, when the chain of the Outer Hebrides, at a distance of a hundred miles, stretched like a strip of sapphire against a pale golden sky. Next morning a white mist spread all over the lower hills like a wide sea, with the higher peaks rising like islets above its level surface. Through all these memories of landscape there runs, as a tender undertone, the recollection of the human interest of the scenes. One's mind recalls the fading relics of ancient paganism, the devoted labours of the Celtic saints who first brought the rudiments of civilisation to these shores, the coming of the vikings from the northern seas, the feuds and massacres of the clans. The landscapes seem to be vocal with the pathos of Celtic legend and song, and with the romance of later literature,

> In each low wind methinks a spirit calls,
> And more than echoes talk along the walls.

The demureness of the Scottish Highlander appears to have been in large measure developed during last century, and especially since the Disruption of the National Church and the domination of the Free Kirk. At the time of the Reformation and for many generations afterwards, he was wont on Sunday to play games—throwing the stone, tossing the

caber, shinty, foot-races, horse-races, together
with music and dance. It was formerly usual
for him to be able to play on some musical
instrument; in older times on the harp and in
later days on the pipes, the fiddle, or at least
the Jew's harp. Writing in 1773 Mrs. Grant
of Laggan averred that in the Great Glen
'there is a musician in every house, and a
poet in every hamlet.' In 1811 she could
still say, 'there are few houses in the Highlands where there is not a violin.'[1] Where-
ever there was a good story-teller, or one
who could recite the old poems, songs, tales,
legends, and histories of former times, the
neighbours would gather round him in the
evenings and listen for hours to his narratives.
These customs continued in practice until the
early part of last century, and some of them
still sparingly survive among the Catholic
islands of the Hebrides. But the Presbyterian clergy in later times have waged ceaseless war against them. 'The good ministers
and the good elders preached against them
and went among the people and besought
them to forsake their follies and to return to
wisdom. They made the people break and

[1] *Letters from the Mountains*, vol. i., p. 112; *Essays on the
Superstitions of the Highlanders of Scotland*, vol. ii., p. 202.

burn their pipes and fiddles. If there was a foolish man here and there who demurred, the good ministers and the good elders themselves broke and burnt their instruments, saying

> Better is the small fire that warms on the little day of peace
> Than the big fire that burns on the great day of wrath.

The people have forsaken their follies and their Sabbath-breaking, and there is no pipe and no fiddle here now.'[1]

The same sympathetic observer from whose pages these words are taken has given the following illustrative example of the clerical methods : 'A famous violin-player died in the island of Eigg a few years ago. He was known for his old-style playing and his old-world airs, which died with him. A preacher denounced him, saying, "Thou art down there behind the door, thou miserable man with thy grey hair, playing thine old fiddle, with the cold hand without, and the devil's fire within." His family pressed the man to burn his fiddle

---

[1] A. Carmichael, *Carmina Gadelica*, 1900, Introduction, p. xxvi. Dr. Norman Macleod, who had no sympathy with this bigotry, relates—'A minister in a remote island parish once informed me that "on religious grounds," he had broken the only fiddle on the island. His notion of religion, I fear, is not rare among his brethren in the far west and north.'— *Reminiscences of a Highland Parish*, p. 35.

and never to play again. A pedlar came round and offered ten shillings for the violin. The instrument had been made by a pupil of Stradivarius, and was famed for its tone. "It was not at all the thing that was got for it," said the old man, "that grieved my heart so sorely, but the parting with it! the parting with it! and that I myself gave the best cow in my father's fold for it when I was young." The voice of the old man faltered, and the tear fell. He was never seen to smile again.'[1] Taught to think their ancient tales foolish and their music and dancing sinful, the people have gradually lost much of the gaiety which with other branches of the Celtic race they once possessed.

One who was familiar with the Highlands in the middle of last century will be struck with the further decay or disappearance of various customs which even then were evidently fading out of use. Of these vanished characteristics, one of the most distinctive, whose loss is most regrettable, was the practice, once universal, of singing Gaelic songs during operations that required a number of men or women, working together, to keep time in their movements. This picturesque usage appears to

---

[1] A. Carmichael, *op. cit.*, p. xxviii.

have died out on the mainland, though it
still survives among the Catholic islands of
the Outer Hebrides. There were many such
songs, each having a marked rhythm, to which
it was easy to adjust the motions of the limbs.
I have already referred to the boat-songs that
kept the rowers in time. Besides these,
there were songs for reaping and other labour
in the field. Indoors, too, each kind of work,
wherein two or more persons had to move in
unison, had its music. Thus when two women
grind corn with the quern or handmill, as they
still do in some of the Outer Isles, they move
to the rhythm of a monotonous chant. When
they thicken (wauk) homespun cloth, they
keep themselves in time by singing—a practice which may also still be heard among the
Catholic parts of the Hebrides. I have only
once seen the quern in use, but when I first
visited Skye, the songs still continued to be
sung, though not as accompaniments to con-
certed movement. In some of the Outer
Hebrides milking-songs are still in use, and
the cows are said to be so fond of them that
in places they will not give their milk without
them, nor occasionally without their favourite
airs being sung to them.[1] There are likewise

[1] A. Carmichael, *op. cit.*, vol. i., pp. 258, 276.

herding-songs sung when the flocks are sent out to the pasture, which, unlike most of the Gaelic music, are joyous ditties appropriate to what was once, over all the Highlands, one of the happiest times of the year.

A notable change among the cottages and houses in the Highlands during the last fifty years is to be seen in the disappearance of some of the old forms of illumination, consequent on the introduction of mineral oil. Candles of course remain, but in former days a common source of light was obtained from the trunks of pine-trees dug out of the peat mosses. The wood of these trunks, being highly resinous, burnt with a bright though smoky flame. Split into long rods it made good torches, or if broken up into laths and splinters, it furnished a ready light when kindled among the embers of a peat-fire. If a bright light was wanted, the piece of wood was held upright with the lighted end at the bottom, when the flame rapidly spread upward. If, on the other hand, it was desired to make a less vivid light last as long as possible, the position of the wood was reversed. Metal stands were made to hold these pine-splinters, the simplest form consisting merely of a slim upright rod of iron

fastened below into a block of stone, and
furnished with a movable arm which slid up
and down, and was furnished at the end
with a clip that would hold the wood at any
angle desired. In Morayshire, these stands
were known as 'puir men.' A few years ago,
Mr. James Linn, of the Geological Survey,
secured from the farms and cots of that district an interesting collection of these objects
which had been thrown aside and neglected,
after they were superseded by cheap oil-
lamps. This collection has since found a
place in the Museum of National Antiquities
at Edinburgh.

Another old Highland characteristic which
has been constantly waning since 1745 has
had its rate of diminution greatly accelerated
since railways and steamboats were multiplied,—the localisation of clansmen in their
own original territories. It is true that the
clan name may still be found predominant
there. In Strathspey, for instance, most
families in the Grantown district are Grants;
Mackays prevail in the Rae country, Campbells
in Argyleshire, Mackinnons in Strath, and
Macleods in the north of Skye. But in all
these old clan districts there is a yearly increasing intermixture of other Highland

names, together with many from the low-lands.

The application of the clan name Macintosh to a waterproof, has sometimes given rise to odd mistakes, real or invented, as where an Englishman, who had got out at one of the stations on the Callander and Oban railway, is reported to have come back to the carriage from which he had descended, and into which four or five stalwart natives had meanwhile mounted, whom he asked, ' Did you see a black Macintosh here?' ' Na,' was the answer, ' we're a' red Macgregors.'

But unquestionably the most momentous of all the changes which have come upon the people of the Highlands is the gradual, but inevitable dwindling of their native spoken language. Ever since the barriers against the free intercourse of Celt and Saxon were broken down, Gaelic has been undergoing a slow process of corruption, more especially in those districts where that intercourse is most active. English words, phrases, and idioms are gradually supplanting their Gaelic equivalents, until the spoken tongue has become in some districts a mongrel compound of the two languages. One may still meet with natives who know, or at least say that they know, no

English. 'Cha 'n-eil Beurla acom, I have no English,' is sometimes a convenient cover for escaping from troublesome questions. But, unless among the more remote parishes and outer islands, the younger generation can generally speak English, at least sufficiently well for cursory conversation.

It is much to be regretted that the Sassenach hardly ever takes the trouble to learn even a smattering of Gaelic. Apart from the pleasure and usefulness of obtaining a firmer hold on the good will of the natives, some little knowledge of the language provides the traveller with an endless source of interest in the meaning and origin of the place-names of the Highlands, which are eminently descriptive, and often point to conditions of landscape, of human occupation, of vegetation and of animal life very different from those that appear to-day. The old Gaels were singularly felicitous and poetical, as well as wonderfully profuse, in their application of topographical names. In my early wanderings over Skye, I used to be astonished to find that every little hummock and hollow had a recognised name, not to be found on any map, yet well known to the inhabitants, who by means of these names could indicate precisely the route to be followed across a trackless moorland or a rough mountain range. Even if no attempt may be made to speak the language, enough acquaintance with it may easily be acquired for the purpose of interpreting a large number of place-names. The same descriptive term will be found continually recurring, with endless varying suffixes and affixes of local significance.

To speak Gaelic, however, without making slips in the pronunciation is difficult. Some of the sounds are hard for Saxon tongues to accomplish, and unless they are accurately given, the uneducated peasant has often too little imagination to divine the word that is intended. Thus, a lady whom I knew on the west side of Cantyre, told me that when she first came to live there, being a stranger to Highland manners and customs, she was desirous at every turn, to increase her knowledge of them. One day she asked her cook, a thorough Highlander, 'Kate, what is a philabeg?' 'A what, mam!' 'A philabeg; I know it's a part of a man's Highland dress.' 'Och, mam, I wass never hearin' of it at all.' Some time afterwards, having meanwhile ascertained what the word signifies, she happened to come into the kitchen when a Highlander in full costume was standing there. 'Oh Kate, I asked you not long ago to tell me what is a philabeg, and you said you had never heard of it. There's a philabeg,' said she, pointing to the man's kilt. 'That, mam! of course, I know that very well, I'm sure. If you'll said pheelabeg, I would be knowin' at once what you wass askin' about. I've knew what is a pheelabeg ever since I wass born.'

It seems hardly possible for a lowlander, unless he begins early in life and has abundant practice, to lose all 'taste of the English' in his Gaelic talk. Thus a pre-Disruption minister with whom I was well acquainted in Argyleshire, and who was not a native Celt, but had learnt Gaelic in his youth, made mistakes in the language up to the end of his long life. One of his co-presbyters so highly appreciated humour that some of the stories he told of my old friend were suspected to be more or less touched up by the narrator. And many were the stories thus circulated through the Synod of Argyle. One of them, I remember, referred to a Gaelic sermon of the minister's in which he meant to tell his hearers that they were all *peacach caillte*, that is, lost sinners; but as pronounced by him the words sounded like *pucach saillte*, which means 'salted cuddies' or coal-fish. On another occasion, being in a hurry to start from a distant inn, he called the waiting-maid, wishing to desire her to have the saddle put to his horse. The Gaelic word for a saddle is *Diollaidich*, and he got the first half of it only, which makes a word with a very different meaning, so that what he did say was, 'put the devil (*diabhol*) on the horse.'

Professor Blackie, who threw himself with all the ardour of his enthusiastic nature into the study of Gaelic, laid the Highlands and all Highlanders under a debt of gratitude to him for his untiring labours on their behalf. He gained an accurate grammatical knowledge of the language, and a consider-able acquaintance with its literature, but he never properly acquired the pronunciation. During a visit I once paid to him at his picturesque home on the hillside near Oban, we crossed over to Kerrera. After ramb-ling along the western and southern shores of that island, the Professor said he would like to call on a farmer's wife who was a friend of his. Accordingly we made our way to the house, where he saluted her in Gaelic. The conversation proceeded for a

little while in that tongue, but at last the
good lady exclaimed, 'Oh, Professor, if you
would speak English I would understand you.'

In my early rambles over Skye, I found
that 'a little Gaelic is a dangerous thing.'
I had sufficient acquaintance with the language
to be able to ask my way, but had made no
attempt to 'drink deep' at the Celtic spring.
On one occasion when passing a night in a
crofter's cottage, I could make out that the
conversation which the inmates were carrying
on, related to myself and my doings. In a
thoughtless moment I made a remark in
Gaelic. It had no reference to the subject
of their talk, but it had the effect of putting
an end to that talk, and of turning a battery
of Gaelic questions on me. In vain I protested that I had no Gaelic. This they good
humouredly refused to believe, repeating again
and again, 'Cha Gaelig gu leor, you have
Gaelic enough, but you don't like to speak it.'

CHAPTER X.

THE Orkney and Shetland Islands present in many respects a strong contrast to the Hebrides. Differing fundamentally in their geological structure, and consequently also in their scenery, they are inhabited by a totally distinct race of people, and the topographical names, instead of being Gaelic, are Norse or English. The natives, descendants of the old Norwegian stock that once ruled the north and west of Scotland, still retain many marks of their Scandinavian origin. Blue eyes and fair hair are common among them. They are strongly built and active, with an energy and enterprise which strike with surprise one who has long been familiar with the west Highland indolence and procrastination. My first descent upon the Orkneys was a brief but interesting expedition, when after a ramble along the north coast of Caithness, I had reached, with my colleague, Mr. B. N. Peach, the little inn of Huna, near John o' Groat's House. For geological purposes we were desirous of visiting the nearest of the Orkney group, Stroma, 'the island of the stream,'—a name which graphically marks its position in the midst of the broad tidal current of the Pentland Firth that sweeps past it like a vast river, and with a flow fully three times faster than that of an ordinary navigable river. We engaged the old ferryman, who used to run the mail-boat from Caithness to Orkney, and were warned by him that, as the weather looked threatening and the tide in the evening would be against us, he could not give us more than an hour on the island, and he would not allow the men to have any whisky on the voyage, since they might need all their wits about them before we got back. The sail across was easily made. Obeying our captain's injunctions to keep within the prescribed hour, we did most of our work running, and succeeded in ascertaining what we wanted to know. On re-embarking, we soon perceived that his prognostication as to the weather was likely to be

fulfilled. The sky had become entirely overcast, and, though no rain fell, ominous moanings
of wind warned us not to linger. The tide
had turned and was beginning to flow west-
wards against the breeze. As it increased in
its rate of flow the surface of the firth began
to curl and boil, streaks of foam were whirled
round in yeasty eddies, while here and there
the water, as if in agony, would rear itself in
swirling columns that burst into spray, which
was swept along by the wind in clouds of
spindrift. Not far off we could see the
'Merry men of Mey,' a tumultuous group
of breakers above a dangerous reef, surging
up into sheets of foam-crested water that
writhed and tossed themselves far up into
the misty air. Our pilot sat at the helm
watching every advancing billow and cleverly
bringing the boat round in time to meet it.
It was a difficult piece of navigation, skilfully
performed. We could then understand why
the men were to be prohibited from tasting
whisky till they got back to Huna. But
arrived in safety, we cheerfully ordered the
stipulated bottle for them.

Subsequently on crossing over into the
Orkney group, I had soon occasion to note
the difference between the boatmen there and

those with whom I was familiar in the west of Scotland. More adventurous and skilful than their Celtic fellow-countrymen, they generally possess larger and stronger boats, which they keep in better trim. Some of their smaller boats are built with sharp sterns, and exactly resemble the common type one sees in Norway. In the eighteenth century, as Boswell mentions, the people in the Inner Hebrides sometimes obtained their boats from Norway. The Orcadians, among other traces of their Scandinavian descent, seem to take to the water as naturally as the seals which they shoot. On several occasions my Orkney boatmen piloted me along the base of cliffs and among rocks against which the heavy Atlantic swell was breaking, where no Skye boatmen I ever met with would have ventured. No one can fully realize the grandeur of the great cliff of Hoy unless he can look up at it from below, as well as from the crest above. Its warm tints of bright yellow and red make it seem aglow with light even in dull weather, and from a distance it looks as if it caught sunbeams which are falling on no other part of the scene. Viewed from its upper edge, this cliff presents a wonderful picture of decay. The horizontal beds of sandstone have been split by the weather into long deep vertical chasms, and etched out into fantastic cusps and cupolas, alcoves and recesses. From the edge of the precipice, which rises a thousand feet above the sea, one looks down on the long Atlantic rollers, seemingly diminished to mere ripples, and their heavy breakers to streaks of foam, while the surge, though it thunders against the rocks, 'cannot be heard so high.' The Old Man of Hoy, which has been left standing as an isolated column in front of this great cliff, is the grandest natural obelisk in the British Islands, for it rises to a height of 450 feet above the waves that beat against its base.

Swept by the salt-laden blasts from the ocean, Orkney and Shetland cannot boast of trees. Hedges of elder grow well enough when under the protection of stone walls, but are shorn off obliquely when they rise above them, as if a scythe or bill-hook had cut them across. A group of low trees, sheltered by the houses at Stromness, appears to be the resort of all the birds within a compass of many miles. There is a story of an American traveller who landed at Kirkwall in the dark, and, after a stroll before breakfast next morning, returned to the hotel amazed at the 'completeness of the clearing' which he supposed the inhabitants had made of their forests. To the geologist, the antiquary, and the lover of cliff scenery, the Orkney islands offer much of great interest. Though it was in the first of these capacities that I was drawn to the islands, the standing stones, brochs, and mounds, as well as the magnificent coast-precipices, were soon found to have irresistible attractions.

Shetland, lying more remote from the rest of Britain, has preserved, even more than Orkney, traces of the Scandinavian occupation. One comes now and then upon an old Norse word in the language of the people, and so foreign are the topographical names that, in hearing them pronounced, one might imagine oneself to be among the fjords of Norway. To this day we may hear a Shetlander, who is about to sail for the south, say that he is going to Scotland, as if he regarded his own islands as part of another kingdom. On my first visit to Shetland I spent some time on the mainland, chiefly on geological errands bent, but not without a glance at the scenic and antiquarian interests of the islands. One of my excursions took me to Papa Stour—a small island lying to

the west, and exposed to the full fury of the
Atlantic storms, which have tunnelled its
cliffs with caverns and gullies. Some of these
perforations have been continued until they
open upward in cauldron-like holes on the
surface of the moorland. During gales from
the west, the sea is driven into these clefts
with a noise like the firing of cannon, and
bursts out in sheets of spray from the
cauldrons on the moor. On this island, as
in so many other parts of Shetland, the
want of fuel is a serious evil. The inhabitants have gradually cut away and burnt
much of the thin coating of turf which
covered the naked rock. Hence over considerable areas there is now no soil,—only
sheets of crumbling stone which supports no
vegetation and cannot be made to yield a
crop of any kind.

On the way back from Papa Stour to Ler-
wick, I availed myself of the kindly offered
hospitality of one of the proprietors on the
mainland. The lady of the house was unfortunately confined to bed, but her daughter
and the governess did the honours of the
house. This young lady was said to be descended from one of the daughters of the
Shetland worthy whose likeness Scott drew

as Magnus Troil in the *Pirate*. At all
events she was a typical Shetlander, as
much at home on the water as on the land.
Mounted on a strong pony, she used to scour
the country far and near, picking her way
across bog and stream in a region where
roads were few. In her boat, she had made
acquaintance with every creek and cavern for
miles along the coast on either side. Some
time before my visit, a vessel with a cargo
of teak had been wrecked in the neighbourhood, and such part of the wood as could
be reached had been removed. But the
young lady, in the true spirit of the wrecker,
knew where every stray log was to be found,
in each little voe and creek into which the
waves had carried it. She had a huge dog
which accompanied her on her rambles, and,
as one of the family, was admitted into the
dining-room at meal-time. During dinner the
animal, instinctively divining that I was fond
of dogs and might be expected to be attentive to him, placed himself at my side, with
his nose resting on the edge of the table
and his eyes directed towards my plate.
Interested beyond measure in the talk of my
young hostess, I forgot my four-footed friend
for a little, and, on turning to continue

operations with knife and fork, found to my astonishment that my plate was empty, and that he was pleasantly looking at me and licking his lips.

In the course of a cruise in the 'Aster' round the Shetland Islands I enjoyed ample opportunities of becoming acquainted with the whole of the wonderful coast-scenery of this archipelago. With a steam yacht it is possible to keep close inshore, and to sail back and forward along the more interesting parts. In this way I was enabled to see the great cliffs of Foula well, and to watch the movements of its 'bonxies' or Great Skuas. With the view of protecting these now rare and almost exter- minated birds, the proprietor of the island many years ago gave strict orders to the natives not to molest them nor take their eggs, and on no account to let any birds'-egg collectors come and help themselves. He was on the steamer one day bound for Scotland, when one of the passengers, entering into conversation with him, began to talk of Foula, and to complain of the incivility of the people of the island. The laird inquired in what way they had been dis- courteous to him. 'Well, you see,' said the bird-man, 'I am a dealer in birds' eggs, and I went to the island to obtain some eggs of the

Great Skua. The natives refused to get me any, and when they saw me preparing to go and hunt for them myself they gathered round and threatened to pitch me over the cliff into the sea.' 'And, by Jove,' exclaimed the laird, 'they would have done it too. They have my orders ; I am the proprietor of Foula.'

As the yacht steamed round St. Magnus Bay and past the extraordinary group of fantastic islets that rise out of its waters, we had the good luck to see a white-tailed eagle winging its way northward, and pursued by a flock of large gulls. This bird is now almost extinct along our coasts. A few pairs are still left. One of these breeds near the top of a cliff 500 feet high, in a group of islets which is a favourite anchorage for the 'Aster.' Last year (1903), besides the two old birds, a third was seen.

Rounding the far headland of Unst, the most northerly point of the British Islands, we ran up a flag to salute the lighthouse on that lonely spot. So seldom does any yacht pass there, and, judging from our experience, so few vessels of any kind come within saluting distance of the place, that the keeper, taken aback apparently at our courtesy, and not wishing to delay his return of it, seized a pair of white trousers that were drying on the parapet rail, and waved them enthusiastically, while his comrade ran to hoist the flag.

One of the greatest obstacles to yachting in these northern seas during summer is the prevalence of fogs. In two cruises to the Faroe Islands, the 'Aster' had to be navigated for most of the way in a dense white mist, with a smooth sea below and blue sky above, but when one end of the vessel was scarcely visible from the other, and the foghorn had to be kept constantly going. So excellently, however, had the course been laid, that after soundings had shown that land could not be far off, we heard the barking of a dog and the firing of a gun. In a few minutes the top of the Lille Dimon could be seen above the fog, and we entered the channel for which we had been steering.

At the time of one of our trips to Faroe, small-pox had been prevalent in Scotland, and when we ran into the sheltered inlet of Trangisvaag, the yellow quarantine flag was run up on the wooden building ashore, and a boat came off to warn us not to land until we had been inspected by the medical man of the place. In a little while he pulled alongside, and after some preliminary conversation asked that the

whole human contents of the yacht should be
mustered on the deck before him. So we all
placed ourselves in a row, while he marched
along and inspected us. It was interesting to
notice the amused and half-contemptuous faces
of the crew at this performance, each man feeling himself as strong and well as youth, sea-
air, and good food could make him. My host
thought that the official should not be allowed
to leave without some refreshment, and called
on the steward to bring it. The Doctor
selected a glass of whisky, evidently without
knowing what it was, for before we could
make any explanation, he tossed it off as if it
had been so much water. But not until it
was well down his throat did he realise the
strength of the liquor. He gave a few gasps,
while his eyes filled with water, and he had
to make an effort to compose himself and go
on with the conversation as if nothing had
happened. If he had never tasted Talisker
whisky before, we believed he would not
forget his first experience of it.

So exactly do the Faroe Islands reproduce
the scenery of the Inner Hebrides that it is
difficult at first to believe that we are not
somehow back again under the cliffs of Skye
or Mull. Green declivities descend from the

interior of these islands to the edge of the cliffs, which then plunge sheer down into the sea. The precipices are built up of nearly level sheets of brown basalt, edged with narrow strips of grassy herbage, cleft into chasms, and eaten out into tunnels and caves by the restless surge. From the horizontal bars of the great cliffs, the eye ranges upward to the brightly verdant slopes above, and marks dark-brown ribs of rock running parallel with these bars in a series of terraces away up to the crests of the ridges and hills. Only in the little bays, which here and there indent the ranges of formidable precipice, does one catch sight of evidence of human occupation.

But, while the topography is so similar, the population presents a singular contrast to that of the Western Isles of Scotland. Everywhere it gives proofs of energy, industry, comfort, cleanliness, and civilisation. Each little community at the head of its cliff-girt inlet has built a hamlet of neat wooden houses, which, with their painted doors, trim windows, and clean white curtains, show that the inhabitants are well-to-do, and not without some of the luxuries of life. Fishing is the main industry, and all the inhabitants are more or less engaged in it—men, women, and children. The men go to sea and bring back the fish. The women look after it as it lies drying in the sun, cover it with tarpaulin if rain comes, and stack it up ready for export. There is usually a chief man or merchant who takes general charge of the trade, and arranges for the steamboats to come and carry off the piles of fish.

To return from such a scene to the west of Skye cannot but fill the heart with sadness as one passes inlet after inlet, either with no inhabitants or with only a handful of them, housed in squalid, miserable, dirty huts, too poor to provide themselves with good sea-going boats, too timid or too lazy and unenterprising to gather the harvest of the sea, as the men do in Faroe, but content to live as their fathers have done, save that now they have become possessed by a greed for more land, which, when they get it, they will doubtless cultivate in the same unskilful and slovenly fashion. In the herring fishing, which is the chief industry among the Western Isles, the boats come largely from the east side of Scotland, and are manned by the stalwart and active seamen of the shores of the Moray Firth and other parts of the coast.

The subject of fish and fishing recalls some

recollections of angling experiences on the mainland. In boyhood I used sometimes to assist at a 'burning o' the water,' when all the shepherds, poachers, and idlers of the district assembled to take part in the fun and excitement of spearing salmon or grilse. The Gala Water on these nights presented a singularly picturesque sight—the lurid glare and smoke of the torches, the cautious movements of the men in the river, the shouts of those on the bank as a successful 'leister,' that had transfixed a fish, was handed over to them, and the chorus of shepherds' dogs that were among the most active and excited of the spectators. The account of the night exploits at Charlie's Hope in *Guy Mannering* is as truthful as it is graphic.

Among the lakes of Sutherland there is one not far from Beinn Griam which, an enthusiastic angler assured me, consists of 'three parts of fish and one water.' Another sporting friend, not to be outdone, lauded the extraordinary abundance of game in his native island. 'There is a stream there,' he would say, 'once so stocked with trout that I never failed to fill a big basket. But now the feathered game has become so abundant that though the fish are as plentiful as ever, I can hardly get any, for almost every time I cast my line I hook a grouse in the air.'

A former well-known witty editor of an Edinburgh newspaper was fond of escaping to the banks of the Yarrow or the Ettrick for a few days' fishing. One Monday morning he was accosted by the clergyman who had been preaching the day before, and who, though a stranger to him, asked a number of questions about his sport. The editor replied civilly to the battery of queries, and at last began to catechise in his turn.

'And are you too a fisher?' he asked.

'Oh no, I have no time for angling. You see I am a fisher of men.'

'And have you had much success in your line?'

'Not nearly as much as I could wish.'

'Ay, I can believe that. I looked into your creel [the church] yesterday and there were very few fish in it.'[1]

There is a story told of an amateur angler who with an attendant was fishing, from the English side, the Carham Burn, which at one part of the border separates the two kingdoms. His hook had caught under the opposite bank,

[1] This anecdote has been variously related; but the version given here is probably the true one.

and he was under the impression that it had
been taken by a large fish which had run up
from the Tweed. His old companion, however, disabused him by drily remarking, 'Ay,
ye hae got a big fish, nae doot; ye hae
heukit auld Scotland.'

Those who are accustomed to salmon which
has been carried in ice a long distance, and
kept for some days before being eaten, do not
always appreciate the newly-killed fish as it
is given in Scotland, with its firm, flaky con-
sistence and fresh curd. A Londoner, who
had taken a house for the summer in Forfarshire, had made the acquaintance of the lessee
of one of the salmon fisheries on the coast of
that county, and asked him one day to be
so good as allow him to have a fish for a
dinner party which he was about to give. A
fine fresh salmon was accordingly sent to the
house. A few weeks afterwards the Englishman came down to the coast again, and after
expressing his thanks for the fish, ventured to
remark that somehow it was harder and more
flaky than what he was accustomed to in
London. He was about to give another
dinner, he said, and would like another salmon.
The lessee, promising that he should have
one quite to his taste, went down to one of

his men and gave the following order:
'Sandy, you'll take that fish and hang it up
in the sun all day. Then after breakfast to-
morrow you'll lay it on a stone and thump it
hard all over with a heavy stick, then hang
it up in the sun again till the afternoon, and
after that send it up to Mr. ——.' The
Londoner in a few days appeared to express
his thanks for the fish which he pronounced
to be exactly what he liked, and what he
was used to in the south.

Trouting streams in this country and in
Western America have distinct peculiarities.
Some years ago I was rambling up Glen
Spean, and along the heathery and rocky
banks of the River Treig with an American
friend, who had spent much of his life in surveying the Western Territories of the United
States. 'What a fine stream,' he remarked,
'not to have trout in it!' I assured him
there were plenty of trout in all the streams
of the district. 'But how can that be?' he
enquired, 'there are no poles growing along
the banks.' He explained that in the Far
West, Providence appeared to have so arranged that fish need not be sought for in
streams on the margins of which no wood
grew, such as would supply a fishing-rod.

The mention of sport in the Highlands brings to recollection another illustration of the curious vitality of some stories, and the singular transformations which they may undergo as they are passed on from mouth to mouth through successive generations. An old legend in the north-west Highlands tells how two men set out to kill a wolf that was destroying the sheep of the crofters of Kintail. One of them entered the animal's den, while the other stood on guard at the entrance. Soon afterwards the wolf returned and made for its cave, when the man at the entrance seized it by the tail as it got inside, and held it fast. His companion within then called out

> One-eyed Gilchrist
> Who closed the hole?

The other answered

> If the rump-tail should break
> Thy skull shall know that.[1]

Probably this tale was carried to Canada by some of the Highland emigrants and became naturalised and localised there, for it has come back in the following guise: Two Scotsmen in a mountainous part of the colony, climbed up

[1] Translated from the Gaelic by A. Carmichael, *Carmina Gadelica*, vol. ii., p. 235.

a rocky slope to the mouth of a narrow cave, into which one of them crawled to discover what might be inside. The other contented himself by lighting his pipe and sitting down outside, but had not been there above a minute or two when a huge she-bear came rushing up the declivity and made straight for the cave. Seeing the danger to his friend he had presence of mind enough to seize the tail of the bear just as the animal had got within the entrance, and to plant his feet firmly against the rock on each side. Presently a voice from the inner recesses shouted out, 'Donald, Donald, fat be darkenin' the hole?' To which Donald replied, 'My faith, Angus, gin the tail break ye'll fin' fat be darkenin' the hole.'[1]

---

[1] In another version the predatory animal has become a wild sow!

CHAPTER XI.

THE shepherds in the pastoral uplands of the
south of Scotland are a strong, active, and
intelligent race. I have spent many a happy
day among them, living in their little shielings, on the friendliest footing with them, their
families, and their dogs. The household at
Talla Linnfoot, in Peeblesshire, was a typical
sample of one of these families. Wattie Dalgleish, the shepherd there when I first went
into the district, was becoming an elderly man,
no longer able for the stiff climbs and long
walks that were needed to look after the whole
of his wide charge. His young and vigorous
son was able to relieve him of the more distant
ground, which was shared with another man,
not of the family, who slept in one of the

outhouses. Wattie's active wife and daughter
looked well after the domestic concerns of the
household. His laugh had the clear, hearty
ring of a frank, honest, and kindly nature. He
delighted to recount his experiences of field
and fell, and his Doric was pure and racy.
One evening I had come up from Tweedsmuir
and described to him a man whom I had seen
at work there, planing a shutter which he
had placed on tressels in the very middle of
the road. This worthy wore large round-eyed
spectacles, a tattered apron in front of him,
and a red-tasselled blue bonnet on his head.
The shepherd recognised the man from my
description, and at once asked, 'And did he
speir (enquire) the inside out o' ye?' He had
certainly put a good many questions. He
turned out to be a kind of factotum down the
valley of the Tweed—'barber, cook, uphol-
sterer, what you please'—of whom I afterwards
heard much. As among his avocations was
that of paper-hanging, he was once employed
by a proprietor in Broughton parish to paper a
bedroom. In the afternoon, when the master
of the house came to see how the work was
getting on, he found that the paper had been
stuck on the walls just as it came, without the
selvages being cut off. 'Tammas, Tammas,'

exclaimed the laird, 'what is the meaning of this? Why have you not cut off these ugly borders?' Tammas looked at the laird for a moment through his great goggles, and then with a toss of his head remarked, 'That may be your taste, sir, but on Tweedside we like it best *this* way,' and went on with his pasting.

Wattie Dalgleish had a collie which, like himself, was getting somewhat aged, and no longer fit for the severer work of the hill. The dog would accompany him in his short rounds and return early in the afternoon to the cottage. Some hours later I would come back from my rambles, and as I descended the steep slope opposite, and came within old 'Tweed's' sight and hearing, he would signify his recognition of me by a loud barking, which I could always distinguish from other canine performances, for it showed neither surprise nor anger, but had an element of kindly welcome in it. As I drew nearer, the barking underwent a curious change into a sort of short intermittent howl of delight, and as I came up to the enclosure, the dear old creature would burst into a loud guffaw. He was the only dog I ever knew that had what one might fairly call a true honest laugh. And how his tail would wag, as if it would surely be twisted off, while he marched in front of me to announce in his own way that the guest of the family had come back.

There were so many dogs in the household that one could study the idiosyncrasies of canine nature on a basis of some breadth. It struck me then that perhaps there might be more truth than one had been inclined to suppose in Butler's facetious remark :

> As some philosophers
> Have well observ'd, beasts that converse
> With man, take after him.

Certainly there did appear to be in that shepherd's shieling a curious similarity of disposition between the dogs and their respective masters. My old friend 'Tweed' was a kind of four-footed duplicate of the honest Wattie, down even to the hearty laugh. On the other hand, the stranger shepherd had a collie that closely reproduced his own characteristics. The man was sullen and taciturn, did not mingle with the family, but sat apart, and retired soon to his own quarters. The dog usually lay below his master's chair, refused to fraternise with the other dogs, receiving them with a snarl or growl when they came too near, and marching off with the shepherd when he retired for the night. I tried hard to be on cordial terms with the man, and still harder to ingratiate myself with the dog, but was equally unsuccessful in both directions.

The Talla valley is narrow and deep, the hills rising steeply from 1000 to 1400 feet above the flat alluvial haugh at the bottom, which is about 900 feet above the sea. It must be sadly changed now, when it has become the site of one of the great Edinburgh water-reservoirs. But in the days of which I am speaking it was a lonely sequestered glen, silent save for the bleat of the sheep or the bark of the dogs. In wet weather the wind drove up or down the defile, separating the rain into long vertical shafts, which chased each other like pale spectres. In the narrower tributary gorge of the Gameshope, these ghost-like forms are even more marked, hence they are known in the district as the 'White Men of Gameshope.' Above Talla Linnfoot, the ground rises steeply up into the heights around Loch Skene and the weird hollows of the White Coomb. With my early school-fellow and colleague in the Geological Survey, the late Professor John Young, of Glasgow University, I have wandered into every recess and over every summit

of that fascinating ground. On one occasion
we extended our ramble to the Yarrow valley,
with the intention of spending the night under
the hospitable roof of Tibbie Shiels, who was
then in still vigorous old age. Next morning
we found the ground buried under some six
inches of snow, which still continued to fall.
As a return over the trackless hills was then
impossible, we were shut up for several days,
during which we shared in various domestic
employments, among the rest in learning to
churn butter. Tibbie encouraged us in our
labours by various recollections of Wilson,
Hogg, and other personages of the *Noctes
Ambrosianae*.

When the storm ceased and the sun shone
out again, the whole landscape was white up to
the crests of the hills, save St. Mary's Loch
and the Loch of the Lowes, between which the
little hostelry stands. These waters were still
unfrozen, and wore a look of inky blackness by
contrast with the surrounding ground. One
unlooked-for effect of the wintry covering was
to reveal the surface features of the hills with a
clearness never before realised. These uplands
in their ordinary guise are so rich in colour,
and the distribution of the varying tints has
so little relation to the forms of the ground, that

most of the minor details of the topography are
lost to the eye. But now that colour was
wholly eliminated, every little dimple and ridge
stood out marked by its delicate violet shadows
in the pure white snow.

One of the notabilities of this district was the
widow of another shepherd who occupied the
little cottage of Birkhill at the head of Moffat-
dale. She had not only lost her husband, but
her son had been smothered in a snow-drift not
many yards from her door. Yet she remained
cheerful and contented, with a kindly welcome
and a warm fireside for wayfarers who sought
her hospitality. Many a time have I slept in
the little box-bed in her 'ben,' and partaken of
her 'scones' and other good cheer. One of
my colleagues in the Survey, who made her
house his station for weeks at a time, discovered
that grouse take some time to get accustomed
to the dangers of a wire-fence. Such a line of
division between two sheep-farms had been run
up the hillside near Birkhill, and the grouse
when flying low would strike against the wires
and be killed on the spot. Coming down in
the evening he used sometimes to bring with
him several brace of dead birds, decapitated or
otherwise mangled, but none the less a welcome
addition to his commissariat.

After my marriage I had occasion to revisit Birkhill, and brought my wife with me. Jenny gave her a kindly greeting, and in parting offered her this piece of friendly advice: ' Noo, my leddy, ye'll mind never to anger him, and ye'll see that he ay has a pair o' dry stockins to put on when he comes hame at nicht.' Poor old soul! She had had some experience of stormy scenes under her own roof, and life in these uplands had taught her that wet boots are the common lot of humanity and the beginning of many ailments.

No one who has sojourned for weeks and months among these pastoral hills can fail to have come more or less under their spell. They show none of the grandeur and ruggedness of the Highlands. The hills, on the whole, have smooth, rounded outlines, save here and there, where some crag of grey rock protrudes from the pervading mantle of green bent and purple heath. Yet the topography is sufficiently varied not to become monotonous, while the slopes in every season of the year glow with colour, spread over them like a delicate sheet of enamel. There is beauty enough in the landscape of itself to please, and even here and there to fascinate. Its attractions, however, are infinitely increased by the human associations which cling to every part of the surface, with a halo of legend, romance, and poetry.

> Meek loveliness is round it spread,
>   A softness still and holy;
> The grace of forest charms decayed
>   And pastoral melancholy.

The houses of Tibbie Shiels and Jenny of Birkhill showed the simplest and most rudimentary form of inns. They varied little from the ordinary shepherds' cottages, the most notable difference being that they sold excisable liquors. They were at least clean, with homely comfort, and simple but wholesome fare.

The want of cleanliness in the Scottish hostelries, even those of the chief towns, in the previous century, is continually referred to by English travellers in the country. Sydney Smith, while praising Scotland and its natives, among whom he made his home near the close of the eighteenth century, confessed that they 'certainly do not understand cleanliness.'

The inns or change-houses in country districts remained still in a state of grievous untidiness and squalor. To many a village

and little town Scott's lines might have been
applied :

> Baron o' Bucklyvie,
> The muckle deevil drive ye,
> And a' to pieces rive ye
> For biggin' sic a town,
> Where there's neither man's meat, nor
> horse meat,
> Nor a chair to sit down.

Nevertheless, already before railways had
spread their network across the kingdom,
when the country roads were more frequented
than now by stage-coaches, post-carriages, and
pedestrians, many modest and comfortable little
inns had come into existence, and were to
be met with by the roadside. These have
now unhappily in great measure disappeared,
or have sunk into mere public-houses, kept
open only for the sake of selling drink. My
impression is that proportionately much more
whisky is now consumed by the artizan and
labouring classes than in those days when
various kinds of light or heavy ale were in
demand. The 'tippeny' of Burns' time, his
'reaming swats that drank divinely,' the ale
that 'richly brown, reams ower the brink in
glorious faem,' were still familiar forms of
'Scotch drink.' But nowadays the labourer
no longer 'sighs for cheerful ale'; when he

enters the public-house, it is usually whisky that he calls for.

In my boyhood a custom still prevailed, which I think must now be obsolete—that of placing a 'spelding,' or dried salt haddock, beside the glass of ale ordered by a caller at a public-house or roadside inn. Bitter beer had not yet come into vogue in Scotland. Instead of it, all the liquors supplied were of native brewing, from the light 'tippeny,' which was a refreshing and innocent drink, up to the strongest Edinburgh ale—a liquor which required to be quaffed with great moderation. When a few drops of it ran down the glass they glued it so firmly to the table that some force was needed to pull it off. The salt fish was, of course, served that it might provoke thirst enough to require more liquid.

Another recollection of these old days brings back the excise-officers who used to be on the watch at the English frontier to examine the luggage of passengers from the north. One of the surviving relics of Scottish independence was to be found in the inland revenue duties, which, as they differed on the two sides of the border until they were equalised in 1855, led to a good deal of smuggling. Whisky was then contraband, and liable to

extra duty when taken into England. At
that time, this liquor was hardly known south
of the Tweed, save to the Scots who imported
it from their native country. But now it has
made its way everywhere, and has almost
completely supplanted the gin that had previously filled its place. It is prescribed by
the medical faculty as, on the whole, a safer
drink than much of the wine that comes from
abroad. The quantity of it made every year
is enormously larger than it was fifty years
ago. Not only is it to be found everywhere
in this country, but on the continent, and indeed wherever English-speaking people travel.
If one were asked to name the two most conspicuous gifts which Scotland has made in
recent times to the United Kingdom, one
could hardly go wrong in answering Whisky
and Golf.

There used to be, and probably still are,
many quiet, unpretending, but remarkably comfortable little inns in Galloway. The innkeepers were also farmers, and probably in
many cases their farms formed the chief and
most profitable part of their avocations. Fresh
farm produce was supplied to their guests with
the amplest liberality—excellent beef and mutton, fowls, eggs, butter, milk, and such cream

U

as one seldom met with in other parts of the country.

A notable reform of the last half century in the Highlands has been seen in the improvement of the inns. I can remember the primitive condition of some of them which have been enlarged into what are now pompously called hotels. Many years ago I had occasion to spend a night or two in one of these antique and uncomfortable houses in Skye. One Sunday morning I was in bed and awake, when the bedroom door was quietly opened, and by degrees a half-dressed female figure stealthily entered. She looked at the bed to see if I were still asleep, and as I kept my eyes half closed, she thought herself unobserved. Stepping gently across to the dressing-table, she opened my razor-case, and having possessed herself of one of the razors, as quietly retreated. I lay conjecturing what use the landlady (for it was she) would make of the implement. Visions of murder floated through my mind, but after a time the door once more opened, and my hostess, as quietly as before, stalked across the room and replaced the razor in the case. She seemed too calm for a murderess, and there had been no noise in the house, but the razor had evidently served some definite purpose.   I got up, dressed, and came down to breakfast.   My host met me at the foot of the staircase with a smile on his face, which on the previous evening had been 'rough and razorable,' but had now lost its stubbly beard of a week's growth.   I then saw one use at least to which my razor had probably been put.   Whether the old lady had any further private manipulations of her own in which the implement played a part, I never found out.

One of the defects of the old Skye inns was the absence of any weights to the window-sashes, and commonly also the want of any means of keeping the windows open.   The glass was seldom cleaned, though the outside surface was washed more or less clean by the battering of the rain.   The doors, too, could not always be fastened, and the visitor who wished to secure privacy might have to barricade the entrance by getting some chairs and his port-manteau piled up against the door.   Even these precautions, however, were sometimes of no effect.   I was once in an inn at Portree where one of the guests, on awaking in the morning, found another head reposing on the pillow near him.   His first impulse was to kick out the intruder, who was sound asleep, but on second thoughts he jumped out of bed and rapidly dressed. Before leaving the room he recognised that the head in question was that of the waiter, who had evidently pushed the door open during the night and got into bed. After taking a walk for an hour the tourist returned to the inn, which he found in great commotion. On enquiring of the landlord, he was told that their waiter, a most respectable and trustworthy man, had disappeared; he had left his clothes in his own room, and must have gone out and drowned himself in the loch, for they had been searching for him everywhere, and he could not be found either in the house or any-where else; if it were not the Sabbath they would have the loch dragged for his body, but they would do that next morning. The visitor, after expressing due sympathy with the distress of the household, asked whether they had looked into his bedroom. 'Your bedroom!' exclaimed the host somewhat angrily, as if he thought fun were being made of him, on such a solemn occasion, 'Your bedroom! No, of course we haven't. What should make us look there?' 'Well,' said his guest, 'you might at least try.' And there sure enough was the somnolent waiter, still asleep, and happily un-conscious of all the stir he had caused. It then turned out that, unknown to the family at the inn, who had recently engaged him, he was liable to occasional fits of sleep-walking. All's well that ends well; but the only consolation the injured visitor ever received from the landlord was the remark, 'What a blessing it was your room; it might else have ruined my business.'

There is a small inn on one of the north-western sea-lochs, where in the year 1860 I spent a night with my old chief, Sir Roderick Murchison. It was in a shocking state of neglect and dirt, with little more in the way of provisions than oatcakes, potatoes, and whisky. It boasted of only one bedroom, which had two beds that did not appear to have been slept in for many a day. Twenty years later I came back to the same inn, hoping that the general improvement would have reached that place too, but I found that as nothing in the way of repair had been done to it in the interval, it was more dilapidated and untidy than ever. I had as a travelling companion a well-known man of science, who, never having been up in that part of Scotland, was glad of the opportunity of seeing it. We occupied the same double-bedded room as I had formerly known. Awaking betimes in the morning, I lay for a while contemplating the ceiling and the undulations and cracks in its plaster. There was a large downward bulge, like a full-bellied sail, right above my friend's head. As I was looking at it, this piece of the plaster suddenly gave way and fell in a mass upon him, with a shower of dust all over the bed. Of course he started up in great alarm, but fortunately he had received no serious injury. It was his first experience of a Highland inn of the old type.

A distinct revival of the roadside inn can be traced to the wide spread of bicycle-riding. Wheelmen appear to be 'drouthy cronies,' who are not sorry to halt for a few minutes at an inviting change-house; but many of them take up their quarters for a night at such places, and this demand for sleeping-room has led to the resuscitation of little inns that had almost gone to decay. It is to be hoped that this revival will continue to spread, and that not only will the old inns come to life again, but that new and better houses of entertainment will be erected in parts of the country where the attractions are many, while the accommodation is but scant.

From inns one naturally turns to drink, which forms the theme of so large a proportion of Scottish stories. It must be admitted

that this prominence is a sad indication of the
extent to which for generations past alcoholic
liquors of all kinds have been consumed in the
country. I used to imagine that the 'trade,'
that is, the calling of publican, was in the hands
of Scotsmen, who were themselves entirely to
blame not only for the drinking, but for the
selling of whisky. On a visit to Antrim, however, I learned that others besides natives of
Scotland have a share in the traffic. In driving
out from Ballymena on an Irish car, my talka-
tive 'jarvie' noticed me looking at a new villa
that was in course of erection not far from the
town.

'That'll be a foin place, sorr,' said he.
'That's Mr. O'Donnel's, sorr.'

'Who is Mr. O'Donnel?' I asked.

'Oh, he was born in Ballymena, and left it
when he was a boy. He went abroad and
made his fortune, and now he's come back and
he's bought the tinnant roight of the land
and he's puttin' up that house and them
greenhouses, and plantin' them trees and layin'
out the garden. Oh, it'll be a foin place, that it
will, sorr.'

'You say he went abroad; where did he go
to?'

'To Scotland, sorr.'

'To Scotland! And how did he come to make his fortune there?'

'Keepin' public-houses, sorr.'

The question is often asked why so much whisky should be consumed in Scotland. One explanation assigns as the reason the moist, chilly climate of the country, and this cause may perhaps be allowed to have some considerable share in producing the national habit. No small proportion of the spirit, especially in the Highlands, is drunk by men who are certainly not at all drunkards, and who can toss off their glass without being any the worse of it, if, indeed, they are not, as they themselves maintain, a good deal the better. But it must be confessed that, especially among the working classes in the Lowlands, tipsiness is a state of pleasure to be looked forward to with avidity, to be gained as rapidly and maintained as long as possible. To many wretched beings it offers a transient escape from the miseries of life, and brings the only moments of comparative happiness which they ever enjoy. They live a double life—one part in the gloom and hardship of the workaday world, and the other in the dreamland into which whisky introduces them. The blacksmith expressed this view of life who, when remonstrated with by his clergyman for drunkenness, asked if his reverend monitor had himself ever been overcome with drink, and, on receiving a negative reply, remarked : 'Ah, sir, if ye was ance richt drunk, ye wadna want ever to be sober again.'

The desire of getting quickly intoxicated is perhaps best illustrated among the miners in the great coal-fields. Thus an Ayrshire collier was heard discoursing to his comrades about a novel way he had found out of getting more rapidly drunk : 'Jist ye putt in thretty draps o' lowdamer (laudanum) into your glass and ye're fine an' fou' in ten minutes.' In the same county a publican advertised the potent quality of the liquor he sold by placing in his window a paper with this announcement : 'Drunk for three bawbees, and mortal for threepence.'

The quality of the whisky is often bad, since much of what is sold is raw-grain spirit, sometimes adulterated with water and then strengthened with some cheap liquid that will give it pungency. There was some truth in the reply of the Highlander to the minister who was warning him against excess, and assuring him that whisky was a very bad thing : ''Deed an' it is, sir, specially baad whusky.' The mere addition of water would do no harm, rather the reverse; but it would be detected at once by the experienced toper. 'This is no' a godly place at all, at all,' said a discontented labourer in the Perthshire Highlands. 'They dinna preach the gospel here—and they wahtter the whusky.'

Strangers are often astonished at the extent of the draughts of undiluted whisky which Highlanders can swallow, without any apparent ill effects. Burt tells us that in his time, that is in the third decade of the eighteenth century, Highland gentlemen could take 'even three or four quarts at a sitting, and that in general the people that can pay the purchase, drink it without moderation.' In the year 1860, in a walk from Kinlochewe through the mountains to Ullapool, I took with me as a guide an old shepherd who had lived there all his life. The distance, as I wished to go, amounted to thirty miles, mostly of rough, trackless ground, and among the refreshments for the journey a bottle of whisky was included. Not being used to the liquor, I hardly tasted it all day, but when we reached the ferry opposite Ullapool, Simon pitched the empty bottle into the loch. He had practically drunk the whole of its contents, and was as cool and collected as when we started in the morning.

All over the Highlands 'a glass' serves as ready-money payment for any small service rendered, such as when a driver has brought a guest to a farm or country-house from some distance, when a workman has completed his repairs and has some miles to walk back to his home, or when a messenger has come from a neighbour and waits to take back your answer. A piper who has marched round behind the chairs of a dinner party at a great Highland laird's, blowing his pipes till it seems as if the windows should be broken, ends his performance by halting at the side of the lady of the house, to whom is brought and from whom he receives a full glass of the native beverage.

It is a characteristic feature of the Scot that, although usually ready for a glass of whisky, he feigns an unwillingness that it should be poured out for him, or at least deprecates that the glass should be filled up to the top. As an illustration of this national habit, the story may be quoted of two Highlanders who were discussing the merits of a gentleman well known to them both. 'Weel, Sandy, ye may say what ye like, but I think he canna be a nice man, whatefer.' 'But what ails ye at him, Donald?' 'Weel, then, I'll just tell ye. I wass in his hoose last week, and he wad be pourin' me out a glass o' whusky; and of course I cried out "Stop, stop!" and wad ye believe it?—he stoppit!'

To prevent any such unwelcome arrest of the liquor, and at the same time to 'save the face' of the would-be participant, he has been known to arrange beforehand with the host or hostess that, while he is to protest as usual against the glass being poured out for him, his scruples are to be peremptorily overcome— 'ye maun gar me tak' it!'

Should any untoward incident deprive a man of a glass plainly intended for him, his annoyance may find loud vent. Among curling circles there is a current anecdote of a well-known adept at the 'roaring play,' who used to be distinguished by a remarkable fur cap which covered not only his head, but his ears. Appearing one day without this conspicuous headgear, he was at once questioned by his friends as to the cause of its disappearance. 'Ay,' said he sadly, 'ye'll never see that cap again; it's been the cause o' a dreadfu' accident.' 'Accident!' exclaimed they; 'where? how? have you been hurt?' 'Weel, I'll no' just say I've been hurtit. But, ye see, the laird o' Dumbreck, they tell me, was ahint me, and he was offerin' me a glass of whisky—— and I never heard him!'

Many stories have been told of the efforts of mistresses of households to avoid the bestowal of strong drink on those employed by them. One of these ladies had supplied a workman with a liberal dinner, but without any whisky or alcoholic liquor. Coming back she found that he had proved a much less efficient trencherman than she supposed he would be, and she rallied him on his bad appetite. His reply was: 'Weel, mem, I canna eat mair, but it wad dae your heart guid to see me drink.'

A whole volume might be filled with the published anecdotes recording in more or less ludicrous form the effects of whisky. I will only give one or two, which I have never seen in print. A man who was wending his way homeward very unsteadily from a lengthened carouse was heard to address the whisky inside of him, 'I could ha' carryit ye easier in a jar.' The quantity of liquor he had consumed may be imagined from the size of the vessel he required to contain it.

Sir Charles Lyell used to tell with great glee a story from his own county of Forfar, belonging to the days of deep potations, when it was the belief that 'drinking largely sobers us again.' A party had met at a country-house, and continued their debauch so long that the laird, Powrie by name, had fallen below the table, while most of the other guests had gone to sleep. Two or three of them, however, who had managed to evade the deepest potations, resolved to play off a trick on the laird. One accordingly climbed up to the roof of the old mansion and, at the risk of his neck, reached the chimney of the dining-room, down which he roared in his loudest voice, 'Powrie, Powrie, it's the Day o' Judgment'; whereupon the laird was heard, by those outside the door, to raise himself on his elbow and hiccup out, 'Eh, Lord forgie me, and me fou'.'

A drunken fellow was found lying at the side of the road by a policeman, who asked him for his name. The answer was, '"My name is Norval, on the Grampian Hills,"——but *Hicks* is on the door.'

With the heavy drinking of those days various connected customs have nearly or wholly disappeared. One still meets with old-fashioned gentlemen, especially at public dinners, who 'take wine with you.' But the rounds of toasts and sentiments, that must have been such an insufferable burden to our grandfathers and grandmothers, have happily vanished. One of the oddest survivals of these toasts was one I heard proposed by the old landlady of a little inn not far from the scene of the Battle of Drumclog. Belonging to the type of landlord

Who takes his chirping pint and cracks his jokes,

she welcomed her chance guests into her roomy and clean kitchen, with its bright coal-fire flanked on either side by an empty arm-chair. Having to spend a night in her house, I was invited to one of these chairs, while she took that on the opposite side of the hearth, and her family attended to the household work. Honoured thus far, I knew my duty would be to call for something 'for the good of the house,' and soon found that my worthy hostess was not unwilling to partake of my 'brew.' Accordingly I made her a glass of toddy of the strength and sweetness she preferred, which she accepted, with the following preface: 'Here's to a' your fouk an' a' oor fouk, an' a' the fouk that's been kind to your fouk an' oor fouk; an' if a' fouk had aye been as kind to fouk as your fouk's been to oor fouk, there wad aye hae been guid fouk i' the warld, sin' fouk's been fouk.'

The change of dinner customs, however, has led to whimsical incidents of another kind from those of the old days of hard drinking. A story is told in Forfarshire of an inexperienced lad who was improvised to do duty at a dinner party, and was instructed by the lady of the house as to what he was to do with the different wines, particularly as to the claret, of which one kind was to be served with the dinner, and the other, of better quality, with the dessert. When the dessert came, she was dismayed to hear him begin at the far end of the table and ask each guest in a loud voice: 'Port, sherry, or inferior clāaret.'

CHAPTER XII.

SCOTTISH humour in relation to death and the grave. Resurrectionists. Tombstone inscriptions. 'Naturals' in
Scotland. Confused thoughts of second childhood. Belief
in witchcraft. Miners and their superstitions. Colliers and
Salters in Scotland were slaves until the end of the eighteenth century. Metal-mining in Scotland.

A NOTABLE feature in Scottish humour is the
frequency with which it deals with death and
the grave. The allusions are sometimes unintentionally ludicrous, not infrequently grim
and ghastly. The subject seems to have a
kind of fascination which has affected people
in every walk of life, more especially the lower
ranks. But like most of the national characteristics, this too appears to be on the wane,
and one has to go back for a generation or
two to find the most pregnant illustrations of
it. Dr. Sloan of Ayr, about forty years ago,
told me that a friend of his had gone not long
before to see the parish minister of Craigie,

X

near Kilmarnock, and finding him for the moment engaged, had turned into the churchyard, where he sauntered past the sexton, who was at work in digging a grave. As the clergyman was detained some time, the visitor walked to and fro along the path, and at length noticed that the sexton's eyes were pretty constantly fixed on him, to the detriment of the excavation on which the man should have been engaged. At last he stopped, and addressing the gravedigger asked, 'What the deil are you staring at me for? You needna tak' the measure o' me, if that's what ye're ettlin' at, for we bury at Riccarton.'

Mr. Thomas Stevenson, father of the novelist, told me that when the gravedigger of Monkton was dying his minister came to see him, and after speaking comfortable words to him for a while, asked if there was anything on his mind that he would like to speak out. The man looked up wistfully and answered, 'Weel, minister, I've put 285 corps in that kirkyard, and I wuss it had been the Lord's wull to let me mak up the 300.'[1]

When Chang, the Chinese giant, was exhibited in Glasgow, an elderly country couple

[1] This story is told with variations in the name of the parish and number of interments.

went to see him. After gazing long at him, they retired without making any observation. At last, as they were going downstairs, the wife first broke silence with the remark: 'Eh, Duncan, whatna coffin he wull tak.'

All over Scotland, and more especially in the lowlands, memorials remain of the time when graves were opened and coffins were rifled of their dead, to supply the needs of the dissecting rooms of the medical schools. In the middle of the eighteenth century, Shenstone, in protesting against this sacrilege, contended that the bodies of convicted malefactors should suffice for the needs of the medical profession—

> If Paean's sons these horrid rites require,
> If Health's fair science be by these refined,
> Let guilty convicts, for their use, expire;
> And let their breathless corse avail mankind.

But though the bodies of executed murderers had for two centuries been handed over to surgeons for dissection, the supply of evildoers must have been still too scanty, even at a time when theft and robbery were capitally punished. The growing success of the medical schools in Scotland increased the demand for human bodies to such a degree as to offer strong temptation to the enterprise of bold and reckless men. So frequent did violations of the tomb become as to lead to extraordinary precautions to prevent them. The graves were protected with heavy iron gratings securely riveted above them, many of which may still be seen in the churchyards of Fife and the Lothians. Watch-houses were likewise erected in the burial-grounds to serve as shelters for the men who in turn every night took their stations there, with guns loaded, on the outlook for any midnight marauders. In a commanding position in the graveyard around the parish church of Crail, one of these houses may still be seen, bearing the suggestive record—

> ERECTED for securing the DEAD
> Ann. Dom. MDCCCXXVI.

The trade of the 'resurrection-men' was finally destroyed by an Act of Parliament passed in the year 1832, in consequence of the murders committed by Burke and Hare in Edinburgh, and Bishop and Williams in London. This measure, by permitting the unclaimed bodies of paupers, dying in poor-houses, to be taken for dissection to the medical schools, provided a supply of subjects which, if not abundant, at least prevented any further violations of the grave.

Of the monumental inscriptions in Scottish graveyards various collections have been published, and to these many more might be added. They have seldom any literary excellence, and their chief interest arises from their oddities of spelling and grammar, and their conceptions of a future state. As an illustrative example of them, I may cite one from the kirkyard of Sweetheart Abbey, in the Stewartry of Kirkcudbright.

> Here lyes The body of Alex
> ander Houston son of Matthe^w
> Houston and Jean Milligan in
> Parish of New Abbay   born
> August ye 12th 1731 died July ye 15th 1763
> Non est mortale quid opto
> Farew^{e}ll my obedient Son
>   of Neighbours well belov'd
> and an Exempler Christian
>   near thirty two remov'd
> Farewell a while my parents bot^h
>   Brothers and Sisters all
> I'll at the Resurrection day
>   obey the Trumpets call.

The insertion of a few words of bad Latin (probably unintelligible to the grieving family), the farewell to the departed, his farewell in response, and the sacrifice of grammar to the exigencies of verse, are characteristic features on the gravestones earlier than the beginning of the last century. Some of these peculiarities are further illustrated by a more ambitious piece of versification which I copied from a tombstone in the churchyard of Berwick-on-Tweed. Though not strictly within the bounds of Scotland, the stone lies at least on the north side of the Tweed, and in its defiance of grammatical niceties is not unworthy of the pen of a northern elegist.

1. The peaceful mansions of the dead
   Are scattered far and near
   But by the stones o'er this yard spread
   Seem numerously here

2. A relative far from his home
   Mindful of men so just
   Reveres this spot inscribes this tomb
   And in his God doth trust

3. That he shall pass a righteous life
   Leve long for sake of seven
   Return in safety to his wife
   And meet them both in heaven

4. God bless the souls departed hence
   This church without a steeple
   The king the clergy and the good sense
   Of all the Berwick people

In connexion with tombstones, I may refer to the frequently rapid decay of the materials of which they are made, in such a climate as that of Scotland. Nearly five-and-twenty years ago I investigated this subject among the old graveyards of Edinburgh and other parts of the country, and found that while some varieties of hard siliceous sandstone retain their inscriptions quite sharp at the end of two centuries, as in the case of Alexander Henderson's tombstone in Greyfriars Church-yard, no marble monument, freely exposed to the elements in a town, will survive in a legible condition for a single century. As an example of this disintegration I cited the handsome monument erected, in that same churchyard, to the memory of the illustrious Joseph Black, who died in 1799. It consisted of a large slab of white marble, let into a massive framework of sandstone. Less than eighty years had sufficed to render the in-scription partly illegible, and the stone, bulging out in the centre and rent by numerous cracks, was evidently doomed to early destruc-tion. Three years ago I returned to see the condition of the tomb, and then found that the marble had disappeared entirely, its place being now taken by a sandstone slab, on which the authorities had with pious care copied the original inscription. Here the

marble, though partially protected by the overhanging masonry of the monument and by a
high wall that screened it in some measure
from the western rains, had fallen into irrepar-
able ruin in less than a hundred years.

A curious attitude of mind towards one
who has died, but is still unburied, is shown
by the use of the word 'corp,' which is
popularly supposed to be the singular of
'corpse.' This usage may be illustrated by
an incident told me by the late Henry
Drummond as having occurred in his own
experience. While attending the funeral of a
man with whom he had had no acquaintance,
he enquired of one of the company what employment the deceased had followed. The
person questioned did not know, but at once
asked his next neighbour, 'I'm sayin', Tam,
what was the corp to trade?'

An old couple were exceedingly annoyed
that they had not been invited to the funeral
of one of their friends. At last the good
wife consoled her husband thus: 'Aweel,
never you mind, Tammas, maybe we'll be
haein' a corp o' our ain before lang, and
we'll no ask them.'

A gentleman came to a railway station
where he found a mourning party. Wishing

to be sympathetic, he enquired of one of the company whether it was a funeral, and received the reply : 'We canna exactly ca' it a funeral, for the corp has missed the railway connection.'

At a funeral in Glasgow, a stranger who had taken his seat in one of the mourning coaches excited the curiosity of the other three occupants, one of whom at last addressed him, 'Ye'll be a brither o' the corp?' 'No, I'm no a brither o' the corp,' was the prompt reply. 'Weel, then, ye'll be his cousin?' 'No, I'm no that.' 'No! then ye'll be at least a frien' o' the corp?' 'No that either. To tell the truth, I've no been that weel mysel', and as my doctor has ordered me some carriage exercise, I thocht this wad be the cheapest way to tak' it.'

It has often been remarked how great an attraction funerals have for some half-witted people. There used to be one of these poor creatures in an Ayrshire village, who, when any one was seriously ill, would from time to time knock at the door and enquire, 'Is she ony waur (worse)?' his hopes rising at any relapse, and the consequent prospect of another interment.

A great change for the better has come

over the usages connected with burials in Scotland. In old days, as already mentioned, the 'lyke-wakes' were often scenes of shocking licence and debauchery. By degrees these painful exhibitions have become less and less objectionable until now, except that there is still sometimes too liberal a dispensing of whisky, there is little that can be found fault with. In country places, where the mourners have often to come from long distances to attend a funeral, refreshments of some kind are perhaps necessary, but it is unfortunate that the average Scot would think such refreshments decidedly 'wairsh' (tasteless) if they did not include an adequate provision of the national drink. Accordingly, it is still too common to think first of seeing that whisky enough has been obtained, even where the claims of pedestrians from a distance have not to be considered. Thus one of the family of an old dying woman was asked, 'Is your Auntie still livin'?' 'Ay,' was the answer, 'she's no just deid yet; but we've gotten in the whusky for the funeral.'

I remember the first funeral I saw fifty years ago in the Highlands. It was in the old graveyard of Kilchrist, Skye, where a large company of crofters had gathered from all parts of the parish of Strath. There was a confused undertone of conversation audible at a little distance as I passed along the public road; and as soon as I came in sight two or three of the mourners at once made for me, carrying bottle, glasses, and a plate of bits of cake. Though I was an entire stranger to them and to the deceased, I knew enough of Highland customs and feelings to be assured that on no account could I be excused from at least tasting the refreshments. The halt of a few minutes showed me that much whisky was being consumed around the ruined kirk.

In former days most parishes in the country possessed one or more 'naturals,' whose lives were embittered by the persecution of the children, though they might be kindly enough treated by the elders, whom they amused by the oddities of their ways and the quaintness of their expressions. Since the establishment of the Lunacy Board, however, they have been mostly drafted into asylums, much to the increase of the decency of the communities, though a little of the picturesqueness of village life has thereby been lost. One of these 'fules' was seen marching along quickly with a gun over his shoulder. Its owner knew it not to be loaded, but he called out, 'Archie, where are you going wi' the gun? You are no' wantin' to shoot yoursell?' 'No,' said he, 'I'm no' jist gaun to shoot mysell, but I'm gaun to gie mysell a deevil o' a fleg (fright).'

Many years ago a half-witted but pawky attendant, perhaps as much knave as fool, was a well-known figure at the old inn of Brodick, in Arran. He was employed in miscellaneous errands and simple bits of work about the inn or the farm, such as suited his capacity, and he was noted for having a specially pronounced love of brandy. One day he was seen by two visitors at the hotel, pushing a boat down the beach and getting the oars ready. They accosted him and asked where he was bound for. He answered that he was going across the bay to Corriegills for a bag or two of potatoes. Their request to be allowed to accompany him was all the more willingly complied with, inasmuch as they at once proposed that they should pull the oars if he would steer. Sandy had not much English, but he employed it to the best of his ability in the hope that it might be the means of gaining him some of his favourite liquor. Having crossed the bay, the boat was pulled towards the large granite boulder that forms so notable a landmark on that part of the shore. He directed the attention of his crew to it, and said :

' D'ye see that muckle stane? Weel, maybe ye'll no' be believin' me, but it's the truth I'm tellin' ye. If onybody wad be climmin' to the tap o' that stane and wad be roarin' as loud as he likes, there's naebody can hear him.'

' Nonsense ; we don't believe a word of it.'

' But I wad wager ye onythin' ye like it's true. I wad be wagerin' ye a bottle o' brandy, if ye like.'

' Very well, we'll try. You jump ashore and get on the stone and roar.'

Sandy with great alacrity sprang out of the boat, and was speedily on the great grey boulder. He opened his mouth and swung his body, as if he were roaring with the strength of ten bulls of Bashan, until he grew purple in the face with his apparent efforts to make a noise. But though he stooped and gesticulated, he took care that never a sound should escape from him.

' Wass you hearin' me?' he asked with a triumphant face when he had come down to the boat again.

' You rascal, you never gave a sound.'

' Ochan, ochan, wass you not seein' that I

was screamin' till I couldna scream ony more, whatefer?'

'Very extraordinary, to be sure. Well, we'll try ourselves.'

So saying they jumped upon the beach, and, with rather less agility than Sandy had shown, clambered up the stone, while he stood beside the boat. When they were both on the top, they proceeded to shout with such vehemence that they might have been heard on the other side of the bay. Sandy, however, as if intent on hearing the faintest sound, put his hand behind each ear in turn, and bent his head now to one side, now to the other. When the two strangers had had enough of this performance, they came down, and indignantly demanded:

'Well, Sandy, do you mean to tell us that you did not hear?'

'Hear ye!' said he. 'Wass you roarin' at all. I was never hearin' wan bit.'

He had a remarkable power of expressing astonishment by his mere looks, and put on a face of child-like innocence when he protested that no sound at all had been heard by him. Feeling that they had been 'sold' by this apparent 'natural,' they left him to fetch his potatoes and pull the boat back himself. But he had his brandy that evening.

Removed into asylums, the village idiots lose the opportunity of giving expression to the memorable sayings which free contact with their kinsfolk and the irritation caused by their young persecutors used to produce. But even there their oddity of phrase comes occasionally forward. My old companion, John Young, already referred to, used to tell how, when he was one of the assistant physicians in the Morningside Asylum at Edinburgh, he was one morning reading prayers. The weather being raw and chilly, he had a cough, which interrupted him at the end of the petition, 'Give us this day our daily bread.' During the pause, one of the patients, sitting in front of him, added in an audible voice, 'and *butter*.'

The second childhood of old age among people who have been sane all their lives sometimes gives rise to confusion of thought and language such as no half-witted creature can rival. I knew an old Scottish lady who used to make curious lapses of this kind. Her nephew met me one day and said, 'I must give you auntie's last. She was in bed, and, calling her maid, said to her: "Jenny, if I'm spared to be taken away soon, I hope my nephew Thomas will get the doctor to open my head, and see if anything canna be done for my hearin'."'

The belief in witchcraft, though it still maintains its hold in the remote districts of the Highlands and Islands, may be regarded as practically extinct in the non-Celtic parts of the country. Yet it flares out now and then in the lowlands, as if it were still smouldering underneath the surface, ready to be awakened once more when the occasion arises to revive it. Forty years ago, in the valley of the Girvan Water, there were some old colliers whose grandmothers had been reputed witches, and who, though they professed to disbelieve the report, had evidently a deep-grounded respect for it. One of these men described to me some of his own experiences in the matter. When still a lad, he was walking one Sunday evening along the road near Kilgrammie with a companion and a fox-terrier. The dog had jumped over a low wall into a field, and they were attracted by its loud barking. Looking over the wall they saw that it was chasing a hare, which, instead of making its escape, seemed to be enjoying the game, and was racing to and fro across the field. The two lads soon leapt over the wall to join in the sport. At last the hare, tired apparently of the exercise, made for a low part of the far wall and scrambled over it. When they got up to the place they were just

in time to see the animal lie down on the door-
step of his grandmother's cottage, pass both its
paws across its nose, and disappear into the
house. It then flashed upon him that as his
grandmother was believed to be able to take
the shape of a hare, he might really have been
chasing her all the while. He added that he
went home as fast as he could.

Another old woman in the neighbouring
village of Dailly, who had been long bed-ridden,
was at last near her end. On the afternoon of
the day she died, the boys of the place were
busy with their games in the street, when a
hare appeared from the country and tried to
pass them. They at once gave chase, and the
animal retreated along the road by which it had
come. Again, a little later, it returned, and
once more attempted to get into the village,
but was again chased away. A third time,
however, when their game had carried the
boys further along the street, puss was successful, and before her enemies could reach
her, gained the outside stair that led up to the
old woman's garret, and disappeared inside the
doorway. The invalid died that evening, and
the hare was believed to be either herself or
one of her accomplices who had come to be
with her at the last.

Y

Let me try to repeat in the vernacular of the district the tale told by the grandson of one of these helpless and harmless old women. 'My grannie was weel kent to be no' canny. She had ways of doin' things and kennin' things that naebody could mak oot. At last she deeit, and she behoved to be buryit i' the Barr, that's a village on the ither side o' the hills, laigh doon by the Stinchar. When the funeral day cam', we carryit the coffin up the steep road, and when we were gettin' near the tap, and hadna muckle breath left, for the coffin was nae licht wecht, a fine-lookin' gentleman, ridin' a fine black horse, made up to us. Nane o' us kennt him or had seen him afore. But he rade alangside o' us, and cracked awa' maist croosely, and cheered us sae that we gaed scrievin' doon the brae on the ither side. Weel, you may jalouse we were a wee bit forfeuchen when we cam' to the kirk-yard, and some o' us thocht we wadna be the waur o' bit drappie afore we gaed on wi' the buryin'. Sae we steppit into the public-hoose. Weel, ye mauna think we bydeit lang there, but losh me! when we cam' oot the coffin wi' my grannie in't was awa', and sae was the man an' the black horse. And to this day I canna tell what cam' ower them.'

Miners are generally a superstitious race. Their subterranean occupation, with its darkness and its dangers, fosters the inborn human instinct to credit the supernatural. Hence old beliefs that have died out in the general community may still be found lingering among them. A miner who meets a woman, when he starts for his work in the morning, will turn back again, as the day has become unlucky for him. Any unexpected event in the mine is sure to awaken all his old-world 'freits.' If any of his comrades should, by the falling of part of the roof of the mine, be crushed to death, he dreads to continue his ordinary work so long as a corpse remains in the pit, and will spare himself no labour until he has tunnelled through the fallen roof. A memorable instance of this devotion has been already alluded to as having taken place in the little coal-field of Dailly, where one of the miners was shut off from all communication with mankind by the crushing down of the roof between him and his fellow-workmen. They toiled day and night to cut a passage through the material, with the view of reaching and removing his body, and they found him actually alive, after being shut up for twenty-three days without food. He died, however, three days after his rescue.[1] Such an incident could not fail to awaken to life all the dormant superstitions and fears of the collier mind. For a long time after, strange sounds and sights were imagined in the mine.

A more ludicrous recollection of that time was narrated to me by a survivor of the tragedy. One of his comrades had returned unexpectedly from work in the forenoon, and, to the surprise of his wife, appeared in front of their cottage. She was in the habit, unknown to him, of solacing herself in the early part of the day with a bottle of porter. On the occasion in question the bottle stood toasting pleasantly before the fire when the form of the 'gudeman' came in sight. In a moment she drove in the cork and thrust the bottle underneath the blankets of the box-bed, when he entered, and, seating himself by the fire, began to light his pipe. In a little while the warmed porter managed to expel the cork, and to escape in a series of very ominous gurgles from underneath the clothes. The poor fellow ran outside at once, crying 'Anither warning, Meg! Rin, rin, the house is fa'ing.' But Meg 'kenn'd what was what fu' brawly,' and made

[1] The story of this entombment alive is told in my *Geological Sketches at Home and Abroad*, p. 71.

for the bed, in time to save only the last dregs of her intended potation.

It is strange to reflect that many people now alive have known natives of Scotland who were born slaves. The colliers and salters had, from time immemorial, been attached for life to the works in which they were engaged. They could not legally remove from them, and if they escaped, could be lawfully pursued, arrested, and brought back to their proprietors. Their children, too, if once employed in any part of their work, became from that very fact bondsmen for life. In my own boyhood I have seen old men and women who were born in such servitude, and worked in the mines of Midlothian. The women were employed in the pits to carry up heavy baskets of coals on their backs from underground to the surface—a laborious and degrading occupation from which they dared not try to escape.

It is related by Robert Chambers that Bald, the mining engineer, about the year 1820, came upon an old miner near Glasgow who had been actually bartered by his master for a pony. When the famous decision was made by the Court of King's Bench in June, 1772, that slavery could not exist in Great Britain, the Court hardly realised that at that very moment there were hundreds of slaves in Scotland who were bought and sold as part of the works on which they and their forbears were employed.

By an act of Parliament of the United Kingdom passed in 1775 (15 George III. cap. 28) the villainage of colliers and salters was meant to be finally abolished. The act, which took effect from 1st July of that year, decreed that all colliers under 21 years of age were to be free in seven years from that date. Those between 21 and 35 were to be released after a further service of ten years from the date of the act, and those between 35 and 45 after a service of seven years, provided that these two classes, if required, should find and sufficiently instruct 'in the art and mystery of coal-hewing or making of salt,' an apprentice of at least 18 years, and on the perfection of such instruction, should then be free from further bondage. All persons above 45 years of age were to be discharged in three years.

Nothing could apparently have been more precise than these stipulations. Unfortunately, however, they were saddled with a provision that before any collier or salter could claim the benefit of the act and gain his freedom, he was compelled to obtain 'a decree of the Sheriff Court of the county in which he resides, finding and declaring that he is entitled unto his freedom under the authority of this act.' It may readily be understood that only a small proportion of the workmen had the means of defraying the cost of such an action at law. As narrated in the subsequent act of 1799, there was 'a general practice among the coal-owners and lessees of coal, of advancing considerable sums to their colliers, or for their behoof, much beyond what the colliers are able to repay; which sums are advanced for the purpose of tempting them to enter into or continue their engagements, notwithstanding the sums so advanced are kept up as debts against the colliers.' Hence, in spite of the legislation, the provision for emancipation remained a dead letter in regard to the great majority of the colliers, who continued to be slaves until their death. It was not until the act of 13th June, 1799 (39 Geo. III. cap. 56) was passed that the shackles were finally broken, and the colliers of Scotland were 'declared to be free from their servitude.'

But though no longer legally bound to these collieries, women continued to be employed in the same laborious and degrading occupation within the coal-mines. Quarter of a century after the act of emancipation was passed, Hugh

Miller, when working as a stone-mason at Niddry, in Midlothian, found the women-toilers still at their task, and he has left the following account of them : ' The collier women of the village, poor over-toiled creatures, who carried up all the coal from underground on their backs by a long turnpike stair inserted in one of the shafts, continued to bear more of the marks of serfdom than even the men. How these poor women did labour, and how thoroughly, even at this time, were they characterised by the slave nature ! It has been estimated that one of their ordinary day's work was equal to the carrying of a hundredweight from the level of the sea to the top of Ben Lomond. They were marked by a peculiar type of mouth. It was wide, open, thick-lipped, projecting equally above and below. . . . I have seen these collier-women crying like children, when toiling under their load along the upper rounds of the wooden stair, and then returning, scarce a minute after, with the empty creel, singing with glee.' Some of these women were still at work when, as a child, I first visited the district. It was not indeed until 10th August, 1842, that the act (5 and 6 Vic. cap. 99) was passed which declared it to be 'unfit that women and girls should be employed in any mine or colliery,' and absolutely prohibited any mine-owner from employing or permitting to be employed underground any female person whatsoever.

Their mole-like operations underground do not wholly eradicate a sense of humour in the colliers. When engaged in a study of the Borrowstouness coal-field, I had occasion to see some of the miners at Kinneil House. One of them remarked to me that they had lately found 'Mother Eve' in one of their pits. I was thereupon shown a large con-cretionary mass of sandstone, having a rude resemblance to a human head and bust. Seeing that this counterfeit presentment of our first parent did not greatly interest me, a younger member of the band, with a sly twinkle in his eye, whispered that besides Eve, they had found the Serpent, and that he was sure I should wish to see that. I was then taken to the back of the house where the 'serpent' lay extended for a length of some ten or twelve feet. The specimen proved to be one of the long tree-roots known as *Stig-maria*, and common among the fossil vegetation of the Coal-measures. Not content with having found the tempter of the Garden of Eden, the miners had resolved to beautify and pre-serve his remains, and had accordingly procured some black lead with which they had burnished him up like a well-polished grate. Of greater interest to me at the time was the remembrance that this same Kinneil House had been the retreat of the illustrious Dugald Stewart during the later years of his life, whence he gave to the world those essays and dissertations which mark so notable an epoch in the history of Scottish philosophy.

Metal-mining, save that of iron, has on the whole, been unsuccessful in Scotland. The experience of Lord Breadalbane in this direction has been that of most proprietors who have sought to discover 'what earth's low entrails hold.' The mines of Leadhills and Wanlockhead are the only examples that have long been worked, and can still be carried on. The history of the metal-mining industry in Scotland is well illustrated by the story told by Chambers of one of the old lairds of Alva, on the flanks of the Ochil Hills. Walking one day with a friend, he pointed to a hole on the hillside, and said he had taken fifty thousand pounds out of it. A little further on he came to another excavation, and added, 'I put it all into *that* hole again.'

CHAPTER XIII.

TOWN-LIFE a hundred years ago presented many contrasts to what it is now in Scotland. Means of locomotion being comparatively scanty and also expensive, communication with England was too serious a matter to be undertaken by any but those who had plenty of money or urgent business. And the number of Englishmen who found their way north of the Tweed was correspondingly small. The Scottish towns, too, though connected by lines of road and stage coaches, were far more cut off from each other than they have now become, since they have been linked together by railways. They still to some extent continued to be centres, to which the landed gentry betook themselves for part of the winter. Hence they retained some old-world ways and local peculiarities, which modern intercourse has more or less completely effaced. They were much smaller in size and more compact, for the vast acres of suburban villadom, now surrounding our cities and larger towns, had hardly begun to come into existence. They were likewise so much less populous, that each of them rather resembled an overgrown family, where everybody of special note was known more or less familiarly to the whole community.

There can be little doubt that Scottish towns were once almost incredibly dirty. Drainage, in the modern sense of the word, was unknown. Edinburgh, especially at night, must have been one of the most evil-smelling towns in Europe, when with shouts of 'Gardyloo' the foul water and garbage of each house were pitched out of the windows. The streets were thus never decently clean, save immediately after a heavy rain had swept the refuse into the central gutter, which then became the channel of a rapid torrent. Laws had indeed been framed against throwing foul water from the windows, and Boswell tells us

that in his time the magistrates had taken to
enforce them, but that owing to the want of
covered drains the odour still continued.
When he walked up the Canongate with
Johnson, who had just arrived, he could have
wished his companion 'to be without one of
his five senses on this occasion;' for he could
not keep the lexicographer from grumbling,
'I smell you in the dark.' In Byron's youth
the same state of things continued, and he
could still say tauntingly to Jeffrey,

> For thee Edina culls her evening sweets,
> And showers their odours on thy candid sheets.

The state of the Edinburgh streets in a
snowy winter must have been deplorable.
Sydney Smith, writing from the town in 1799,
after a thaw, remarked that 'except the morning after the Flood was over, I should doubt
if Edinburgh had ever been dirtier.' By the
time that proper sanitary arrangements came
into practice, the well-to-do citizens had forsaken their abodes in the high tenements of
the Old Town, and the houses came to be
tenanted by a poorer class. Although the noc-
turnal cascades were prohibited, the refuse was
carried down and deposited in the streets. I
can remember when these thoroughfares were

still disgustingly odoriferous and unsightly, until the dustman had been round with his cart and a perfunctory brush, which seemed never to find its way into the narrow closes.

The domestic habits of the townsmen were in many respects less luxurious and more homely than they are now-a-days, and people saw more of each other in a friendly unostentatious way. Instead of the modern stiff, ceremonious dinner party, receding further and further into the late hours of the evening, there was the simple and often frugal supper, the praises of which have been so enthusiastically recorded by Cockburn. It was customary to ask friends, especially strangers, to breakfast, a usage which still survived in my youth, especially among the University Professors. As already mentioned, long after I had left college, I used to enjoy the breakfasts given by Pillans, and the company he gathered round his table for that meal.

The people of an older generation gave themselves to social intercourse much more freely and simply than we do now. One feature of town-life, formerly conspicuous in Scotland, is now almost gone—the multiplication of convivial clubs. During the seventeenth and the early part of the eighteenth century, every town in the country had its clubs, to which the male inhabitants would adjourn once a week, or even every evening. In the larger towns these gatherings included the most intellectual and well-born members of the community, who met for the discussion of literary, philosophical or scientific topics, as well as for free social companionship. But no doubt in these towns and in the smaller centres of population throughout the country, there were many associations which had no such laudable aims, but fully deserved Butler's description of them:

> The jolly members of a toping club,
> Like pipe-staves, are but hooped into a tub;
> And in a close confederacy link
> For nothing else but only to hold drink.

The clubs, whatever might be their object, did not then number in each case hundreds of members, most of them unknown to one another, and frequenting a luxuriously furnished mansion, such as the word club suggests now, but consisted of mere handfuls of men, all knowing each other, and meeting in a tavern. These associations often boasted of jocular names, which referred to their origin or customs. Thus, in Edinburgh, the *Antemanum Club* was so named from its members declaring their hands of cards before beginning play, or as has been suggested, because they 'paid their lawing' before they began to consume the liquor. The *Pious Club* was so named because it met every night in a pie-house. The *Spendthrift Club* received its title from its members disbursing as much as fourpence-halfpenny each night. Then there were the *Oyster Club*, the *Dirty Club*, the *Mirror Club*, the *Friday Club* (so called because they met on Sunday), and many others. Robert Chambers, in his *Traditions of Edinburgh*, has preserved some interesting reminiscences of these institutions.

Lord Cockburn has left a graphic picture of a scene in his boyhood when he saw the Duke of Buccleuch, with a dozen more of the aristocracy of Midlothian, assembled in the low-roofed room of a wretched ale-house in the country, and spending the evening in roaring, laughing, and rapidly pushing round the claret. As an illustration of the way in which even the most intellectual members of society would forsake their own homes for convivial intercourse in a tavern, the following anecdote may be given. Among the citizens of Edinburgh none were more illustrious than Joseph Black, the discoverer of carbonic acid, and

James Hutton, the author of the *Theory of the Earth*. These two men, who were intimate friends, and took a keen interest in their social meetings, were once deputed by a number of their literary acquaintances to look out for a suitable meeting-place in which they might all assemble once a week. The two philosophers accordingly ' sallied out for this purpose, and seeing on the South Bridge a sign with the words, " Stewart, Vintner down stairs," they immediately went into the house and demanded a sight of their best room, which was accordingly shown to them, and which pleased them much. Without further enquiry the meetings were fixed by them to be held in this house, and the club assembled there during the greater part of the winter, till one evening Dr. Hutton, being rather late, was surprised, when going in, to see a whole bevy of well-dressed but somewhat brazen-faced young ladies brush past him, and take refuge in an adjoining apartment. He then for the first time began to think that all was not right, and communicated his suspicions to the rest of the company. Next morning the notable discovery was made, that our amiable philosophers had introduced their friends to one of the most disreputable houses in the city.'

z

The record of another incident in the close intercourse of Black and Hutton has been preserved, and may be inserted here. 'These attached friends agreed in their opposition to the usual vulgar prejudices, and frequently discoursed together upon the absurdity of many generally received opinions, especially in regard to diet. On one occasion they had a disquisition upon the inconveniency of abstaining from feeding on the testaceous creatures of the land, while those of the sea were considered as delicacies. Snails, for instance—why not use them as articles of food? They were well known to be nutritious and wholesome—even sanative in some cases. The epicures, in olden time, esteemed as a most delicate treat the snails fed in the marble quarries of Lucca. The Italians still hold them in esteem. The two philosophers, perfectly satisfied that their countrymen were acting most absurdly in not making snails an ordinary article of food, resolved themselves to set an example; and accordingly, having procured a number, caused them to be stewed for dinner. No guests were invited to the banquet. The snails were in due season served up; but, alas! great is the difference between theory and practice. So far from exciting the appetite, the smoking dish acted in a diametrically opposite manner, and neither party felt much inclination to partake of its contents. Nevertheless, if they looked on the snails with disgust, they retained their awe for each other ; so that each, conceiving the symptoms of internal revolt to be peculiar to himself, began with infinite exertion to swallow, in very small quantities, the mess which he internally loathed. Dr. Black at length broke the ice, but in a delicate manner, as if to sound the opinion of his messmate :— "Doctor," he said in his precise and quiet manner, " Doctor, do you not think that they taste a little—a very little—queer ? " " D—— queer ! d—— queer, indeed !—tak' them awa', tak' them awa ! " vociferated Dr. Hutton, starting up from the table, and giving full vent to his feelings of abhorrence.' [1]

The most noted survivor of these old social gatherings in Edinburgh is the ' Royal Society Club,' to which allusion has already been made. This association was founded to promote good fellowship among the fellows of the Royal Society and to ensure a nucleus for the evening meetings. The club has from the beginning been limited in numbers, but has always included the most distinguished and

[1] Kay's *Edinburgh Portraits*, vol. i. p. 57.

'clubbable' of the fellows. It meets in some hotel on the evenings on which the Society's meetings are held, and after a pleasant dinner, with talk and songs, its members adjourn in time to take their places in the Society's hall. When Neaves, Maclagan, Blackie, Christison, and Macnee were present, it will be understood how joyous such gatherings were. Many a good song was written for these occasions, and many an excellent story was told. A favourite ditty by Maclagan, sung by him with great effect, ended with the following verse, which illustrates the delightful mixture of science and fun with which the professor was wont to regale us :

Lyon Playfair last winter took up a whole hour
To prove so much mutton is just so much power;
He might have done all that he did twice as well
By an hour of good feeding in Slaney's Hotel;
And instead of the tables he hung on the wall,
Have referred to the table in this festive hall;
And as for his facts—have more clearly got at 'em
From us than from Sappers and Miners at Chatham;

Whilst like jolly good souls
We emptied our bowls,
And so washed down our grub
In a style worth the name,
Wealth, honour, and fame
Of the Royal Society Club.

Dr. Terrot, Bishop of Edinburgh, and Professor Pillans were members of this club. The bishop used to be a pretty constant attendant both at the dinners and at the Society's meetings afterwards. Pillans, on the other hand, while he came to the dinner, shirked the meeting, the subjects discussed being usually scientific and not especially intelligible or interesting to him. He would say to those who rallied him for his absence, ' I enjoy the play [meaning the dinner] very much ; but I can't stand the *farce* [F.R.S.] that comes after it.'

The change to modern domestic habits, more especially the increasing lateness of the dinner hour, has gradually extinguished most of the social clubs that used to make so prominent a feature in the society of the larger towns of Scotland. An effort was made in Edinburgh some thirty years ago to start a new club at which the literary, artistic, and scientific workers in the city might informally meet and enjoy each other's company and conversation over a glass of whisky and water, with a pipe, cigar or cigarette. Its meetings were fixed for Saturday evening, so as to avoid, as far as might be, dinner engagements, which were less frequently fixed for that than for the other evenings of the week. It began with considerable success, and continued for a number of years to be a chief centre of cultivated intercourse. But it too has now gone the way of its predecessors.

The proverbial patriotism of a Scot shows itself not merely in his love of his country. His attachment binds him still more closely to his shire, to his town, or even to his parish. This intense devotion to the natal district could not be more forcibly illustrated than by the remark of an Aberdonian who, in a company of his fellow townsmen met together in Edinburgh, appealed to them by asking, 'Tak' awa' Aberdeen and twal mile round about, an' faure are ye?' There are times and places, however, where even the most perfervid Scot, Aberdonian or other, is compelled to be candid. Another native of the granite city, in his first visit to London, was taken into St. Paul's Cathedral. He gazed around for a few moments in silent astonishment, and at last exclaimed to the friend who accompanied him, 'My certy, but this makes a perfect feel (fool) o' the Kirk o' Foot Dee.'

Local patriotism was fostered by the multiplication of clubs, even in small towns. But in these places also the advance of the modern

spirit seems to have destroyed the old club-
life. There remain, however, the trade cor-
porations, or guilds, and the magistracy, which
in the old burghs still form centres round
which much of the life and human interests
of these communities cluster. To be a bailie,
still more to attain to the dignity of provost,
has long been an object of ambition, even in
the most insignificant place, and much schem-
ing and string-pulling continue to be carried on
in order to obtain the coveted position :

For never title yet so mean could prove
But there was eke a mind which did that title love.

The old proverb expresses a truth which
has been time-out-of-mind exemplified in every
burgh in the country : 'Ance a bailie, aye a
bailie ; ance a provost, aye My Lord.' Many
anecdotes have been related of the consequential airs assumed by local magnates, who have
been as fair game for the caustic remarks
of outsiders as even ministers themselves.
An English traveller on board of a Clyde
steamer, sailing down the firth, got into talk
with a native on deck, who good-naturedly
pointed out the various places of interest along
the coast. When they were passing Largs, the
stranger asked some questions about the town.

'It seems a nice large place. Have they magistrates there?' 'Ow ay; they have a provost and bailies at the Lairgs.' 'And do these magistrates when they meet wear chains of office, as they do with us in England?' 'Chains! no, no, bless your sowl, they aye gang lowse.'[1]

During the last forty years the steamboat traffic down the Clyde has so enormously increased, locomotion is so much easier, cheaper, and more rapid, that the temptation to escape from Glasgow to the pleasant shores of the Firth has grown strong in all classes of society. Villages on the coast have accordingly grown into towns, until an almost continuous row of villas and cottages has grown up on both sides of the estuary. Hence, as the older towns have been invaded and increased by a population from the outside, they have lost most of their former peculiarities. Rothesay furnishes a good illustration of this growth and transformation. I can remember it as a place with an individuality of its own, when everybody might be said to know everybody else. But it has

---

[1] There are various versions of this story; and different towns are assigned as that to which it refers. I heard it more than forty years ago in the form given above.

now become almost a kind of marine suburb of Glasgow. When I first came to it, one of its conspicuous inhabitants was known familiarly as 'the Bishop,' not from any ecclesiastical office which he filled, but on account of his somewhat pompous and consequential manner. He was in many respects a worthy man, glad to take his share in any useful work, and to be on friendly terms with everybody. One of his peculiarities consisted in the misuse of words, and as he had no hesitation about speaking in public, his mistakes often gave great amusement. His daughter had been shipwrecked, and in referring to her experiences he declared her to be a 'perfect heron, for she was the last man to leave the ship.' The Free Church congregation at Ascog had been for some time without a pastor. When at last one was chosen, a soiree was held to celebrate the event, and the 'Bishop' was invited to it. In the speech which he made on the occasion he congratulated the meeting, and expressed the hope that 'now that they had got a new *incumbrance*, they would have a long time of prosperity and peace.'

When the parliamentary representation of Bute was contested by Mr. Boyle, afterwards Earl of Glasgow, and Mr. Lamont of Knock-dhu, the 'Bishop' acted as one of Mr. Lamont's committee in Rothesay. The ballot had not then come into use, and as the result of the polling in Rothesay, Mr. Lamont at the end of the day obtained a majority of votes. On the other hand, Mr. Boyle had an excess of supporters in Cumbrae. All depended on the result of the voting in Arran, and the arrival of the steamer from that island was anxiously awaited. Mr. Lamont's committee were sitting in their room when at last the news arrived. The majority in Arran for Mr. Boyle proved to be so large as to turn the scale, and decide the election in his favour. The silence of disappointment hung for a few moments over the committee. The first man to break it was the 'Bishop,' who consoled his colleagues with these words, 'Well, well, what can we say? what can we say? but that God always overdoes everything.' He probably meant 'overrules.'

One of the most familiar objects on the Clyde and in Rothesay Bay fifty years ago was the little sailing yacht of James Smith, of Jordanhill. During the summer he lived on the water, and took a share in all that was going on around him there. As far back as 1839 he was the first to detect, in the clays along the shores of the Kyles of Bute, remains of Arctic shells which no longer live in our seas, but still flourish in the north of Norway, and in the Arctic ocean. When I made his acquaintance, he had long ceased to carry on original scientific researches, or at least to publish anything new, but he retained his interest in the subjects which had early engaged his attention. In his little cabin he had a shelf of geological and other scientific books as his travelling companions, and kept himself in touch with the progress of enquiry in his own department. But it was in yachting all round the Firth of Clyde and its islands that he found the chief employment and solace of his old age. I shall treasure as long as I live the recollection of him in his yacht, attired as a genuine old seaman, his face ruddy with sun and sea-air, and beaming with the heartiest good nature.

On the east side of the kingdom it has long been noted how tenaciously the fisher folk cling to their old habits and customs. Red-tiled, corby-stepped houses, thrusting their gables into the street, climbing one above another up the steep slope that rises from the beach, and crowned by the picturesque old church or town hall with its quaint spire, give a picturesqueness to the shores of the Forth such as no other part of the coast-line can boast. Then the little harbours with their fleets of strong fishing boats, rich brown sails, 'hard coils of cordage, swarthy fishing nets,' and piles of barrels and baskets, bear witness to the staple industry of the inhabitants. The men are square, strongly built, and bronzed with exposure to sea-air. The women may be seen sitting in groups at their doors, mending nets or baiting the lines for next night's fishing. Such places as St. Monans, Pittenweem, Anstruther, Crail, and St. Andrews, afford endless subjects for the artist, whether he selects the buildings or their inhabitants. These places lie outside the main lines of traffic through the country; they have only in recent years been connected together by a line of railway, and have thus been brought into direct touch with the outer world. Thanks to this seclusion, they have preserved their antique character, and their natives are among the most old-fashioned Scots in the lowlands. An anecdote told by Dr. Hanna serves to illustrate the state of backwardness in some of these coast villages. A clergyman, in the course of a marriage ceremony at Buckhaven, repeated several times to the bridegroom the question whether he would promise to be a faithful, loving, and indulgent husband, but got no response from the man, who remained all the while stiff and erect. At last a neighbour, who had learnt a little more of the ways of the world, was so provoked by the clownishness of his friend that he came forward, and giving him a vigorous thump on the back, indignantly exclaimed, 'Ye brute, can ye no boo to the minister?' Dr. Chalmers' comment on this scene was—'the heavings of incipient civilisation!'[1]

On the south side of the Forth the fishwives of Newhaven, Fisherrow, and Musselburgh have long been famous for their conservatism in the matter of the picturesque costume which they wear. Dunbar, once a busy port, and the centre of an important herring fishery, used to boast a number of queer oddities among its sea-faring population. One of these men would now and then indulge in a prolonged carouse at the public-house. After perhaps a day or two thus spent, he would return to his home, and, standing at the door, would take off one of his large fisherman's boots, which he would pitch into the house, with the exclamation, 'Peace or war, Meg?' If the goodwife still 'nursed her wrath to keep it warm,' she would summarily eject the boot into the street. Whereupon the husband, knowing that this was

---

[1] *Life of Chalmers*, iv. p. 462.

Meg's signal of war, returned to his cronies. If, on the contrary, the boot was allowed to remain, he might hope for forgiveness, and crept quietly into the house.

Another of these Dunbar worthies had arranged with old Mr. Jeffray, the parish minister, to have his infant baptised at the manse. On the evening fixed he duly made his appearance, but not until after he had fortified himself for the occasion by sundry applications to the whisky bottle. When he stood with the child in his arms, he seemed so unsteady that the minister solemnly addressed him, 'John, you are not fit to hold up that child.' The stalwart sailor, thinking his personal prowess called in question, indignantly answered, 'Haud up the bairn, I could fling't ower the kirk,' the church being the loftiest building and most prominent landmark in the burgh.

A fisherman from another hamlet in the same district had found a set of bladders at sea which he claimed as his property. The owner of them, however, sued him for restitution of the property, which bore, in large letters, P.S.M., the initials of his name and seaport, as proof of his assertion. The East Lothian man, nothing daunted, exclaimed loudly to the presiding bailie, 'Naething o' the kind, sir, P.S. stands for Willie Miller, and M. for for the Cove.'

These lowland regions of the Lothians and Fife, with their strips of sand-hills and links along the shore, have for centuries been the headquarters of Golf—a game which has now naturalised itself over the whole civilised globe. Golfing anecdotes are innumerable and form a group by themselves, of which only one or two samples may be culled here.

A landed proprietor and his son were playing at North Berwick when the young man drove a ball close to his father's head. The observant caddie remarked quietly to him, 'Ye maunna kill Pa!' and then after a pause added, 'Maybe ye'll be the eldest son?'

Strong language appears to be a natural accompaniment of the game. A laird in trying to get his ball out of a 'bunker' swore so dreadfully that his caddie threw down the bundle of clubs on the ground exclaiming, 'Damn it, sir, I wunna carry clubs for a man that swears like you.'

An English caddie on a links in Kent, who was listening to a discussion among the players as to the proper way of spelling the word 'golf,' broke into the conversation with the remark, 'Surely there's no h'*l* in it' (aspirating the letter in Cockney fashion). 'Is there not?' exclaimed a young Scotswoman, 'You should just hear my father on the St. Andrews links.'

A marked and regrettable change has passed and is passing over lowland Scotland—the decay of the old national language—the Doric of Burns and Scott. The local accents, indeed, still remain fairly well-marked. The Aberdonian is probably as distinguishable as ever from a Paisley 'body,' and the citizen of Edinburgh from his neighbour of Glasgow. But the old national words have almost all dropped out of the current vocabulary of the towns. Even in the country districts, though a good many remain, they are fast becoming obsolete and unintelligible to the younger generation. It is sad to find how small a proportion of the sons and daughters of middle aged parents in Scotland can read Burns without constant reference to the glossary. A similar inevitable change was in progress for many centuries on the south side of the Tweed, though it has become extremely slow now:

> Our sons their fathers' failing language see,
> And such as Chaucer is, shall Dryden be.

I can remember men and women in good society, who if they did not ordinarily speak pure Scots, at least habitually introduced

Scots words and phrases, laying emphasis on them as telling expressions, for which they knew no English equivalents. I have watched the gradual vanishing of these national elements from ordinary conversation, until now one hardly ever hears them. Lord Cockburn used to lament the decay of the old speech in his day; it has made huge strides since then.

Not only have the old words and phrases disappeared, but there has arisen an affectation of what is supposed to be English pronunciation, which is sometimes irresistibly ludicrous. The broad, open vowels, the rolling r's and the strongly aspirated gutturals, so characteristic of the old tongue, are softened down to a milk and water lingo, which is only a vulgarised and debased English. There was unconscious satire in the answer given by a housemaid to her mistress who was puzzled to conjecture how far the girl could be intelligible in London whence she had returned to Scotland.

'You speak such broad Scotch, Kate, that I wonder how they could understand you in London.'

'O but, mam, I aye spak' English there.'

'Did you? And how did you manage that?'

'O, mam, there's naethin' easier. Ye maun spit oot a' the r's and gi'e the words a bit chow in the middle.'

CHAPTER XIV.

As it has been in pursuit of geological investigation that I have been enabled to see so much of Scotland, I hope the reader will not think it inappropriate that a few of the pages of this volume of reminiscences should be devoted to some recollections of Scottish geologists, more especially of those with whom I have been personally acquainted, and to some illustrations of my own experiences of the life of a field-geologist in Scotland. Let me preface this chapter with a brief reference to the rise of the Scottish School of Geology.

The intellectual society for which Edinburgh was distinguished in the later decades of the eighteenth and the early years of the nineteenth century, besides its brilliant company of literary men, included also some of the founders of modern science. To three of these men reference has already been made—Joseph Black, one of the pioneers of modern chemistry; James Hutton, the father of modern physical geology; and John Playfair, who first revealed to the general public the far-reaching scope of Hutton's philosophy. With these illustrious men there was likewise associated Sir James Hall of Dunglass, who introduced experimental research as a potent method of testing geological speculation. A striking characteristic of this group of men was shown in their indifference to the opinion of the world outside, and to the making of converts to their views. It was not until some years after Hutton's death in 1797 that his teaching was recognised as the initiation of a new school of thought, which bade fair to rival or even to supersede that of Werner at Freiberg, who was then attracting pupils from all parts of the world. This Scottish school, inasmuch as it laid great stress on the importance taken by the internal heat of the earth in geological history, came to be known as the Vulcanist.

While these men were at work in Scotland, by a curious irony of fate one of Werner's most distinguished pupils returned to Edinburgh, and in 1804 was appointed to the Chair of Natural History in the University there. Robert Jameson, like the other disciples of the Saxon teacher, was fired with zeal to spread the doctrines of his master, and as these doctrines were diametrically opposed to those of Hutton, there began a lively controversy which for a number of years had its chief battlefield in the Scottish metropolis. Werner claimed that by far the most important part in the history of the earth had been taken by water. His system was accordingly known as the Neptunist. It is difficult now to realise the fierceness of this warfare. The rocks round Edinburgh were appealed to with equal confidence by both sides, and many a lively discussion arose upon them. After a good many years, however, Jameson came to see that his master's theory offered but a partial explanation of the phenomena of nature, and that essentially the Vulcanists were right. He publicly recanted his early opinions, and the defection of their leading protagonist led to the extinction of the Scottish Neptunists. With the dying out of the fires of controversy, a kind of languor seems to have settled down upon the progress of geological science in Scotland. There was no longer an active resident school of geologists, and though many Scotsmen had acquired renown as geologists, it was mainly by work in other countries, rather than in their own. In an address which he gave to the Royal Society of Edinburgh in 1862, James David Forbes expressed himself as follows : ' It is a fact which admits of no doubt, that the Scottish Geological School, which once made Edinburgh famous, especially when the Vulcanist and Neptunian war raged simultaneously in the hall of this Society and in the class-rooms of the University, may almost be said to have been transported bodily to Burlington House [London]. Roderick Murchison, Charles Lyell, Leonard Horner, are Scottish names, and the bearers of them are Scottish in everything save residence. . . . Our younger men are drafted off as soon as their acquirements become known. . . . Of all the changes which have befallen Scottish science during the last half-century, that which I most deeply deplore, and at the same time wonder at, is the progressive decay of our once illustrious Geological School. Centralisation may account for it in part, but not entirely.'[1]

Notwithstanding this somewhat gloomy retrospect, there were still a few able men in Scotland, who continued to hold aloft the torch of geological progress. The illustrious Principal Forbes himself was widely known to the geological world for his researches on the glaciers of the Alps and of Norway, and on Earth-temperature. As one saw him in the street or in the class-room, he looked singularly fragile, and it was not easy to realise how such a seemingly frail body could have undergone the physical exertion required for his notable Alpine ascents. His tall spare figure might be seen striding from the University to the rooms of the Royal Society, of which for many years he was the active Secretary. His clear brown eyes wore a wistful expression, and his pale face and sunken cheeks

---

[1] Opening Address to Royal Society of Edinburgh, 1st December, 1862. The distinguished author expresses regret that a certain feeling of patriotism did not still keep a portion of the labours of the Scottish geologists for the Transactions of the Scottish Royal Society, and he makes a kindly and half prophetic allusion to my own probable removal to London. I may here say that I never forgot his words, and that I have considered it a duty as well as a pleasure, even when no longer resident in Scotland, to send some of the results of my researches to the Royal Society of Edinburgh.

showed how his well-chiselled features had
been preyed on by serious illness. Round his
long neck he always wore one of the large
neckcloths then in vogue, and above this, when
out of doors, he carried a thick muffler, from
under which, as one passed him, one might
hear now and then the cough that told of
the malady from which he was suffering. In
his own house, especially when showing some
of the beautifully artistic water-colour draw-
ings which he had made in the course of his
wanderings, the thin, white, almost transparent,
hands told the same tale of suffering. And
yet, in spite of all these visible signs of increasing bodily feebleness, his mind remained to
the last clear and bright, his memory, even
for minute details, perfect, his interest in men
and things, more particularly in scientific progress, as keen as ever, and his kindly help-
fulness to those whom he could assist as
prompt and effective as of old. He was one
of the most beautiful and interesting person-
alities whom I have ever known.

Two of the ablest resident Scottish geologists
were editors of leading Edinburgh newspapers
—Charles Maclaren and Hugh Miller—and to
both of them science was the recreation of
such leisure hours as they could snatch from

literary labour and political controversy. Maclaren was the founder, and for a quarter of a century, editor of the *Scotsman*, from which, as far back as 1845, he had retired to spend his later years in a delightful retreat on the southern outskirts of Edinburgh. His editorial task had been relieved by many a pleasant geological excursion among the rocks around that city, and he had worked out the volcanic history of the district with a minuteness, accuracy, and breadth of view which no one had attempted before him. After passing the results of his researches through the columns of his newspaper, he collected them into a small volume entitled *Geology of Fife and the Lothians*, which, though little known to the general reader, has long ago taken its place among the classics of Scottish geology.

Maclaren had acquired a command of clear, forcible English, and was a great admirer of good style in literature. I remember a conversation with him, in which he enlarged on the tendency of the age to pile up intensitives in description, both in ordinary conversation and in writing. The words 'awful' and 'awfully' were then beginning to come into vogue in the familiar slang. He strongly objected to such tasteless misuse of terms, holding with Pope that expletives give but a feeble aid in composition. 'Take my advice,' he said, 'after the experience of a long life, and be careful to strike out the word "very" in almost every place where you find it in your manuscript. You will discover that this excision will really strengthen your style, in the same proportion that the frequent repetition of the word would weaken it.'

Hugh Miller, as editor of the *Witness* newspaper, the accredited organ of the Free Church, was one of the living forces of Scotland during the last sixteen years of his life. He threw himself with great ardour into all the controversies, political and ecclesiastical, of the time, and his articles were read with eager interest from one end of the country to the other. His establishment in the editorial chair, however, and the consciousness of the influence which his pen enabled him to wield over the minds of his fellow-countrymen, never led him to put into the background the fact that he had been a journeyman mason. His appearance on the streets was certainly most uneditorial. Above the middle height, strongly built, with broad shoulders, a shock of sandy hair, large bushy whiskers, and dressed in rough tweeds, with a shepherd's plaid across his shoulder, he might have been taken for one of the hill-farmers who, on market days, come to Edinburgh from the uplands of the Lothians. He had the true 'Highlandman's ling'—the elastic, springy and swift step of the mountaineer, accustomed to traverse shaking bog and rough moor. As he swung down the North Bridge, wielding a stout walking stick, looking straight before him, his eyes apparently fixed on vacancy and his lips compressed, one could hardly help turning to look after him and to wonder what manner of man he could be. His, however, was a familiar figure on the line of streets and roads that led from the *Witness* office to his home in Portobello. His fellow citizens were proud of him as one of their literary lions, who had also made for himself in science a name which was known all over the English-speaking world.

To Hugh Miller I owe much, and am glad of every opportunity of acknowledging my indebtedness. His *Old Red Sandstone* kindled in me, as it has done in so many others, an enthusiasm for the science to which he devoted his leisure hours, and an admiration for the well of English undefiled to be found in every page of his writing. He personally encouraged

me in my earliest efforts at original observation.
He introduced me to Murchison, and thus
opened the way for my entry into the Geological Survey.

At the end of each summer we met at his
house to talk over the results of our geological
wanderings. The last note I had from him,
written on 9th October, 1856, only a few weeks
before his sudden and tragic end, asked me to
'drop in upon him on the evening of Saturday
first, and have a quiet cup of tea.' He added,
'my explorations this season have been chiefly
in the Pleistocene and the Old Red. I have
now got boreal shells in the very middle of
Scotland, about equally removed from the
eastern and western seas. But the details of
our respective explorations we shall discuss at
our meeting.' That discussion duly took place,
and full of interest it was to me. He displayed
on the table the shells he had gathered, and he
looked forward with keen pleasure to the task
of describing them, and showing the important
bearing they had on the geological history of
the country. It proved to be his last excursion,
as that evening was also the last of our intercourse, for before the end of the year I followed
him to his resting place, near to his great hero
Chalmers, in the Grange Cemetery.

Another literary man in Edinburgh who had also made some interesting contributions to geology was Robert Chambers. He especially concerned himself with the later phases of geological history, more particularly the proofs that Britain had been overspread with ice, and that important changes of level had taken place along the coasts of Scotland and northern Norway. He was also generally believed to be the author of the famous *Vestiges of Creation*—a belief which was fully confirmed after his death. When he heard that I purposed to become a member of the Geological Survey he gave me, I remember, an account of a recent excursion which he had made with a party of the Survey in North Wales. 'Being the oldest member of the company,' he said, ' I was voted into the chair, and had to carve. A leg of Welsh mutton was placed before me, from which I was kept supplying the demands of the geologists, until there was nothing left on the dish but a bare bone. So if you join the Survey, my young friend, you must be prepared for the development of a portentous appetite.'

The house of Robert Chambers in Edinburgh was one of the chief centres at which literary and scientific strangers met the intellectual society of the town. He was an excellent host. His fund of anecdote and reminiscence went back to near the beginning of the century. When no more than twenty years of age he had published a volume illustrative of the Waverley novels, followed next year by two volumes of *Traditions of Edinburgh*, which astonished Scott, who wondered where the boy could have picked up all the information.

Besides the geologists here enumerated there were others contemporary with them who did good service, but with whom my acquaintance was too slight to furnish me now with any personal reminiscences of them. Dr. John Fleming, author of the well-known *Philosophy of Zoology*, was trained as a Wernerian, and never quite adopted the views of modern geologists. I remember him as a tall rather grim figure, full of personal kindness, and gifted with keen critical power. He seemed never to be happier than when he had an opportunity of exercising that power in sarcastically demolishing the arguments of those to whom he was opposed. James Nicol, after he became Professor in Aberdeen in 1853, devoted himself with much enthusiasm and success to the study of the Highland rocks, and I only met him occasionally at the meetings of the British Association, where his tall figure, his abundant sandy-coloured hair, and pronounced south-country accent, made him a prominent personage.

In the early decades of last century a few students from foreign countries were attracted to Scotland for the purpose of examining the rocks, which since the days of the Huttonian and Wernerian controversy had become famous on the Continent. In my journeys abroad I met three of these veterans, each of whom retained a vivid recollection of his stay in this country.

W. Haidinger, who was long at the head of the Austrian Geological Survey and Museum in Vienna, had established his reputation as an able mineralogist, and came to Scotland to study the various cabinets of minerals, public and private, to be found in the country. When I saw him in Vienna in 1869, he had retired from all official duties, and as he sat in his study, surrounded with his books and papers, presented a singularly picturesque appearance, not unlike that in which Faust is usually represented on the stage before transformation into youth by Mephistopheles. Enveloped in a long dressing gown, he sat in an easy chair, his white beard flowing down his breast, and his head covered with an equal exuberance of snowy hair (which, however, was said to be a wig), while his feet were encased in large warm slippers. He remembered well the various mineral collections he had studied in Scotland, and was interested in hearing about the places he had seen, and the survivors of the acquaintances he had made.

H. von Dechen came to Scotland in 1827, and travelled over a good deal of the country, of which he subsequently gave an account in one of the German scientific journals. I first met him in Bonn, where he had a large house commanding fine views up to the Siebenge-birge, which he had studied so minutely and described so carefully. His age, the number and excellence of his geological writings, and his friendly interest in the career of younger men made him the popular Nestor of Prussian geologists. The last time I met him was in Berlin on the occasion of the meeting of the International Geological Congress in 1885, of which he was president. There was one lady member present at his address, and the audience was amused by the formal courtesy with which he began—'Lady and Gentlemen.'

Ami Boué had an interesting history. He was descended from a French family which could trace its pedigree back for some 400 years. In the reign of Louis XIV, his ancestor, being Protestant, had to escape from Bordeaux in a barrel. Boué himself was born in Hamburg. His mother had been educated in Geneva, and French was the language she used in her family circle. His early education was also given in Geneva, but as the French armies had overrun Europe, and the family property in Hamburg consisted largely of houses, which might at any moment be destroyed in the political convulsions, it was considered desirable that Ami should have a profession to fall back upon, in case of any such catastrophe. He was accordingly sent to Edinburgh to study medicine. As he long after remarked to me, 'I really went to Scotland to escape from Napoleon.' But although, when Napoleon was finally crushed at Waterloo, the Hamburg property was saved, Boué determined to continue his medical studies and to take his degree, which he gained in 1817.

During his residence in Scotland he became greatly interested in geological pursuits, and travelled over a good deal of the country, examining its rocks. When he returned to the Continent, he settled for a time in Paris, where he wrote his *Esquisse Géologique sur l'Écosse*— a most valuable treatise which in many respects was far in advance of its time. Subsequently, after wandering over much of Europe, he finally fixed his home in Austria.

Having occasion in some of my own early writings to refer appreciatively to Boué's work, I one day received a letter written in broken English and in a minute, cramped calligraphy, the lines slanting obliquely across the page. To my astonishment the letter bore the signature Ami Boué. This was the beginning of a correspondence which lasted up to the time of his death. I paid him a visit in 1869, and spent some time with him at his pleasant country-house on the last spurs of the Alps near Vöslau, where he had planted quinces, almond-trees, peaches, apples, and vines, and where I found his recollections of Edinburgh and Scotland as vivid as if he had only returned from that region a few years before.

Boué was singular in this respect, that he never thoroughly mastered any language. Although French was the tongue that in early life came most naturally to him, his French sometimes betrayed his German connections. In German he only acquired fluency after middle life, when he had settled in Vienna, and it was in German that all his later contributions to science were written. English he never learned to speak or write correctly.

2 B

But he was rather proud of what he thought to be his facility in that language, and all his letters to me, extending over a period of thirteen years, were written in broken English. As a specimen of the way in which he expressed himself, I may quote a sentence from a letter written by him on 21st November, 1870, during the calamitous Franco-German war. 'The dreadful war-pre-occupations did take me all time for thinking at scientific matter, and now perhaps that distress will approach till nearer our abode! When you will know that I have very good and near parents in both armies and you perceive the possibility of parents killing themselves without recognizing themselves, nor having the opportunity to do so, you will understand that I have often headach when I ride the newspapers or hear from the quite useless slaughters, which have been provocated only by those men at the head of the human society.'

The life of a field-geologist, being spent to a large extent in the open air, brings him into contact with various classes of the people, to whom his occupation is exceedingly mysterious. They see him marching up and down the face of a rocky declivity, chipping the rock here and there, putting the chips up to his eye, scrutinising them narrowly through his lens, which is popularly supposed to be an eye-glass for extremely short sight, then perhaps wrapping them up in paper and putting them in his pocket, or in a bag slung across his shoulder. They watch him taking out a map and marking down something upon it, or whipping out a note-book and writing in it, perhaps for so long a time that the patience of the watchers behind a neighbouring wall or hedge is nearly exhausted, when off he marches again, or comes back to the place he started from, as if he had left something behind him, or had hopelessly lost his way.

A member of the Geological Survey, whose daily avocation consists in such pursuits, is of course specially liable to become the victim of curiosity and suspicion. He carries his accoutrements about his person in such a manner that they do not attract notice, so that his object and actions become extremely puzzling to the country people among whom he has taken quarters for a time. He finds himself set down now for a postman, now for a doctor, for a farmer, a cattle dealer, a travelling showman, a country gentleman, a gamekeeper, a poacher, an itinerant lecturer, a gauger, a clergyman, a playactor, and often as a generally suspicious character. A member of the Survey, who afterwards became a University Professor, received and posted many a letter entrusted to him in the belief that he was the authorised bearer of Her Majesty's mails. Another member, also subsequently Professor, was taken for a policeman in plain clothes, and could not for some time make out why a poor woman poured into his ears a long story about her son, who had been taken up for something that he had not done, and did quite unintentionally, and was quite justified in doing.[1]

Gamekeepers are sometimes sorely at a loss what to make of the Geological Survey trespasser: afraid to challenge him lest he prove to be a friend of their master, and yet afraid to let him go his way for fear he be on poaching thoughts intent, though the absence of a visible gun piques their curiosity. One member of the staff, who had taken up his quarters in a coast town in Fife, was watched by the police on suspicion of having been concerned in a recent burglary. Another was stalked as a suspect who had been setting

[1] This and the next paragraph are taken with some alterations from my *Life of A. C. Ramsay*.

fire to farm buildings. A third was watched hammering by himself in the bed of a stream near Girvan, and as he gave vent to some strong expression when the obstinate boulder refused to part with a splinter, the onlooker on the other side of an adjoining hedge fled in terror to the village and reported that this strange man who had come among them was stark mad, and should not be left to go by himself. Sometimes the laugh goes distinctly against the geologist, as in the case of one of the most distinguished of the staff who, poking about to see the rocks exposed on the out-skirts of a village in Cumberland, was greeted by an old woman as the 'sanitary 'spector.' He modestly disclaimed the honour, but notic-ing that the place was very filthy, ventured to hint that such an official would find some-thing to do there. And he thereupon began to enlarge on the evils of accumulating filth, resulting, among other things, in an unhealthy and stunted population. His auditor heard him out, and then, calmly surveying him from head to foot, remarked : 'Well, young man, all I have to tell ye is, that the men o' this place are a deal bigger and stronger and handsomer nor you.' She bore no malice, for she offered him a cup of tea, but, like Falstaff, he was 'as crestfallen as a dried pear,' and could not face her any longer.

Professor James Geikie supplies me with the following record of his experience when he was on the staff of the Survey: 'One warm summer day I was laboriously forcing my way up a narrow ravine or "cleugh" in the hills south of Colmonel, in Ayrshire. The geology being somewhat complicated, it was necessary to use my hammer at almost every step, and for this purpose I had to keep the bed of the burn where the rocks were best seen. The cleugh was not only narrow and steep, but choked in places with blackthorn, so that progress was both slow and painful. Being far from the madding crowd, there was no reason why, under a broiling sun, I should affect a philosophical coolness which I was far from feeling, and it is probable, therefore, that from time to time I may have sought relief by addressing the obnoxious thorns in vehement language. At the head of the cleugh I came upon a tall farmer-looking man, who told me he had been watching my movements, and wondering who and what I was. When he heard I was trying to find out how the world was made, he expressed no astonishment, but showed keen interest as I pointed out the evidence of glacial work—striated rocks, morainic debris, and large erratics—all of which happened to be well displayed on the hill-side where we stood. As he seemed really anxious to know the meaning of the evidence, I explained it as well as I could, and then we parted. A few weeks afterwards I was dining with an old friend—the late Mr. Cathcart of Knock-dolian—who told me he was quite sure I must have been recently in his neighbourhood. "Only yesterday," he said, "I met the old farmer of G——," who had a strange tale to tell me. "Dod! Mr. Caithcart," he began, "I ran across the queerest body the ither day. As I was comin' by the head o' the cleugh I thocht I heard a wheen tinkers quarrellin', but whan I lookit doon there was jist ae wee stoot man. Whiles he was chappin' the rocks wi' a hammer : whiles he was writin' in a book, whiles fechtin' wi' the thorns, and miscain' them for a' that was bad. When he cam up frae the burn, him and me had a long confab. Dod! he tell't me a' aboot the stanes, and hoo they showed that Scotland was ance like Greenland, smoored in ice. A vary enterteenin' body, Mr. Caithcart, but—an awfu' leear." '

Among my own geological experiences in Scotland I may mention that on one of

my excursions, when, with a large party of
my students, I was passing along the sea-
front of a fishing village in Fife, I heard
a stalwart matron ask her gossip at the next
door, 'Whae's aucht them?'—that is, who
owns them, or has charge of them? She
evidently believed the company to be lunatic
patients, but could not see any one among
their number who seemed to her sane enough
to be probably their keeper.

On another occasion in the same district
I had been engaged for some days in geological exploration with a colleague, and had
several times come upon a travelling show,
which was slowly making its way through
the country. On entering one of the little
coast-towns we found that we were immediately behind this show, which, with its
cavalcade of waggons, had preceded us by
only a few minutes. The women were still
standing at their doors, making remarks on
the new arrival, when my companion and I
came up. As we passed a couple of them,
we heard the one remark to the other, 'Na
noo, arena thae twa daicent-lookin' chiels to
be play-actin' blackguards!'

If, fifty years ago, the ongoings of a field-
geologist gave rise to much curiosity and

speculation in the lowlands, it may be imagined how strange his occupation would seem to the natives of the Highlands, especially among the Western Isles, and in districts where little English was spoken, and where, consequently, he might be the subject of audible remarks that he did not understand or could not reply to. When I first set foot in Skye, most of my rambles there had geological pursuits as their aim. The general character and succession of the rocks of the island had been made known by Macculloch in his classic *Description of the Western Islands of Scotland*. I found that he was still remembered by some of the older inhabitants, but less as a geologist than as a writer who had maligned them. In his four volumes of letters to Sir Walter Scott on *The Highlands and Western Isles of Scotland*—on the whole a somewhat tedious work, though often amusing and occasionally even brilliant—he had given an account of his experiences as a traveller and geologist in the Highlands. This account was angrily resented by the natives as exaggerated, and even untruthful. They had entertained him in their houses, furnished him with boats, carriages, men, and other assistance, and he repaid them by satirising their households and holding their manners and customs up to public ridicule. Old Mackinnon of Corriehatachan was so indignant that the next time he went to Glasgow after the publication of the book, he took the engraved portrait of its author to a crockery-dealer and commissioned a set of earthenware with Macculloch's likeness on each. These articles were distributed over Skye, and I have been told that some of them are still to be seen.

Subsequently Skye was visited in 1827 by Murchison and Sedgwick, who came to Strath. The familiar anecdote of the geologist who entrusted his bag of specimens to a lad to be carried some miles to his inn, and who found that the bag had been emptied and refilled with stones picked up near the door, is told of Hugh Miller, of Sedgwick and of Murchison. I was assured in Skye that the trick was played on Macculloch. But to contrive to escape from the apparently unnecessary fatigue of carrying a heavy bag a long distance is so natural that we can believe it may have been carried out with all these worthies. I heard the anecdote in Skye, from the late Dr. Donald Mackinnon. But the most circumstantial account of it I have met with is that of Dr. Norman Macleod. 'A shepherd, while smoking his cutty-pipe at a small Highland inn, was communicating to another in Gaelic his experiences of "mad Englishmen," as he called them. "There was one," said he, "who once gave me his bag to carry to the inn by a short cut across the hills, while he walked by another road. I was wondering myself why it was so dreadfully heavy, and when I got out of his sight I was determined to see what was in it. I opened it, and what do you think it was? But I need not ask you to guess, for you would never find out. It was stones!" "Stones!" exclaimed his companion, opening his eyes, "Stones! well, well, that beats all I ever knew or heard of them! and did you carry it?" "Carry it! Do you think I was as mad as himself? No! I emptied them all out, but I filled the bag again from the cairn near the house, and gave him good measure for his money"!'

Another well-known story to the detriment of a geologist, is also claimed for Skye. I was assured that it was Sedgwick, who, when chipping a rock by the roadside as he went along on a Sunday, was stopped by a Strath man with the query, 'Do you know what you are doing?' and, on answering that he was breaking a stone, was told, 'Ay, you are doing mair than that; you are breakin' the Sabbath.' But here, again, the remark is so obvious in a Sabbatarian country that it may have been made by independent censors on more occasions than one.

The memory of the visits of these early geological pioneers had faded away when I came to Skye. It seemed that no geologist since their day had been seen in Strath, so that the appearance of a lad wandering about alone and, as it looked, aimlessly, with a hammer in his hand and a bag over his shoulder, gave rise to much wonderment and conjecture among the crofters. They knew me by the name of *Gille na Clach*, or the 'Lad of the Stones,' and came in the end to see that I was harmless. But now and then they would express their convictions or their pity. Once, when passing some huts on the shore of Loch Slapin, I stopped to break off a fragment from a projecting rock in front of them. As usual, I looked at the chip with my lens, and, having satisfied myself as to the nature of the rock, was resuming my walk, when I heard two old crones at their doors speaking of me. I knew very little Gaelic, but I caught up the emphatic remark that closed the conversation—'As a cheill.' When I returned to

Kilbride I asked the tutor of the family the meaning of the expression, and learnt that it was, 'He's wrong in the head.'

One of my earliest excursions from Kilbride led me to the island of Pabba, which lies like a flat green meadow in front of Broadford Bay. Hugh Miller had described to me its richly fossiliferous Liassic shales, and I went with the determination to spend some time on the island, and make a good collection of its fossils. The only habitation in the place was one small hut, tenanted by Charles Mackinnon and his family, who looked after the cattle sent across from the farm of Corrie. Coming with the recommendation of their master, I was cordially welcomed. But the resources of the island were slender. My sleeping quarters were a heap of heather in a corner of the upper floor of a barn, while for my dining-room I had the use of the 'ben' or inner room in Charles' hut. The food consisted chiefly of potatoes, oat-cakes, milk, and tea, with an occasional herring or an egg. After a day's work along the shore, I would spend the evening in the hut, labelling and wrapping up my specimens, while Mackinnon, who knew a little English, sat by the side of the peat fire, and gave me his company. We had been engaged in this way for some time the first evening, when the door opened, and his wife looked in. After watching me for a few moments arranging my bits of stone, she made a remark in Gaelic which drew an angry reproof from her 'goodman,' who ordered her to go away. With some difficulty I drew from him the admission that the poor woman had only said 'if she wassna kennin' ye had sense, she wad be thinking ye wass a terrible eediot.'

When it was time to retire for the night, my hostess would take a live peat between the tongs in one hand and a candle in the other, and sally out into the night, then up an outside stair, without any rail, to my barn, where she lit the candle, and left me. I shall never forget the moaning of the wind through the open louver-boards that served for windows, the gusts that swept through the place and nearly blew out the candle, and the shrieking of the sea-fowl, like the agonised cries of drowning seamen. But the heather was soft, the blankets warm, and with youth on one's side one slept soundly till the morning.

At my departure I pressed my kind host and hostess to accept remuneration for their services, but they rejected the notion almost with indignation. At last Charles was persuaded to let me send him some remembrance when I got back to the south country. He said he would prefer a book, and when asked to choose his book, he timidly enquired whether he might have '*Josaiphus.*' Although his knowledge of English was scanty, he used to read English books aloud to his children, but I am afraid that much of what he read must have been unintelligible both to him and to them. However, I procured and sent him an illustrated copy of *Josephus*, which, I was told, he used to show with pride as the largest book on his shelf.

A more distant excursion took me to the extreme north-eastern part of Skye. After spending some time on the shore of Loch Staffin and making a collection of the well-preserved fossils to be obtained there, I started late one afternoon for the hamlet of Lonfern, in which my friends at the Manse of Snizort, told me I would get a warm welcome at Mrs. Nicolson's, if I mentioned that I came from them. The distance was only a few miles, but there was much to interest me by the way, so that the gloaming had set in, and still no sign could be seen of the hamlet. At last I came upon a man returning from the hill with a creel of peats on his back, and asked him the path to Lonfern, when a conversation ensued, which may here be given as an illustration of crofter inquisitiveness.

'Lonfern! Are you gaun to Lonfern? And where hae ye come frae?'

'I have come this evening from Loch Staffin.'

'Frae Loch Staffin! and ye'll be a marchant?'

'No, I'm not a merchant.'

'Not a marchant! and what is't that ye'll be carryin' in your bag?'

'My bag is full of stones.'

'Full of *stones*! Ochan, ochan! d'ye tell me that? Stones in your bag. And what wull ye be doin' wi' the stones?'

'Well, I mean to take them south and look at them all very carefully.'

'Lookin' at stones! Well, well! And have ye no stones in your ain countrie?'

'O yes, plenty of them; but they are not the same as you have in Skye. But will you not tell me how I am to go to reach Lonfern.'

'To Lonfern! Ow ay, to be sure, the way to Lonfern. But what use are the stones to you?'

'Well, I told you, I wished to have samples of the Skye stones beside me.'

'To think o' a man keepin' stones to look at them! But are they worth onythin'? Can you make onythin' oot o' them?'

'Yes to me they are worth a great deal, for they show me what Skye was like long, long ago. But it is getting dark now, and I really must push on to Lonfern, if you will point out the track.'

'Ay, ay; well, well, that's queer enough. To think that ye wud be comin' all the way frae the south country to pick up a wheen stanes at Loch Staffin. And I'll warrant the bag's heavy too. So it is, whatever' (gently lifting it from my back).

'Well, my friend, I must say good night, if you won't help me to find Lonfern.'

'Ow ay, but I wull that. D'ye see thae twa peat-stacks. Weel then, ye'll be keepin' round by them to the burn, and ye'll be coming to the wood plank across the burn, and ye'll cross over there, and then ye'll be keepin' straught on by the side o' the dyke, and in a wee while you will be seein' Lonfern forenenst you.'

'Thank you, thank you, and good night.'

'Gude nicht, and I'm wussin' ye safe hame wi' that bag.'

I had been told by my Snizort friends that Jessie Nicolson's cottage could easily be

2 C

found, for it was the largest of the row that formed the hamlet. But by the time I arrived there, the darkness had settled down, so that only by stooping, in order to get the outline of the roofs against the western sky, could one judge of the relative size of the huts. At last I selected what seemed to be the right one, and knocked at the door. There was no answer for a time, and while waiting I could hear, to the left hand, under the same roof, the heavy breathing and crunching noises of the cows. After a second knock, the door was eventually opened, and the figure of an elderly woman appeared against the faint light of a candle in the room to the right hand. I asked if this was Mrs. Nicolson's. Instead of answering, she began to pass her hand over my face, neck, and shoulders. Not knowing whether she might be deaf and dumb, I shouted out that I had come from the Manse of Snizort. At the sound of these words, she took me by the arm and almost dragged me into the room with the light. 'Frae the Manse o' Snizort, are ye?' she exclaimed. 'And very welcome here.' Planting me down by the side of the peat fire, which she raked together and stacked up with more fuel, she plied me with questions as to how they all were at the manse, and at every additional detail of news, her joy seemed to increase. By degrees her family of well-grown sons and daughters began to assemble, and to every one I was introduced afresh as from the Manse of Snizort, and had to answer a similar round of questions. Meanwhile the old lady, from a handsome brass-bound chest of drawers (perhaps a marriage gift from her friends at Snizort) which stood on one side of the room, took out a tablecloth of beautiful snow-white linen, and spread it on the table. One of the sons had come in from the bay with a fresh salmon, which, cut up into steaks, formed part of an excellent supper, enlivened with much talk, wherein the Manse of Snizort and its inmates played a large part.

In this same room there were two beds, one of which was spread afresh for me, while the other was occupied by one of the sons. My experience among the crofters had accustomed me to peat-reek, but its pungency this evening surpassed anything I had previously undergone. After the family had retired, and I had lain down between the soft white sheets, it was some time before the smarting of the closed eyelids would allow of sleep.

The architecture of one of these houses is of the simplest kind. On one side of the door is the division reserved for the cattle. On the other is the part occupied by the human inmates, which in the smallest huts may consist of a single room. Where there are more rooms than one, they are joined on to each other, with only a thin wattled or blanket partition between them. There is no separate passage, so that from the innermost room it is necessary to pass through the others to reach the outside. The doors between the rooms often consist only of a blanket hung across the opening, and pushed aside when one wishes to enter or to leave. On the morning following my arrival I was awakened by the footsteps of some one passing through my room, and noticed a female skirt disappearing beyond the blanket. In a few moments the eldest daughter of the house entered bearing a tray laden with bottles and glasses, which she brought up to my bedside, in order that, as she said, I might 'taste something before I got up.' Not being used to such a matutinal habit, I declined her offer with my best thanks. But she grew quite serious over my refusal, assuring me that my tasting would give me an appetite. In vain I maintained that at breakfast time she would see that I stood in no need of any help of that kind. She only the more ran over the choice of good appetising things she had brought me. 'Some whusky nate? some whusky and wahtter? some whusky and milk? some acetates?' This last I conjectured to be a decoction of bitter roots in whisky, often to be found on Highland sideboards in the morning. Seeing that a persistent refusal would have displeased her, I consented at last to have some milk and whisky, but I did not discover that the draught in any way improved my breakfast.

There are few meals in the world more enjoyable than a true Highland breakfast. It presupposes, however, good health, a good digestion, and freedom from the daily visits of the penny post. The porridge and cream at the beginning provide a sensible substratum on which the later viands can be built up. Even if you confine your efforts to only one or two of these viands, the variety of the whole table, redolent of the hillside and the moor, and so unlike the typical morning repast of ordinary southerners, imparts a sense of plenty and freedom, and renews the longing to be out once more in the glen or on the mountain. Christopher North, who more than most men appreciated the merits of this repast, used to say, after having made a good meal, 'now is the time to pitch in a few eggs.'

Johnson, too, who liked good living, admitted that the Scots, both Lowland and Highland, excel the English in breakfast. 'If an epicure,' he says, 'could remove by a wish, in quest of sensual gratification, wherever he had supped, he would breakfast in Scotland.'[1]

The breakfast at Lonfern was worthy of the supper of the evening before. When I had to address myself to my journey to Portree those kindly folk gathered round me with expressions of the most affectionate interest, as if I had been an old friend instead of an unknown stranger. They would not hear of my starting off by myself. It was a walk of eighteen miles, they said, and the track was rough, and in many places not easy to find. Besides, there was a high cliff on the left hand, and if mist came on I might fall over into the sea, several hundred feet below, and there were deep slacks (ravines) to cross, and many burns which might be swollen, together with other dangers which were duly detailed. So one of the sons must accompany me all the way, and carry my bag. To refuse the escort would have given offence; so we parted with the heartiest good wishes on both sides, and I had unlooked for companionship through the moors and boggy tracts that

[1] *Journey of a Tour to the Western Islands*, 1757, p. 124.

lie between the edge of the sea-washed precipices and the steep hillsides of Trotternish.

During my earlier visits to Skye, the Admiralty survey of the surrounding seas and coasts
was in progress, under the direction of Captain
Wood, R.N. He used to be a welcome guest
at Kilbride, and he sometimes took the house
party on board his gunboat for a sail down
Loch Slapin. On one of these occasions we
visited the Spar Cave, and, with the help
of the sailors and Bengal lights, we saw
that famous cavern more completely than perhaps it had ever been seen before. But its
glory was gone. A couple of generations of
Sassenach tourists, aided by the hammers,
candles, and torches of ignorant Celts, had
defaced the place beyond belief, shorn it of
the beauty of its white crystalline pillars, and
left it mangled and smoke-streaked. In the
course of centuries, if left undisturbed, 'Nature,
softening and concealing, and busy with a
hand of healing,' would doubtless repair the
damage. But the ruthless iconoclast should
in the meantime be debarred access to the
grotto, until the 'sweet benefit of time' has
renewed the former glories of the place.

We went on to Loch Scavaig, landed at
the head of that gloomy fjord, and walked

over to Coruisk. I have often been there since, but have never a second time witnessed a sight which was provided for us by the tars of the gunboat. As everybody knows, who has been to this most sombre of Scottish lakes, the declivities around the water are dotted over with boulders of all sizes, left there by the glacier which once filled the basin of Loch Coruisk and passed down Loch Scavaig out to sea. Some of these blocks of stone stand perched in the most perilous positions, on steep slopes and on the edge of cliffs, whence from a little distance it seems as if a mere touch would suffice to send them bounding into the lake below. Their number and situation evidently interested the sailors, who, as a change from their usual boating and sounding for the marine survey, dashed off for the nearest hill, along the profile of which the boulders lay in especial abundance. We had not noticed at first in which direction the men moved, when our attention was attracted by a thundering noise from the hill in question, followed by a loud splash in the lake below. The tars had found some of the perched blocks capable of being moved, and no doubt they dislodged as many as they could. But, fortunately for the sake of geolo-

gists, they could not succeed with the larger
and finer boulders, which still remain where
the melting ice allowed them to rest.

In recent years, while the 'Aster' has been
cruising along these coasts, it has several times
anchored for the night at the head of Loch
Scavaig, and a more impressive anchorage can
hardly be imagined. The precipices on either
side plunge almost perpendicularly into the
water, and mount upwards, crag over crag,
into the far black, splintered crests and pinnacles that surround Coruisk. The tints of
sunset flame along these peaks, while the
evening shadows creep slowly upwards, and
deepen into such darkness below that one
cannot tell where land and water meet. The
sea, though tidal, may be motionless as the
calmest lake. The stillness is only broken
by the hoarse roar of the torrents that tumble
in white cascades through rifts in the black
rocks. In the long summer nights the northern
sky remains full of light, and even at midnight the striking outlines of the surrounding
mountains stand out sharp and clear against
it. Now and then a sea-gull may circle
slowly past and disappear in the gloom, but
for the most part there is little sign of life
at these hours.

CHAPTER XV.

INFLUENCE of Topography on the people of Scotland.   Distribution and ancient antagonism of Celt and Saxon.   Caithness
and its grin.   Legends and place-names.   Popular explanation of boulders.   Cliff-portraits.   Fairy-stones and supposed
human footprints.   Imitative forms of flint.   Scottish climate
and its influence on the people.   Indifference of the Highlander to rain.   'Dry rain.'   Wind in Scotland.   Shakespeare
on the climate of Morayland.   Influence of environment on
the Highlander.

IT is impossible to wander with attentive eyes
over Scotland without recognising how powerfully the topography of the country has con-
trolled the distribution of the races that have
successively peopled it, and how seriously the
combined influences of topography and climate
have come to affect the national temperament
and imagination.   As I have elsewhere discussed this subject, I will only refer briefly to
it here as an appropriate ending to these
chapters of a geologist's reminiscences.

I. First as regards the Topography.   Confining our attention to the Saxon and Celtic elements of the population, we can readily see from the mere form of the ground why the two races have been distributed as we now find them. On the west side of the country the Norse sea-rovers seized upon the islands and the narrow strips of cultivable land along the coasts of the mainland. They were 'vikings' or baysmen, at home on the sea and unwilling to wander far from its margin. They had no inducement to quit their harbours and surrounding farms in order to penetrate into the bleak mountainous fastnesses of the interior which they left in possession of the older Celtic people. When the Norwegian sway came to an end, and the invaders returned to the cradle of their race in the north, they left behind them some of their own stock who had intermarried with the Gaels, and as a still more enduring memorial of their presence, abundant Norse names, which still cling to hamlet, island, promontory, bay, and hill. But the selvage of coast-line which they had occupied was so narrow, and the chain of islands lay so near, that the mountaineers would have little difficulty in moving down from the high grounds, overspreading the Norse settlements, and mingling with their inhabitants. The spoken language of the vikings disappeared, and Gaelic once more became the native tongue of the whole district.

On the east side of the country, however, the conditions were somewhat different. In that region the mountains here and there retire so far from the sea as to leave wide stretches of lowland. On these spaces of comparatively fertile land the early Teutonic invaders found more ample room for their settlements. They accordingly possessed themselves of these tracts from Caithness southward, along the shores of the Moray Firth to Aberdeen, and thence round the eastern end of the Grampian range into the broad valley of central Scotland. They seem to have in large measure driven out the earlier Celtic people who, on this side of the island also, were left to live as best they could among the mountains. The topography which enabled the invaders to possess themselves of this territory has sufficed ever since to keep the races apart. Gradually, indeed, along their mutual boundaries, though apparently less distinctly than on the West Coast, they came to intermingle with each other. But the ancient antagonism between Celt and Saxon lasted down through the centuries, and in an attenuated form almost to our own day. The Highlander, when he used to raid the cattle and burn the farms of the Lowlander, was avenging the wrongs which his remote ancestors had suffered at the hands of the hated Sassenach. The Lowlander, on the other hand, who found himself often powerless to ward off or revenge these outrages, and had to pay blackmail to prevent their repetition, solaced himself by losing no opportunity of expressing his contempt for his Celtic neighbour. The word 'Highland' actually came to have an opprobrious meaning, summing up, as it did, all the bad qualities of the race to which it was applied. More particularly, the imperfect knowledge of English on the part of the mountaineers, and their slowness or inability to understand what was said to them in that language, led their Saxon fellow-countrymen to the foolish conclusion that this apparent dullness arose from innate stupidity. The poor Celts, in their efforts to express themselves in the language of the Lowlands, naturally made use of the words they heard there, so that a Highlander who was warned against doing what would have been a foolish action, could innocently exclaim, 'She's no sae tam Heelan' to do that.' I can remember in my boyhood, being much struck by coming across some survivals of this use of the word, and of the feelings of contempt with which it was employed. There were then many stories current illustrative of what was thought to be the dense stolidity and ignorance of the Celts. The type of conceited Lowlander, so well represented in Bailie Nicol Jarvie, never realised his own vulgarity, or recognised the innate gentlemanliness of even the poorest and least educated Highlander who had escaped Sassenach contamination. But these misunderstandings have been buried and forgotten.

Probably the best district of the country for the purpose of marking the topographical conditions that determined the limits within which the two races are confined, is to be found on the east side of Sutherland and Ross, and in the county of Caithness. To this day these limits remain fairly well marked. The low ground forms but a narrow strip along the coast from the Moray Firth to the Ord. On that strip, and through the Black Isle to Tarbat Ness, the people are Teutonic, but as we penetrate into the hills, the squalid cabins, poor crofts, peat reek, and sounds of the Gaelic tongue, tell unmistakeably that we have entered upon the domain of the Celt. Caithness offers

one of the most singular pieces of topography
in Scotland. Looking at the map, one would
naturally regard it as a continuation of the
highlands of Sutherland, and expect its population to be also Gaelic. But in actual fact,
it belongs not to the mountains, but to the
lowlands, and has been for many centuries in
possession of the Scandinavian stock. It consists of a flat platform or tableland, in places
not more than 100 feet above the sea, into
which it descends in an almost continuous line
of abrupt precipices. The contrast between the
varied and picturesque coast-line and the tame
monotony of the featureless interior is singularly striking, and again, that between the
wide, moory, peat-covered plain, and the bold
Sutherland mountains that spring up from its
border. The names of places over this plain
and along the shore bear witness to the long
occupation of the territory by the descendants
of the Norsemen. But as soon as we enter
the hills, Gaelic names appear, and we find
ourselves among a population that still speaks
Gaelic.

As a consequence of the flatness of the
interior of Caithness, the few roads which cross
the county run for miles in straight lines.
Their rectilinear direction is said to have had

a curious effect on the physiognomy of the inhabitants. Two men coming from opposite quarters recognise each other long before they can come within speaking distance. A smile of recognition, however, begins to form itself on their faces, and this lasts so long, before they actually meet, that it becomes stereotyped into a kind of grin, which is alleged to be characteristic of the most typical natives of Caithness.

That the topographical features of Scotland have influenced the national imagination is well indicated by the legends and place-names that have been attached to them. A deep cleft on a mountain-crest, a bowl-shaped hollow scooped out of a hillside, a profound ravine, a conical mound or a group of such mounds, rising conspicuously above a bare moorland, a solitary boulder of gigantic size, or a line of large boulders—these and many other prominent elements in the scenery, alike of the Lowlands and the Highlands, have arrested attention from the earliest times. As they appear so exceptional in the general topography, exceptional causes have been sought to explain them, and they have given rise to legendary beliefs that have been gradually interwoven in the mythology and superstition of the races that have dwelt among them. That these apparently abnormal features owed their origin to some form of direct supernatural agency has been tacitly assumed as their only possible explanation. Now and then they are referred to the immediate action of the Deity. Thus all over the hills and valleys of the south of Ayrshire, an incredible number of boulders of grey granite have been scattered. So abundant are they in some places as, when seen from a distance, to look like flocks of sheep, and so distinct are they in form, colour, and composition from any of the rocks round about them, that they could not fail to excite the imagination in trying to account for them. A stonebreaker who was asked how he supposed they had come to lie where they are, after a pause gave the following picturesque explanation, 'Weel ye see, when the Almichtie flang the warld out, He maun hae putten thae stanes upon her to keep her steady.'

More usually the popular fancy has fixed on the Devil, with his copartnery of wizards, warlocks, witches and carlines, as the authors of the more singular parts of a landscape. I have already referred to this aspect of diabolic agency, and by way of further illustration may cite here an example of the kind of legend

2 D

which has grown up in all parts of the country. I was once directed to a shoemaker in the village of Carnwath as possessing more local knowledge of his district than anyone else. By a piece of bad luck for himself, but of good fortune for me, on the day of my call upon him the man had so injured a finger that he could not at the moment continue to ply his trade. He was accordingly delighted to accompany me over the ground, and point out some of the changes which it had undergone within his own memory. A conspicuous feature in the district was furnished by a number of boulders of dark stone scattered over the surface between the River Clyde and the Yelping Craig, about two miles to the east. Before farming operations had reached their present development there, the number of these blocks was so much greater than at present that one place was known familiarly as 'Hell Stanes Gate' (road), and another as 'Hell Stanes Loan.' The tradition runs that Michael Scott, the famous wizard, had entered into a compact with the Devil and a band of witches to dam back the Clyde with masses of stone to be carried from the Yelping Craig. It was one of the conditions of such pacts that the name of the Supreme Being should never on any account be mentioned from the beginning to the end of the transaction. All went well for a while, some of the stronger carlines having brought their burden of boulders to within a few yards from the river, when one of the younger members of the company, staggering under the weight of a huge block of green-stone, exclaimed, 'O Lord! but I'm tired.' Instantly every boulder tumbled to the ground, nor could witch, warlock, or devil move a single stone one yard further. And there the blocks had lain for many a long century, until the modern farmers blasted some of them with gunpowder to furnish material for dykes and road-metal, and got rid of others by tumbling them into holes dug to receive them.

The shoemaker, however, though he enjoyed the popular explanation, had got far beyond the thraldom of old superstition, and had made some acquaintance with modern science. When I asked him how he would himself account for the scattering of these blocks of stone over the district, he replied at once, 'O, ye ken, they cam on the backs o' the icebairges,' and he proceeded to give me a graphic picture of what he supposed must have been the condition of Clydesdale when it lay below an icy sea, across which the stones were transported and were left where they now lie.

In many cases the origin of striking local features is referred to the doings of powerful witches alone, as in the case of Ailsa Craig, which is said to be the work of

A witch so strong
That could control the moon, make flows and ebbs.

The legend relates that for some purpose she designed to carry over a hill to Ireland, and selected one near Colmonell. Having lifted it up in her apron, she set off on her broomstick through the air, but unfortunately, when some miles out over the firth, her apron-strings broke, and the huge mass fell into the water, where its upper part has projected ever since as the well-known 'craggy ocean-pyramid.' In proof of the truth of this tale, the hollow is pointed out from which the rock was removed.

Even among the minor topographical features of the country, the natural play of the imagination may be seen where the instinctive feeling for the detection of resemblances has led to the recognition of so many likenesses to men and to animals, sometimes obvious, sometimes far-fetched, among the outlines of hills and crags. This tendency may be seen at work in every country. Anyone can perceive the strikingly lion-like aspect of Arthur's Seat, which seems to sit watching over Edinburgh, ready to spring at a foe. The profile of Samuel Johnson's (some say Lord Brougham's) face and his portly body have long been familiar on the southern front of Salisbury Crags, though it seems to me that the mouth is wider open and the chin hangs a little more than when I used to admire it as a boy. The 'tooth of time' is incessantly gnawing at all such cliffs, and while some fancied resemblances are gradually effaced, others are brought into existence. Travellers up Loch Carron see in front of them on the summit of the mountain Fuar Thol a gigantic recumbent profile, which from generation to generation is likened to that of some contemporary personage. At present it is spoken of as the face of a well-known politician whose features are familiar in the pages of *Punch*. Our grandchildren will find a likeness in it to some one of their own time. In the little anchorage of the Shiant Isles, the face of one of the surrounding cliffs presents the outline of a man in the attitude so often depicted in the background of Teniers' pictures.

Further illustration of this universal habit of mind may be gathered from even the smaller objects in nature. Children delight to recognise resemblances in things; the grown man learns to detect differences. Yet in regard to things that are unfamiliar, the man's first instincts are those of the child. He seizes on the likeness which the newly observed objects bear to some already known to him, and he may even go so far as to mistake similarity for identity. Perhaps in no department of nature does this habit of mind manifest itself more flagrantly than in the mineral kingdom. People who know little or nothing of minerals or rocks, readily enough perceive a resemblance between some pieces of stone and certain plants, animals or inanimate objects, with which they at once compare or even identify them. In the vast majority of cases, there is no real connection between the stone and the object which it resembles. The likeness is merely accidental and external. Among the multitudinous shapes which concretions of mineral matter have assumed, a curious collection might be made of imitative forms. The 'fairy stones' of Scotland, found as concretions among deposits of clay, present endless rude figures of manikins, or portions of the human body, of fishes, birds, plants, cannon-balls, snuff-boxes, shoes, and innumerable familiar objects. Similar concretions occur all over the world, and have long attracted popular notice.

An Orkney laird once wrote to me that his people, while removing flagstones from the shore of his island, had made an extraordinary discovery, no less than 'the footprints of men, women, children and animals,' all impressed on the solid stone and in excellent preservation, and he courteously offered to send me some specimens of these interesting remains. The identification of the impressions as human relics was of course out of the question, for the rock that contained them belonged to the Old Red Sandstone, which was deposited long before any trace of man appeared upon the earth. Nevertheless, as there was just a possibility that among the specimens, there might be some new fossils, which might add to our knowledge of the flora or fauna of that ancient formation, I asked the proprietor to be good enough to send a few examples of the 'find.' In due course one or two large boxes arrived containing several hundredweight of stone. But every one of the specimens was merely the cast of a mineral concretion. Yet they were curiously like footprints. One looked as if a young man, in going out to a ball, had stepped with his dress-boot upon soft mud, into which he had sunk about an inch. Another seemed as if it might have been made by a rough-shod farmer, springing from his dog-cart upon the surface of a muddy pool. There were prints resembling misshapen female feet, and one or two might, with a little imagination, have been taken for prints of infants, whose fond mothers were trying to make them stand on a soft clay floor. But not a single one of them had anything to do with a human being, or with any fossil plant or animal.

The flints which lie dispersed through the chalk, and which are distributed in such profusion over the surface of parts of the north-east of Scotland, present many curiously imitative shapes, either belonging to them originally, or brought about by the irregular fracturing and rolling which the stones have undergone under the sea or on the beds of rivers. The following letter, written to me by a workman in the south of England, where chalk-flints are immensely abundant, and are largely used for road making and other purposes, may be taken as an illustration of the popular view of these objects.   It is given *verbatim et literatim.*

I have a collection of flints In fantastic Shapes of a human Race such as leg with foot also feet harms legs Hand with finger also finger skul and other Parts of Human frame about 50 Pieces weight nearley One hundred I have also Kelt harrow heds speer heds and set. My Collection of the Human Race is a splended one and I dont think they Can be beeten they look as natrel as the boddy they or far sale and honestly worth a thousand Pounds I will take a Reasonable Offer for them they are on View at my House and I should like to find a Home for them. Faithfully yours, ——— Gravel Thrower.

II. Not less important than the topography of a country, as a factor in the bodily and mental development of a people, is the Climate. Alike in prose and verse the climates of northern countries have been abundantly maligned, though it has been generally allowed that they produce men of mark both in body and mind. We are told that the sun 'ripens spirits in cold northern climes,' and that courage, strength, and endurance may be looked for in people inured to exertion in these regions. In English literature the climate of Scotland has naturally offered a convenient butt for sarcasm and abuse, coupled occasionally with an admission that, at all events, it has fostered a sturdy race. Waller, in order to enhance his praise of the doings of Cromwell in Scotland, speaks of his successes over

> A race unconquered, by their clime made bold,
> The Caledonians, arm'd with want and cold.

There can be no doubt that most of this dispraise of the climate has been based on mere hear-say report, and that where it has been grounded on actual personal observation in Scotland, it has generally been the result of exceedingly brief experience, during short excursions into the country. It has in large measure arisen from the confounding of climate with weather. A man who comes into a country for a few weeks, and is unlucky enough to meet with a spell of bad weather which lasts most of the time of his visit, may be pardoned if he abuses what he has himself suffered from, but he has no right to pass any judgment on the climate of the country. Climate is the average of all the variations of weather during a long succession of years, and cannot be tested by any mere summer tour. A Scot may fairly claim that his country can boast of two or three climates, tolerably well marked off from each other, but all of

them healthy, and on the whole, not dis-
agreeable.   There is the oceanic climate of
the western isles and firths, under which in
sheltered places many flowering shrubs and
evergreens flourish luxuriantly, which can
scarcely be grown elsewhere in the country
save under glass.   The eastern climate, being
further removed from the warm Atlantic
waters, and more directly exposed to the chilly
east-wind, is less genial.   The central climate
of the mountains is one of greater extremes,
the summer temperature in the valleys being
sometimes high, while the frosts in winter are
often severe, and the snow-rifts remain un-
melted in the shaded corries all the summer.
To these might perhaps be added the Shetland climate, characterised by the prevalence
of winds and sea-fogs.   The winds are there
fierce, and always more or less laden with
salt from the spindrift of the surrounding
ocean, so that shrubs cannot grow above the
limit of their sheltering wall, and true trees
are not to be seen.   The white sea-fogs spread
rapidly over the islands during summer,
and though dense enough to blot out the view,
are not always so thick as wholly to obscure
the sun.

To one accustomed to more southern latitudes

the chief defect of the Scottish climate is the want of sunshine. The *nimbus Britannicus* spreads too frequently as a grey pall across the sky. But the native who has been used to this canopy all his life, and has never seen the continuous unclouded blue of a southern clime, manages to enjoy good health, lives often a long and active life, and resents imputations on the meteorology of his country, though he reserves to himself, especially if he be a farmer, the privilege of a good grumble, when no stranger is at hand to overhear it.

Most people shun a shower, and think themselves worthy of pity if one should overtake them when they can find no shelter, or have no umbrella to protect them. But to ordinary Highlanders exposure to heavy rain is a matter of indifference, even if not a source of real pleasure. On any wet day you may see these men standing together in pouring rain, although a shed or other shelter may be close at hand. They get soaked to the skin, but it does not seem to do them any harm. In fact, they say themselves that the wet thickens the cloth of their raiment and keeps them warm. And that they are often really warm is obvious enough when the steam may be seen rising from them, as if they were drying themselves before a fire. The only concession I ever noticed a Highlander make is now and then to take off his cap, if the water is trickling from it down his neck, and to wring the rain out of it before putting it on again. As an illustration of how strong and persistent this national trait is, it may be mentioned that about the middle of the eighteenth century a Highlander from the forest of Mam More emigrated to Canada, where after some years he was visited by an old friend from Scotland who, when the man was out of the way, asked his wife and daughters whether he ever talked of the Highlands. They said he frequently did so, and though he was fairly content with his home in the colony, he would often complain that there was not rain enough. When a good heavy shower came, he would go out and stand in it till he was quite drenched; and returning into the house, dripping wet, but with a smile of satisfaction on his face, he would say, 'What a comfortable thing rain is!'[1]

A lady of my acquaintance on the west coast, to whom I remarked that it was a pity for ordinary mortals that so much rain fell

[1] Burt's *Letters*, vol. ii., p. 28.

there, immediately answered me, 'O, but you must remember, it is *dry* rain.' The remark appears stupidly absurd, but she was an intelligent and observant person, who would not have made an idiotic statement. I learnt that what she referred to was the rapidity with which the rain disappeared from the surface of the ground and from the garments of those exposed to it. She maintained that, owing to the more genial climate of the west, the rain, as it fell, was warmer than on the east side of the country, and owing to more rapid evaporation, and perhaps to greater porousness of the soil, it vanished out of sight sooner. Certainly from my own experience, I do not think one catches cold from severe wetting so readily on the west as on the east coast.

In the year 1728, Aaron Hill, who is now chiefly remembered because of his connection with Pope, became popular in the north of Scotland owing to the vigorous, but ultimately unsuccessful efforts, he made to cut and float down timber on the Spey, for the uses of the navy. He was entertained by the nobles and magistrates, and received the freedom of the town of Inverness. But he must have happened upon a spell of bad weather, for when he halted at Berwick he wrote on the window of the inn the following lines:

> Scotland! thy weather's like a modish wife;
> Thy winds and rains for ever are at strife;
> So Termagant a while her thunder tries,
> And when she can no longer scold—she cries.[1]

More trying to the temper than the rain is the wind that too often sweeps across the country. Men who have to 'strive with all the tempest in their teeth,' acquire a certain compression of the lips and look of determination which sometimes, by the end of a long and weather-beaten life, may become permanent. Edinburgh, built on ridges exposed to the breeze from all quarters, is said to be distinguished by the 'windy walk' of its inhabitants. Ami Boué was struck with the wall that ran along the middle of the earthen mound which was thrown across the central valley, in order to connect the old and the new town of that city, and he tells us that pedestrians chose one or other side of this wall

---

[1] Burt in his *Letters* says that he found these lines scribbled on the window with the initials A. H. at the end of them, and he conjectured them to be Hill's. They were afterwards included in the poems of that writer, who seems to have had a passion for thus disfiguring window-panes, for he has collected a series of his verses 'written on windows in several parts of the kingdom in a journey to Scotland.'

according to the quarter from which the continual and often violent winds blew. 'How many hats,' he exclaims, 'were lost there in a year! I wore out more umbrellas in my four years of residence in Great Britain than during all the rest of my life. Macintoshes had not been invented.'[1]

To any one intent on some definite employment out-of-doors, such as fishing, sketching, botanising, geological mapping, or any pursuit where quiet air is necessary, nothing can be more exasperating than a struggle against the ceaseless driving of the blast. Mere heavy rain, if it fall straight, can be endured, for it allows one to stand, to turn round, and if an umbrella be used, to consult a map or guide-book. With a furious wind, however, you can do nothing but

> Grow sick, and damn the climate—like a lord.

In Scotland, as in other countries having a variable climate, the weather has long been a

---

[1] From Boué's *Autobiography*, which he wrote in French some time before his death, and printed in Vienna. It abounds in misprints, over and above those of which he appends a long list, and reminds one of the French of his *Esquisse Géologique sur l'Écosse*. He addressed copies of the work in his own handwriting to his friends, to be distributed after his death. Mine was not only inscribed to me inside, but the postal cover was also addressed by him, and I received it by post shortly after the news came that he had passed away.

staple subject with which to introduce a conversation. And it is curious that even when the sky is overcast, with a threatening of rain, the usual greeting, 'It's a fine day,' may not infrequently be heard as the beginning of the colloquy. So inveterate is this habit that the observation is apt to escape from the lips, even when the meteorological conditions make it grotesquely out of place, as in the case of the man who made use of it on a day of howling tempest, but immediately corrected himself: 'It's a fine day,' said he,—'but coorse.'

Remarks about the weather have been known to be resented on Sundays as an unbecoming topic of conversation for that solemn season. When the usual salutation had been made to one of the more strait-laced elders, he testily answered, 'Ay, but whatna a day's this, to be speakin' about days?'

Still more gruff was the Aberdonian response to the ordinary greeting of a stranger on a country road, 'Ou ay, fae's findin' faut wi' the day. There's some folk wad fecht wi' a stane wa'.'

The number of days in a year when an outdoor walk is impracticable on account of the weather is in Scotland far smaller than people might imagine. Of course there come storms of wind and rain that will keep one a prisoner for a day or so at a time. But even in these storms there are not infrequently lulls, when a brisk walk may be enjoyed before the tempest begins again. Geological surveying affords a good test of climate, and I have found it quite possible to carry this work on the whole year through. Snow puts a stop to it, but many winters come and go without leaving snow on the lowlands at all, or at least for more than a day or two altogether.

Those who are familiar with the peculiarly genial and healthy climate of the southern shores of the Moray Firth have sometimes thought that as good an argument as many that have been brought forward to prove that Shakespeare visited Scotland, might be based on the extraordinarily minute and accurate description which he gives of the climate of that region.

> The air
> Nimbly and sweetly recommends itself
> Unto our gentle senses. This guest of summer,
> The temple-haunting martlet, does approve
> By his loved mansionry that the heaven's breath
> Smells wooingly here: no jutty, frieze,
> Buttress nor coign of vantage, but this bird

Hath made his bed and procreant cradle ;
Where they most breed and haunt I have observed
The air is delicate.

The salubrity of the climate has been recognised for many years by medical men, who, as already mentioned, send their patients from the south of England to these northern shores.

The most suggestive illustration of the influence of environment upon the character of the people is probably to be found in the Highlands. There can be no doubt that the Celtic inhabitants of that region belong to the same stock as those of Ireland. We know, indeed, as a historical fact, that the south-western districts of Scotland were actually peopled from Ireland. Yet no one familiar with the population of the two countries can fail to recognise the contrasts which they present to each other, both in general physique and in habits and temperament. Neither race has kept itself pure and unmixed, but in each case the foreign infusion has been of the same kind in varying proportions. Norsemen, Danes, Normans, English, have mingled with the Celtic stock in both islands. The Irishman, however, has had the advantage of, on the whole, a better climate. His country possesses

far more level ground and a much larger proportion of arable soil. His mountains rise
up for the most part as islands out of a vast
plain, and thus have offered little serious
impediment to the free intercourse of the
people from one end of the island to the
other. Hence he has been able to sow and
reap his crops, and to rear his sheep, cattle
and horses, with comparatively little opposition
from nature. Moreover, he has escaped the
shadow of the Calvinistic gloom. His religion
has not repressed his natural liveliness of temperament. His clergy have not set themselves
to eradicate all his superstitions and usages,
habits and customs, but have allowed these
free play where they were not clearly opposed
to the cause of morality. And thus his gaiety,
if it has not been greatly promoted by the
cheerfulness of his surroundings, has at least
not been always and everywhere dimmed and
chastened by a contest with his environment
for the means of subsistence, save where the
population has increased beyond the capacity
of the ground to support it, nor by a stern
and inquisitorial interference on the part of
his priesthood.

The fate of the Celt in the Highlands has
been far different. There he has found himself

in a region of mountains too rugged and lofty for cultivation, save along their bases, and too continuous to permit easy access from one district to another, yet not sufficiently impassable to prevent the sudden irruption of some hostile clan of mountaineers, carrying with it slaughter and spoliation. Shut in among long, narrow, and deep glens, he has cultivated their strips of alluvium, but has too often found the thin stony soil to yield but a poor return for his labour. For many a long century he had to defend his flocks and herds from the wolf, the fox, and the wild cat.[1] The gloom of his valleys is deepened by the canopy of cloud which for so large a part of the year rests upon the mountain-ridges and cuts off the light and heat of the sun. Hence his harvests are often thrown into the late autumn, and in many a season his thin and scanty crops rot on the ground, leaving

[1] The last wolf is believed to have been killed in Scotland about the year 1743 in the forest of Tarnaway, Morayland, by Macqueen of Pall-a'-Chrocain, a deer-stalker of great stature and strength (Chambers' *Domestic Annals of Scotland*, Vol. III. p. 609). The fox is still common in many districts, where it is hunted with dogs and rifles. The wild-cat is becoming scarce, but continues to haunt some of the mountainous tracts of the Highlands. A number of captive individuals are kept in confinement at the Earl of Seaforth's residence in Glen Urquhart.

him face to face with starvation and an in-
clement winter. Under these adverse conditions he could hardly fail to become more
or less subdued and grim. But he has likewise
been exposed, more irresistibly than his fellow-
countrymen of the Lowlands, to the mis-
guided solicitude and sombre fanaticism of
kirk-sessions and Presbyteries. His tales, his
legends, and his superstitions have been de-
rided by his ecclesiastical guides as foolish
fables; his songs, his instrumental music, and
his dances, have been stigmatised as vain and
unworthy exhibitions, his musical instruments
have been broken and burnt. His natural
and innocent ebullitions of joy and mirth have
been checked and repressed as unbecoming in
a being who is journeying onward to eternity.

Need it be matter for wonder if under
these various restraining influences the gaiety
which the Highlander doubtless shared originally with his brother in Ireland, has been in
large measure replaced by a serious sedate-
ness, passing even into depression. When he
chooses to solace himself with music, its sad
cadences seem to re-echo the monotonous
melancholy of the winds that sough past his
roughly-built cot, or howl down his glens and
across his wastes of barren moorland. But

while the lighter side of his nature has thus suffered, his higher qualities have probably been only further fostered and developed. His struggle with climate and soil has strengthened in him a spirit of stubborn endurance and self-reliance, which his moral training has directed towards praiseworthy ends. This spirit finds its freest scope in the life of a soldier. In that career, also, the instincts and traditions of his race meet with their fullest realisation. And thus it has come that for more than a century and a half the British Army has had no braver or more loyal body of men than those of the Highland regiments. On many a hard-fought field, in all parts of the world, wherever deeds of heroism had to be done, the pibroch has thrilled and the tartan has waved in the front.

INDEX.

GLASGOW: PRINTED AT THE UNIVERSITY PRESS BY ROBERT MACLEHOSE AND CO. LTD.